Portraits of
Palestinian
Women

Portraits of Palestinian Women

ORAYB AREF NAJJAR

with Kitty Warnock

INTRODUCTION BY

Rosemary Sayigh

UNIVERSITY OF UTAH PRESS
Salt Lake City

Copyright © 1992 University of Utah Press
All rights reserved
Photographs by Orayb Aref Najjar
A portion of the Salima Kumsiyya chapter was published in *The Christian Century*, August 1982.

∞ This symbol indicates books printed on paper that meets the minimum requirements of American National Standard for Information Services— Permanence of Paper for Printed Library Materials, ANSI A39.38–1984.

LIBRARY OF CONGRESS CATALOGING-IN-PUBLICATION DATA

Najjar, Orayb Aref.
     Portraits of palestinian women / Obayb Aref Najjar with Kitty Warnock; introduction by Rosemary Sayigh.
        p.   cm.
     Includes bibliographical references and index.
     ISBN 0–87480–385–3   (alk. paper)
     1. Women, Palestinian Arab—Biography. 2. Jewish-Arab relations. 3. Israel— Ethnic relations. I. Warnock, Kitty. II. Title.

HQ1728.5.N35   1992
305.42'095694—dc20   91–51099
                                                                       CIP

To Palestinian women in the occupied territories and in the diaspora, a book that covers at least some of their varied experiences,

To my extended family and my sisters and brothers,

To my late grandmother Fattum, who encouraged her daughters and her granddaughters to spend money on education and not on "rags" (clothes),

To my late aunt Arifa, who did volunteer work in refugee camps in the 1950s,

To my late mother, Salwa Madi Najjar, a writer and artist, and a hard act to follow, and to aunt Samira Abu Ni'meh, who raised us,

To my mother's family in Haifa, from whom we were separated by the Mandelbaum gate in Jerusalem, the "gate of tears,"

To my father, Aref Najjar, who when I was ten, told me I was going to university,

To my husband, Tomis Kapitan—because he is such a good father, I had time to work on this book,

To our daughter Rima, hoping that when she grows up, she will come to know and appreciate the type of women introduced in this book.

CONTENTS

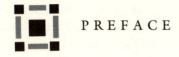

PREFACE

In the winter of 1984 a group of women met in East Jerusalem to collect studies about Palestinian women for the Nairobi "End of the Decade" conference of 1985. We found that not much current material was available. Women's demonstrations, sit-ins and detentions are regularly reported in the Palestinian press, but there were few studies about gender relations, and fewer still in which women describe how they feel about the Palestinian experience. The group assigned research tasks to the women present, and Kitty Warnock and I, who at that time were teaching at Birzeit University, were asked to "write something in English about women – quickly!"

Each of us wrote the life histories of four women, photocopied them, and sent them to the conference. Shortly after that, Kitty returned to England and I went to the United States to do graduate study. Several events encouraged me to interview nine more women for this book and continue to work on it on my own after Kitty's return to England: The Israeli military government forbade the most important heads of women's organizations from leaving the country to represent Palestinians at Nairobi; and then in December 1987, the Intifada* started and women

*Intifada (uprising) comes from the Arabic word *yantafed*, to shake off.

ix

were more active than they had ever been in resisting Israeli occupation. I went to the West Bank in the summer of 1989. There, I interviewed some of the leaders who were forbidden to leave for Nairobi. I also updated the 1984–1986 interviews and discussed with the women their roles in the Intifada and added some new women to the book.

Initially, Kitty and I decided which facets of Palestinian life we wanted to cover and then interviewed women we knew or of whom we had heard. The selection of the women was very important. Each was invited to talk about a subject she was most familiar with, or felt most strongly about, or had some expertise in. We wanted to write about the refugee experience, so Kitty chose Umm Ibrahim Shawabkeh. I sought out Aisheh Shamlawi because I wanted to cover land confiscations. Although I planned to interview Na'imah al-As'ad about the teachers' union, the nature of the talk changed when I found her with a lawyer after the arrest of her husband and the "search" of her house. On one occasion, meeting a woman made me add a segment to the book. In 1989, while I was looking for a friend who teaches at Birzeit University, I found Tahani Ali working at a computer. Tahani's experience with education was so different from that of Fadwa Hussein, a former student Kitty interviewed in the same village in 1985, that I decided to compare the two.

While not every "type" of Palestinian woman is represented, we made an effort to include women of different ages who have been through various periods of Palestinian history (British, Jordanian, Israeli, and Intifada) and women with different kinds of experiences and educational levels. We included illiterate women, educated women, some who are deeply involved in the struggle against the Israeli occupation, as well as others who are merely struggling to get by or get an education.

On some subjects, we had several potential interviewees. I asked Salima Kumsiyya to tell the story of the demolition of her home as collective punishment. I could have written about another Beit Sahur twenty-one–member extended family whose home was demolished the same night. I could have interviewed a woman who was forced to leave her home with her ten-day-old baby on a cold night in November 1981 as punishment for an act about which she knew nothing. But the story of Salima Kumsiyya was compelling because it symbolized the Palestinian experience. There was the struggle of building the house, stone by stone over a period of fourteen years. There was the community solidarity that made the rebuilding of the house possible. And, over the years, there was evidence of the growing political sophistication of Mrs. Kumsiyya. But most important, Mrs. Kumsiyya was a great storyteller and singer of traditional Palestinian songs (to which she added new material), and a person with untapped leadership potential, as she had occasion to discover when she was forced to confront Israeli soldiers and officials.

Kitty, who understands Arabic and can speak it, sometimes interviewed women directly, but at other times asked questions through an interpreter. She taped all her interviews and worked from the transcripts. Most of my 1985 and 1986 interviews were tape-recorded. The updates and the 1989 interviews were written from carefully recorded notes. The footnotes to each chapter provide more information about the language used in the interviews and how the narratives were collected and written.

Most of my interviews were conducted in Arabic. I tried to preserve each women's style in translation. I was especially careful to do that with rural women. Umm Ayyash speaks mostly in matter-of-fact short sentences: "Mother kept to herself. She did not visit many people, and she did not gossip." Some of the "organized" city women express themselves in long sentences and use ideological formulations, as exemplified by Zahira Kamal, a leader of a women's committee:

> The uprising is the Palestinian answer to the inequities inflicted by Israeli rule. For the first time since 1967, Israel has started to realize that there are moral and financial costs to the occupation. At first, the Israeli army believed that all it needed was more time and more instruments of repression to crush the uprising, but the army failed because the Intifada is fighting the occupation on many different levels, none of which force can affect.

There were times, of course, where grammar stood in the way of rendering the sentence as is, but an effort was made to catch both meaning and style. Kitty handled the material in the same manner.

Not every woman asked agreed to talk to us, and two changed their minds after they were interviewed. One M.D. first allowed Kitty to use her name, then asked to be quoted anonymously, and so was replaced by Dr. Rita Giacaman. Another, a divorced fortune-teller, who with her seventeen-year-old married daughter would have made an excellent cover for the book, was pressured by her neighbors to drop out; she explained, "A divorced woman has to be careful about her reputation." She did, however, read my coffee cup.

I sought leaders from women's committees not included in the book, but some declined and one was out of the country in the summer of 1989. One female activist agreed to be interviewed anonymously, but we had decided to talk only to those who were willing to reveal their identities. We had a good reason: Palestinian literary critics have pointed out that Palestinians often lose sight of the real women behind the symbols they use to depict them. Palestinian women are often seen as symbols of the land (although, often, they do not own it) and as symbols of fertility (although prenatal care is not readily available to the most "fertile"). Women are often called the "mothers of sons" (although about 50 percent of the time they bear daughters), "the sisters of men" (although they themselves have brothers), and the widows of heroes (although they are often heroines in thousands of ways), but yet when it is their turn to ask for their reward in Palestinian society, they are asked to wait because the Palestinian struggle for self-determination has not yet been won. Part of their problem is their invisibility. We did not want "a community activist," we needed one who was willing to stand up and be counted, one with a name.

Palestinian women have a different problem in the Western world. Somewhere out there in the land of Middle East Studies live "Arab–Muslim–Middle-Eastern women." As a Muslim Arab who has lived in the Middle East, I do not know the women about whom most Middle East "experts" write. They are not like the farmers I know; neither are they like the office workers. And although Palestinian women are deeply involved in the nationalist Palestinian struggle, perhaps sometimes at the expense of their demands as women, the West knows them only as shadowy veiled figures with no interest in politics. But home demolition is politics, and so is refugee status, and women *are* involved, thus the need for a book that goes beyond the stereotypes. In *Portraits of Palestinian Women*, women appear as themselves in the hope that they will cease to be invisible as women and as Palestinians and that they will be put "on stage," as novelist Sahar Khalifah insists they deserve to be.

This book also sheds light on the Palestinian men some of these women know. Again, not all of them fit the stereotype of the Arab male, and some, like my own father, are more supportive of women's ambitions than their traditional male upbringing could account for.

Often, the interviews and the documents gathered on a woman consisted of hundreds of pages (as in the case of Mrs. Samiha Salameh Khalil), so the question of selection came up. Every account, whether it is sociological, anthropological, or journalistic, is a selective rendition of a story. Only raw data is really a personal account. Organizing information into a coherent story imposes a structure on the information, a fact Gerbner pointed out when he said, "The introduction (or elimination) of a character, a scene, an event, has functional consequences. It changes other things in the story. It makes the whole work 'work' differently" (Gerbner 1985: 19). The need to shorten accounts also removes important parts of the stories. In a letter dated 2 July 1991, Kitty Warnock wrote me, "P.S. It's very sad working through my vast pile of notes and transcripts, remembering everybody and seeing what a lot of wonderful material I was not able to use!" Knowing how much we had to edit out, both Kitty and I tried to be sensitive to what each woman considered important.

The theme of each narrative often emerged from what each woman stressed. I interviewed Siham Barghuti because she was one of the founding members of a women's committee. But her description of the difficulty of having a normal married life under occupation because of repeated separation from her husband made that an important theme in the final product. I had read many interviews with political activists about their town arrests. But the reality of the practice was brought home to me only when I saw it through the eyes of Zahira's nieces when she casually mentioned them. I felt readers would feel the way I did about the practice and chose to include the reaction of Zahira's family to her town arrest. To do so, I had to leave out more solidly political material.

In the case of the leaders, if one gave a lengthy account of an aspect of her nationalist work, and that account was similar to one given by another woman, I kept it in but shortened it considerably, thus appearing to give it less emphasis. Although the theme of imprisonment and death of a relative or acquaintance could be found in almost every story, I did not feel I needed to include every prisoner or every Palestinian killed that the women had mentioned. I hope the readers will read one such account, learn from the footnotes how pervasive the practice of imprisoning and killing Palestinians is, and then understand what thousands of families are going through. This type of editing was done because the function of this text is not to tell the story of an individual woman's life, but for the stories, *taken together*, to depict the Palestinian experience over the last ninety years.

Not all Palestinian regions are represented. Although Gaza women share the Palestinian experience and live under worse conditions than women in the West Bank, Kitty and I have decided not to include Gaza since both of us have visited but have never lived there. We believe that others with more extensive experience in Gaza can do it more justice than we can.

Updating the women's stories added depth to the understanding of their lives because it allowed readers to compare what women said they wanted to do and what they had to settle for or what they had accomplished. Assia Habash, a pioneer in preschool education, had a clear goal in 1986, and in May 1991 we saw that she had achieved her objectives. Others were not as lucky.

In many cases, women confided in marvellous detail their experiences in the uprising, information I was asked not to reveal. I have complied with those requests, hoping that the day will come when those details can be added to the accounts published in this book.

The book also includes a bibliography, the most comprehensive list published on Palestinian women. It was first suggested and compiled by Rosemary Sayigh, one to which I later added, paying special attention to publications of the Occupied Territories.

Over the years, anthropologist Rosemary Sayigh has written very perceptive analyses on Palestinian women, and we are pleased that she has joined us in this enterprise. Her seeing some value in our manuscript in its early stages and her willingness to write the introduction for it encouraged me to do something with it despite my other commitments. I reasoned that if Rosemary can pull that manuscript out from under her bed, dust it off, and write despite the bombardment of Beirut and the ensuing chaos, I can pull the manuscript off my shelf in the safe area where I live and write. More than anything, Rosemary's involvement has encouraged me to turn this "write something in English" manuscript into a book.

ABBREVIATIONS

FA   *Al-Fajr* (Arabic), published in East Jerusalem
FE   *Al-Fajr* (English), published in East Jerusalem
GUPW   General Union of Palestinian Women
JP   *Jerusalem Post*
JP (Int.)   *Jerusalem Post*, International Edition
JPS   *Journal of Palestine Studies*
MEI   *Middle East International* (London)
MEJ   *Middle East Journal* (USA)
PFWAC   Palestinian Federation of Women's Action Committees (for-
            merly PUWWC)
PRM   Palestine Resistance Movement
PUWWC   Palestinian Union of Working Women's Committee, the first
            committee established in the West Bank in 1978
PWC   Palestinian Women's Committee, established in 1982
UNRWA   United Nations Relief and Works Agency
UPWWC   Union of Palestinian Working Women's Committee, established
            in 1981
WCSW   Women's Committee for Social Work, established 1982/83

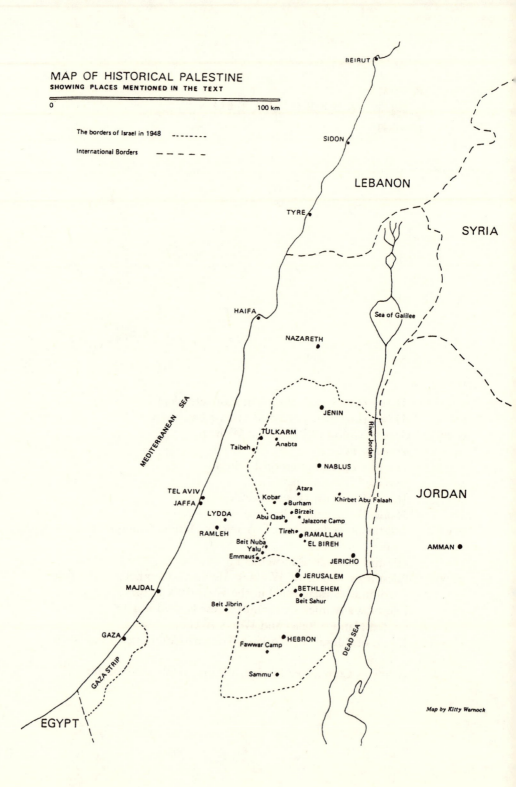

MAP OF HISTORICAL PALESTINE
SHOWING PLACES MENTIONED IN THE TEXT

0   100 km

The borders of Israel in 1948   - - - - - - - -

International Borders   — — — — —

BEIRUT

SIDON

LEBANON

TYRE

SYRIA

HAIFA

Sea of Galilee

NAZARETH

MEDITERRANEAN SEA

JENIN

TULKARM

Taibeh   Anabta

NABLUS

River Jordan

JORDAN

TEL AVIV   Atara
JAFFA   Kobar   Khirbet Abu Falaah
        Burham
LYDDA   Birzeit
    Abu Qash   Jalazone Camp
RAMLEH   Tireh   RAMALLAH
    Beit Nuba   EL BIREH
    Yalu   AMMAN
Emmaus   JERICHO
MAJDAL   JERUSALEM
    BETHLEHEM
    Beit Jibrin   Beit Sahur

GAZA   HEBRON
    Fawwar Camp   DEAD SEA
GAZA STRIP
    Sammu'

Map by Kitty Warnock

EGYPT

Palestinian Women
A Case of Neglect

Rosemary Sayigh

This morning, as on other mornings, Mouna awoke before the rest of the family. . . . In a refugee camp, you're surrounded every second by others. . . . Mouna finds peace and solitude only when her seven younger brother and sisters, mother and grandparents are asleep. That is when she reads political papers, books, and pamphlets published by the PLO on the Palestinian struggle. But there are only two books on Palestinian women. She has to find her examples of fighting women in the USSR and the Third World (Bendt and Downing 1982:28).

Despite a growing recent literature, a deep disparity exists between the rich history of Palestinian women's involvement in their people's struggle and the recording of that history. Work done so far is fragmented in approach, diverse in language, and uncertain of the historical roots of today's activist women. These women have received scant recognition even in the Arab World, where only the names of a few militants and martyrs are widely known. In the non-Arab world the idea endures that Palestinian women have not been as active as Algerian women, and though the Intifada brought women onto the television screen and newspaper page, girls such as Mouna still lack comprehensive accounts. This "blind spot" has persisted in spite of a renaissance of Palestinian history and in spite of a "herstory" born out of the Western feminist movement.

A scanning of women's studies symposia and journals reveals the extent of the absence of Palestinian women even when the focus is on the Third World.[1] They are also as absent from most symposia on Arab/Middle Eastern/Muslim women as they are from mainstream journals.[2] It is to small progressive presses and publications such as *MERIP Reports, Khamsin, Race and Class*, and *Peuples Méditerranéens* that we must turn for consistent attention to this subject.

The neglect of women by Palestinian research and publishing centers is more surprising and calls for a detailed analysis that cannot be given here. Sanbar has pointed to the psychocultural effects of Palestine's "deconstruction" on the generation of intellectuals that began to work after 1948, focusing their efforts on understanding the power of the Zionist movement and its international backing.[3] Research into Palestinian history, society, and culture appeared of secondary importance; even major episodes such as the Great Rebellion of 1936–38 and the war of 1947–48 were not studied. In such a context, the neglect of "muted" groups such as peasants and women was merely a reflection of their absence from "official" history.[4]

With the rise of the Palestinian resistance movement,[5] the General Union of Palestinian Women (GUPW) began to play an important part in the "diplomatic struggle," calling for the production of information material about the Palestinian women's movement. To satisfy these needs a number of pamphlets were produced between 1974 and 1982 in Lebanon by various sectors in the Palestine Liberation Organization (PLO). Most of such material was produced in haste for immediate conference consumption. A more serious study of attitudes to the resistance movement by women in Bourj al-Barajneh camp was published by the PLO Research Center (al-Khalili 1977), and the GUPW published a critical evaluation of the experience of women within the Palestinian resistance movement (Abu Ali 1975). However, as the crisis in Lebanon mounted, the GUPW's cultural program, which included collecting archives, researching the women's movement history, and publishing a magazine, was pushed aside by emergency tasks. A survey of Palestinian media of the period reveals interviews with militants, theoretical discussions of the "woman question," speeches honoring International Women's Day, and papers produced for GUPW seminars; but though the phrases "women's reality" and "the woman question" are often used, they are seldom worked out.

It is against this background of absence that Najjar and Warnock's collection of life histories of women in the West Bank takes on its significance as a breakthrough. The women chosen for this study span differences of generation, class, locality, occupation, and family situation. All are articulate, but only four are women's movement leaders. Younger, university-educated professional women are strongly represented, but so also are "ordinary" women from villages, small towns, and camps. In the book, we meet a refugee who was unable to pull herself and her children out of the cycle of poverty caused by her uprooting, but we also meet a woman from another refugee camp who has gone to graduate school and is now helping others through volunteer work. The inclusion of Mary Shehadeh, a woman in her nineties, pushes the book's time span back to the late Ottoman and early Mandate period. Excerpts from two of Mrs. Shehadeh's speeches remind us how early Palestinian women launched into speechmaking and journalism, while the stories of two young women from West Bank villages point to struggles still being waged with families in conservative milieus. A variety of family backgrounds and relations emerges – liberal and authoritarian fathers, strong and submissive mothers, conventional and unconventional husbands – belying the notion of an archetypal Arab/Muslim family. We recognize the strength women often possess where their freedom is limited; feminists among us are forced to think more carefully about the question of women's power and powerlessness.

This is not primarily a book about Palestinian-Israeli politics, nor is the book about the Palestinian national or women's movement, though it is a source for understanding both. By giving free scope to both private and public aspects of women's lives, Najjar and Warnock shed light on how these interact within the context of a national struggle. They have produced vital, substantial, resonant texts that tell us what it is like to be Palestinian, female, and live under Israeli occupation.

The Palestinian Women's Movement: An Overview

First, a correction: One cannot properly speak of "the" women's movement. From the beginning it has been characterized by a pluralism that before 1948 reflected a Palestinian society with its ethnic/sectarian mix and strong regional and local associations; after 1948, dispersion forced Palestinians to organize under disparate laws and regimes. Within the national movement, different ideologies and factions also separate women. Thus today, beside the main national framework, the General Union of Palestinian Women (GUPW), we find women active in still-surviving branches of the pre-1948 Palestine Arab Women's Union (PAWU),[6] in resistance groups, in other PLO mass unions (students', workers', etc.), in numerous social associations, in the four women's work committees of the Occupied Territories, and in the Democratic Women's Movement and other parties in Israel.[7] Informal ties of kinship, locality, and friendship as well as women's mobility across the diaspora crosshatch the boundaries of these disparate organizational frameworks.

It must be noticed, too, that much of the Palestinian women's political action is spontaneous, erupting outside the scope of formal organization. This has been particularly true of women of the peasant class, who took part in anti-British street demonstrations as early as 1921, and played a many-sided, still-unresearched role in the Great Rebellion.[8] To widen the lens further, we need to take account of actions that are not directly political but, by being carried out in a particular place and time, carry a political charge, for example, carrying on lives in conditions like those of Israeli occupation or in camps in Lebanon. The unique difficulty of the Palestinian struggle, its imbalance of forces, make *sumoud* (steadfastness, staying put) an essential form of resistance on a level with political and military struggle. In addition, Palestinian women have been in the forefront of institution building, social work, and cultural production. To focus then only on "organized" women would be to miss these other kinds of struggle.

Pre-1948

An excellent source for the beginning of Palestinian women's organizing is Mogannam, first published in 1937 in England, and recently republished in the United States (Mogannam 1976); another is Touby's brief biographies of outstanding Palestinian women, published after 1948 but going back to early in the century (Touby 1948). From these, it is clear that there were women's social associations (mainly sectarian) from late Ottoman times. The first political, cross-sectarian women's unions appear in Jerusalem and Haifa in 1921, soon after the beginning of British rule; Jaffa's Arab Women's Union is said to date from before World War I. In 1929, a year of widespread nationalist protest, the first national women's organization was formed, the Palestine Arab Women's Congress (later

PAWU), after a founding congress in Jerusalem attended by 200 delegates from all over the country. The PAWA spread rapidly to large and small urban centers.

Mogannam's account conveys the dynamism and originality of early PAWA activities, but ends in 1932; no one has researched its subsequent history. Interviews conducted with a few surviving leaders emphasize continued activity in the face of mounting violence and insecurity. Many questions call for further exploration, for example, the class origins of PAWA leaders and members, its mode of recruitment, its outlook towards social issues and the "woman question," the effect on it of factional splits, the position of the PAWA in the national movement as a whole, and the relations between its leaders and the national leadership. Views of the PAWA constructed after 1948 have assumed that its role was purely auxiliary and supportive; but the Palestinian historian A. W. Kayyali gives indications that women, along with students and intellectuals, formed a vanguard within the national movement, pressing the leadership to take more militant action.[9]

Alternative frameworks for women existed during the Mandate period. Important but unresearched, the Rifaqat Qassam (Companions of Qassam) were limited to the Haifa area but, unlike the PAWA, reached out to peasant women. Girls' schools in urban areas became an arena of nationalist mobilization. As violence escalated in 1947, women in some urban areas formed secret paramilitary cells, the Uqhuwan.[10]

The interest of this lost history is suggested by the story of a long-dead, unknown Haifa woman, Fatimeh Araqeel. Keeper of a public Turkish bath, she was one of the principal figures in the 1936–38 insurrection in the West Galilee area, passing on messages between mountain and urban guerrillas through women clients. This fragment, preserved by women from Haifa in a Damascus camp, was picked up by Palestinian resistance movement women activists and passed on to this writer in the course of a casual visit.

1948–1967

Loss of country and dispersion were stunning blows to both national and women's movements; one can hardly overestimate their effects in rupturing women's lives and organizations. Poverty or reduced income confined women to their homes or forced them out to work; the number available for "national work" was drastically reduced. Nevertheless the impression given in official literature of a gap between 1943 and the forming of the GUPW in 1964–65 is incorrect. There was continuity in spite of rupture and dispersion, and there were also new forms of activism.

First, several PAWU branches survived. Mainly these were in what remained of historic Palestine (Jerusalem, the West Bank, Gaza), but a few branches were carried outside and re-formed in the diaspora: Sadej Nassar from Haifa continued to be active in Damascus; Wadia Khartabeel from Toulkarm and Evelyn Homsi from Jaffa formed a new union in Beirut; in Cairo, too, a new union was formed by Samira Abu Ghazaleh. However, political obstacles rapidly appeared. Zuleikha Shehabi, chairwoman of the Jerusalem branch of the PAWU, was not allowed by the Jordanian government to represent Palestine at an Arab women's conference held soon after 1948. The Syrian government closed down the union office in Damascus in 1957 (Sadej Nassar kept on working from her home). But these and other leading women formed a vocal lobby calling for a Palestinian entity, and several participated in the meetings that gave birth to the PLO. This continuity also passed from mother to daughter. Samiha Khalil's mother worked in Toulkarm with Wadia Khartabeel. Mrs. Khalil herself worked with several women's associations in the 1950s before founding In'ash al-Usra, but she was also there for the founding of the GUPW. Mrs. Khalil demonstrated against the British in the 1930s, against British influence in Jordan in the 1950s, and is now still struggling against the Israeli occupation. Her daughter Saida is active in Palestinian politics.

The scale of the refugee disaster also brought more women into relief, social care, and income-generating projects.[11] At least nine new social associations were established between 1948 and 1967, almost all by women.[12] Many women also carried out social work in small informal groups or as individuals. A very different reaction, coming from younger, educated, unmarried women from other social strata, was to join opposition parties such as the Ba'th, PPS, Jordanian Communist party, and Arab Nationalist Movement or, in Israel, Rakah and al-'Ard.[13] This was a new step since, in Palestine, women had not joined "mixed" (male and female) political entities. Such recruitment found its motivation in the scale of the 1948 disaster, and was facilitated by the weakening of family control over girls as they entered university, worked outside the home, and traveled. A well-known example is Leila Khaled (Khaled 1973). Another is Raja Abu Ammasheh, killed in Jerusalem in 1955 while leading demonstrations against the Baghdad Pact. Several PPS and ANM women were arrested in Jordan. In Israel, Samira Khoury joined the Communist party and became active in the teachers' syndicate.[14]

With the beginning of *feda'yyiin* operations in the early sixties, some women became supporters of the still clandestine resistance organizations; open recruitment of women only began after the Battle of Karameh in 1968.[15]

Though only a small minority of women were politically active during the 1948–67 period, their importance as a vanguard went far beyond their numbers. Few before 1967, their number increased sharply after the shock of the 1967 Arab-Israeli war through which Israel completed its occupation of all of historic Palestine, creating 300,000 new refugees.

1967 to the Present
The defeat of the Arab armies in 1967 and subsequent emergence of the Palestinian resistance movement engendered a series of radical transformations that formed an entirely new context for the organizing of Palestinian women. The effect of the resistance movement on women, as on Palestinians generally, was one of activation and "recentering," drawing them into Palestinian frameworks: the resistance groups, the PLO mass unions, and the institutions of the embryo state. Since then, Palestinian nationalism has spread throughout the diaspora, making it a unified political field despite distance, national boundaries, and interresistance group conflict. Setbacks suffered in Jordan, Syria, and Lebanon as the Arab governments sought to restore their tutelage have only strengthened Palestinian self-reliance, as did failure of any Arab government to come to the aid of the resistance movement when Israel invaded Lebanon in 1982.

Since the center of gravity of the resistance movement has shifted throughout this period from one region to another, with each period and region having specific characteristics for the organization of women, I shall briefly review each phase.

GAZA AND THE WEST BANK, 1967 TO 1971. Israeli occupation was followed by a sharp rise in women's participation in all kinds of resistance, from demonstrations and sit-ins to sabotage. In Gaza, women participated in a continuous insurrection between 1968 and 1971. They were killed and imprisoned. Many who were imprisoned were also tortured (Fatmeh Bernawi, Widad Guevara, Aisheh Odeh, Abla Taha, Myriam al-

Shakhshir, Lutfiyya Harari, Therese Halasa); others were deported, including 'Issam Abdul Hadi, chairwoman of the GUPW's Executive Committee. Though brief, this period gave the women's movement new heroes and leaders. Their acts of resistance were carried out in small groups or individually, without strong mass participation except in Gaza. Temporarily crushed in the Occupied Territories, resistance group organizing, still in its infancy, moved to Jordan.

JORDAN, 1968 TO 1970. After the Battle of Karameh, the resistance movement was free openly to recruit, train, and carry on military operations against Israel. Women were now for the first time admitted to full membership in resistance organizations and fighting units with men, though in the main group, Fateh, political meetings and military training were segregated. Mass mobilization programs began in refugee camps. Women were also recruited into building the social infrastructure of the PLO/resistance movement. This phase of the "people's war" ended in Black September 1970, followed the next year by the transfer of the resistance movement headquarters to Lebanon.

LEBANON, 1969 TO 1982. Here the resistance movement enjoyed its longest period of autonomy and popular support, though subject to continual attack. Women continued to join the resistance groups, with membership spreading from urban, educated women to those in camps. Female cadres carried out crucial tasks of mass mobilization, and some women reached the central committee level. The GUPW was active in diplomacy, but its programs for the masses suffered from lack of trained cadres and from interresistance group conflict. Women also continued to be active in independent social associations, running productive, cultural, and social-care projects in the camps alongside those of the GUPW and Palestinian resistance movement. In spite of their activism, their weight as a sector within the national movement was weakened by their organizational dispersion; only slight progress was made towards defining women's issues or articulating them to national struggle.[16]

1982 TO THE PRESENT. With the withdrawal of the Palestinian resistance movement from Beirut and the dispersion of its institutions and fighters, a period of crisis began, first signaled by the split in Fateh, followed by the formation of an anti-Arafat front supported by Syria. These and other developments in the Palestinian and Arab arenas ultimately had the effect of recentering Palestinian resistance away from the diaspora and back to the Occupied Territories, leading towards the Intifada of 9 December 1987. Politically, the Intifada is a reaction to Palestinian isolation and a deepening of Israeli repression under the Likud Party. It also draws on structural, cultural, and demographic changes in the Palestinian population since 1967. Organizationally, its sustained, mass character owes much to the organizing by women and youth that preceded it. Since the organizing by women in the West Bank and Gaza, while sharing historical roots with the movement outside, differs somewhat in its context, structure, programs, and outlook, the following section examines it more carefully.

The Women's Movement in the Occupied Territories

More than twenty years of Israeli occupation have pushed the women's movement here into directions that differentiate it structurally and programmatically both from its forerunner unions and charitable societies and from the movement in the diaspora. On the one hand it has evolved towards a national, mass structure that the older, locally based groups did not aim at. On the other, it is more autonomous and decentralized than the movement outside (whether GUPW or women's sections of resistance groups). Conditions under Israeli occupation have given women's groups greater national importance than they have had outside.

Israeli occupation works through an interlocking apparatus of coercion. Local leadership has been tolerated only if considered moderate, and women's associations thus have been among the very few organizations permitted to survive.[17] In a valuable paper on the West Bank women's movement, Rita Giacaman notes how local charitable associations filled the gap in public services under British and Jordanian rule.[18] At least thirty-two such associations were operating before 1967; by 1976, in spite of the occupation, they had grown to thirty-eight. Their programs included: health care, nursery schools, orphanages, care for the aged, relief, and some income-generating activities. Signs of nationalist motivation for such social work is the fact that eight of the associations use "Arab Women's Union" as a part of their titles, while fifteen were set up in 1965, the year of the GUPW's founding conference.

Established during 1964–65, the General Union of Palestinian Women was at first firmly based on Palestinian territory. Its founding conference was held in Jerusalem and its first executive committee was composed of representatives from women's groups and from regions, with Palestinian districts outweighing those of the diaspora. Banned by both Israel and Jordan in 1967, loss of its core territory was a blow from which the GUPW did not recover until its second national conference in 1974 in Lebanon. Operating from the diaspora made the union more dependent on, and subordinate to, PLO/resistance movement structures.[19] Though most organized women believe that "organic unity" between the GUPW and the resistance movement is a progressive step, it is arguable that the union was damaged by it structurally and programmatically.[20]

In the Occupied Territories, the vacuum in national leadership created by Israeli repression spurred the women's social associations to revise their concept of their task and expand their efforts. Their guiding idea became *sumoud,* a concept with economic, social, cultural, and political dimensions, calling for larger income-generating projects as well as efforts to sustain national culture.

A feature common to women's social associations in the Occupied Territories and the diaspora has been their direction by urban, educated middle-class women. Centers and projects have been urban based, neglecting villages and camps where the majority of the population lives. The social associations have approached women of other classes as clients and beneficiaries rather than as full members with a role to play in choosing and running projects. Legal restrictions imposed by other governments (British, Jordanian, Israeli, Lebanese, etc.) have played a part in limiting their aims, structure, and membership.

Dissatisfaction with the social associations pressed a group of younger women into discussions from which, in 1978, emerged the first women's work committee in Ramallah (Palestinian Union of Women's Work Committee, PUWWC). Those who launched it came from much the same class background as the social association women, but they were younger, more highly educated, and more radical in their stand towards class and gender. Rita Giacaman describes some of them as politically committed, others as nationalistic and socially aware. Some had worked among women in camps and discovered that, if mobilization is to be effective, class boundaries have to be broken down: It must no longer be "*us* (bourgeois women) working for *them* (needy women)" (Siham Barghuti); women in all classes and milieus must become active participants in deciding their future. What was needed was a "mass organization directed towards the radical solution of the women's and the national problem."

One of the first actions of the Palestinian Union of Women's Work Committee (PUWWC) was a study of women workers in Ramallah factories intended to encourage them to join workers' unions.[21] Siham Barghuti explains that the short working life of most women workers convinced the PUWWC that they must turn their efforts to the housewife majority. Women in villages, camps, and work settings were encouraged to form work committees like the parent one, with membership limited to thirty so as to allow local leadership to emerge and local priorities to be expressed.

Three other committees have followed the first, expressing different political affiliations and sometimes stressing the recruitment of different sectors of women.[22] To overcome competition inherent in such ties, the four have formed "The Higher Council of Women," which also includes leaders of social associations. The council provides a loose unifying framework for the women's movement as a whole.

Without the option of becoming open members or cadres of resistance groups, women in the Occupied Territories have been forced to organizè on a segregated basis. This has given them space to define their own issues and to emphasize social developmental as distinct from resistance group priorities. At the same time, each of the four committees has continued to lend support to the goals of its group through mass mobilization in support of its policies. Policy differences among the constituent groups of the PLO sharpen divisions among the women even though all groups have similar programs.

The strategy of mass organization has taken the committees into rural and poor urban areas where poverty intensifies gender inequality and where families generally remain more conservative than among the urban middle class.

Although the GUPW in Lebanon aimed at incorporating all women, it fell short of this goal for a number of reasons, among them overcentralization, lack of training for local leaders, and interresistance group conflict. The GUPW's program in camps did contain a developmental component (adult literacy, health education, professional training, and income-generating projects), but activities such as these were neglected; priority went to political mobilization and emergency-related tasks. GUPW committees in camps represented resistance groups rather than women themselves. Built up from the grass-roots level, all committees in the Occupied Territories are better adapted to choosing projects that women at this level

need. National politics are no less important to women inside the Occupied Territories than to women outside, but so are projects such as providing dental care to children in village kindergartens. It is true that
women activists in the Occupied Territories have earned public respect
because, like men, they have been arrested and imprisoned; however,
respect also comes from recognition that they perform valued functions in
society.

Their wide mass basis and relative autonomy also give the four new
committees a strong position from which to develop ideas and action
around women's issues. In Lebanon during the period of PLO/resistance
movement autonomy the main slogan of the GUPW was, "Women will
achieve their liberation through participation in national struggle." In the
Occupied Territories women activists started with this slogan and continue to stress it in their publications, but they now realize that the
conditions in which rural and poor urban women live makes it "impossible to effectively mobilize them in national struggle." This discovery led
to goals different from those formulated from inside PLO/resistance movement structures, i.e., that "women need to organize around their own
problems" and to "adopt specific programs aimed at improving (their)
lot." In the diaspora women have been activated by the Palestinian resistance movement but not empowered; inside the Occupied Territories,
through developing their own structures and programs, women have
begun to define issues and articulate them in the national struggle.

Conditions of Israeli Occupation

After more than twenty years of occupation, Israeli repression figures in
these texts not in the form of denunciations but as a fact of daily existence. Though no one is unaffected, repression hits most systematically
those who try to "do something." Samiha Khalil, head of In'ash al-Usra,
has been imprisoned six times, has been placed under town arrest, and
during 1988–89 faced charges of incitement and sedition. Zahira Kamal, a
founding member of the first PUWWC, has spent six years under town
arrest. Siham Barghuti, another PUWWC founder, spent two and a half
years in prison after breaking town arrest.

To represent the women killed during the Intifada, the writers have
chosen the first martyr, Haniyyeh Ghazawneh, an unmarried young
woman from a poor family. Haniyyeh, twenty-five, was shot trying to

rescue a fourteen-year-old boy from an Israeli soldier. A spontaneous action such as this characterizes Palestinian women from before the British Mandate and doubtless has its parallel in other Arab countries under foreign occupation. Haniyyeh was not organized and had had little schooling. Her father had gone as a work migrant to the United States and her mother had raised the children alone, like thousands of other Palestinian mothers, hunched over a sewing machine.

Even before the Intifada, effects of the occupation on ordinary women were far-reaching. Many have faced difficulties like those Umm Ibrahim describes, forced into unskilled wage labor because of the imprisonment of husbands or sons. Family separation is a common experience of activist women: Siham Barghuti was separated from her husband when he was deported during their honeymoon. But nonactivists as well face separation from husband, children, and family as the economic subjugation of the Occupied Territories forces Palestinians to migrate in search of work. Reunions across such a wide diaspora are expensive and most families can afford them only rarely.

Curfew affects women in a special way, as Mona Rishmawi, a lawyer, points out in her narrative:

> During the Intifada, when a whole refugee camp is placed under curfew for up to forty days . . . a woman has to cope not only with food shortages, but with six to ten children out of school, underfoot, for extended periods of time in a two-room house.

Najah Manasrah, a psychiatric nurse, has to go looking for women traumatized by events because they do not know help is available. Assia Habash supplies kindergarten teachers with booklets telling parents how to deal with children terrified by Israeli nighttime raids.

The low level of medical, educational, and public services perpetuated by the occupation also affects women in specific ways. When villages are deprived of running water and electricity, domestic labor becomes more backbreaking. Lack of public transport in rural areas keeps girls out of secondary school and university, prolonging the disparity between urban and rural areas. The scarcity of medical services in rural areas increases the burden of caring for the sick, as well as keeping women last in terms of medical attention. Repression by national planning authorities and the closure of institutions and unions by the occupation means that not only can the population's need for services not be *met*, it cannot even be *measured*.[23]

Collected before and after the Intifada, some of these life histories reflect the escalation of repression that has been Israel's response. Tahani Ali, a student of physics at Birzeit University, entered the university in 1983 and was still there seven years later. "Indefinite closure is psychologically debilitating because it puts the future on hold"–the tone is reflective, almost clinical, as Tahani describes the changes caused in her own and other peoples' lives as repression intensifies: classes have been reorganized at off-campus locations, and students such as Tahani help teach schoolchildren the way she had been taught when her high school was closed years earlier; people knit sweaters for prisoners, boycott Israeli products, grow their own vegetables, and hoist Palestinian flags to the top of cypress trees; and Israeli soldiers enter villages wearing Arab kufiyas and driving Arab-owned cars to avoid detection. Tahani doesn't sound terrorized, though she sleeps in a dressing gown in case Israeli soldiers again break into her bedroom in the middle of the night. In her orderly account, they seem like creatures from another planet, unclassifiable: "What kind of mind will send you a bill for imprisoning your son?"

Women and Culture

Orientalism has nurtured a set of misperceptions about Arab/Middle Eastern/Muslim women that the role of Palestinian women in cultural production forces us to revise. The first of these is that schooling for women began thanks to the efforts of missionaries and colonial administrations. Within this misperception lies a second: that culture is identical with literacy and schooling, that is, lack of education means exclusion from culture.

Schools for girls already existed in Ottoman Palestine, and though many were mission-run schools (including the earliest, in 1837, in Jerusalem), by the end of the century there was an expansion in the number of Turkish-speaking government schools as well as private, communal ones (Christian, Muslim, and Jewish). In 1882 in Jerusalem there were thirteen girls' schools as compared to sixty-eight for boys; if only Muslim and Christian schools are counted, the gender imbalance is reduced: twelve schools for girls with 926 students as against twenty-five for boys with 1,221 students.[24] There were also girls in Ottoman government schools: in 1914, out of 8,249 students, 1,480 (19 percent) were girls.[25]

Under the British Mandate, public education suffered severe financial neglect. The Mandate government claimed that it was "handicapped in its endeavours to extend the field of female education both in towns and villages by the traditional disfavour with which, until comparatively recent times, the education of girls has been regarded by the majority of the population of Palestine."[26] Though it had pledged early to "equip all Arab areas with primary schools," the Mandate failed to fulfill even this limited aim. By 1944–45 government primary schools had been built in only 400 of Palestine's over 800 villages; of these, forty-six were for girls. Thus three kinds of inequality were reinforced: (1) between the Arab and Jewish sectors of the population (Arabs depending more than Jews on government schooling); (2) between Arabs in urban and rural areas (75 percent of Arabs were rural while all secondary schools were in towns); and (3) between male and female sectors of the Arab population (most rural Palestinians opposed sending girls to mixed schools). Of the development of education for Arabs that did take place under the Mandate, most was due to private and community funding. As for girls, the government's claim that the population disfavored their education is belied by the expansion of private girls' schools during Mandate times. Mogannam's notes on this subject point to the role of pioneer women educators. Some of the early women's associations also ran schools for girls.

The texts collected here awaken the reader to the way the double disadvantage of being Palestinian and female has spurred successive generations of women to succeed in educational endeavors. They also illustrate the sharp unevenness of opportunity between regions and classes, and the way different family contexts help or hinder.

Even before World War I, Mary Shehadeh's father in the coastal city of Jaffa encouraged her to read, sent her to the Friends' School in Ramallah, and would have let her go to Greece for medical training had not the war intervened. Samiha Khalil's father on the other hand pulled her out of that same mixed-sex school when she reached the tenth grade. Girls schools continued to be concentrated in Jerusalem, Ramallah, and the coastal cities; during the Mandate it became usual for middle-class girls in these regions, Muslim as well as Christian, to complete the entire school program. However, lack of a national university, both before and for many years after 1948, held back the professionalization of women, limiting access to the few whose families had sufficient means and a liberal enough outlook to let them study abroad.[27]

In this situation, family standards become a decisive factor. Several women in this book were lucky enough to have parents who encouraged their ambitions. Assia Habash's father supported her studying in Beirut in the fifties, in a mixed rather than a segregated college. In Zahira Kamal's household, limited savings were reserved for the education of her brothers, but Zahira's hunger strike convinced her father to let her attend a university in Egypt. In Najah Manasrah's case, it was her father who advised her to put emotions aside and do graduate work in the United States so that she and her husband could have a better life.

A disaster for Palestinians as a whole, 1948 had far-reaching effects on education for women. Pockets of deprivation remained, but in refugee camps free schooling from six to sixteen was offered to girls as well as boys, while state universities in most "host" countries became accessible. At the same time, the trauma of dispersion and economic deprivation altered family attitudes towards employment of women. Development in the Arab oil-producing countries opened up jobs for women with qualifications in teaching, health care, and public and business administration. As Palestinian women won esteem in such posts, their success helped make families readier to invest in, or agree to, university education for their daughters. Egypt's opening of its universities to Palestinian students particularly benefited women in Gaza and the West Bank whose families could not afford to send them to private universities elsewhere.

High educational achievement of an urban minority of Palestinian women must be set against low overall literacy levels. Women in adult literacy classes give some of the reasons: household chores, social pressure, poverty, sex discrimination, lack of transportation.

The stories of Samar Suleiman and Fadwa Hussein, both from small West Bank villages, illustrate the way poverty, lack of schools, and social prejudice interact to block ambitions. Both were fatherless and lived in villages that had no secondary schools for girls. Getting educated was a struggle: Samar's schooling stopped at age fifteen when she was sent to Brazil to marry. Fadwa graduated from Birzeit University only to find that there was no employment for her in Burham. In rural communities such as these, women are still obliged to marry young and bear many children; household labor is harder than in the cities, and there are still few jobs available for educated women.

Schools mean progress, no schools mean backwardness: this is deeply etched into the collective Palestinian consciousness. Like other Third World national liberation struggles, the Palestinian one carries within it aspirations for social, economic, and cultural development. An often-heard explanation for the Zionist victory in 1948 is "our backwardness," and this belief has added a nationalist drive to individual need for job qualifications. Esteem for education has led to Palestinians having the highest per capita proportion of university graduates in the Middle East.[28] What has been women's share in this drive? Dispersion makes it difficult to give a precise answer. However, in the five colleges of the Occupied Territories, women formed 36 percent of students in Birzeit, 37 percent in al-Najah, 45 percent in Bethlehem, 55 percent in Hebron, and 38 percent in Gaza in 1981–82.[29] These are high ratios and support the idea that getting to a university has gender as well as national implications for Palestinian women. Nonetheless, justifiable nationalist pride in this narrowing of the gender gap in the sphere of education can lead to other errors. One is to forget the still narrow demographic base from which women reach the university, with the secondary levels that prepare for it unavailable to most Palestinians, women in particular.[30]

A second error caused by enthusiasm for formal education is to perceive that noneducated women are excluded from politics and culture. Too strong an emphasis on the intellectual and professional achievements of today's Palestinian women risks obscuring the strong role noneducated women, especially peasants and nomads, have had in various types of cultural production.

One of these is oral poetry. Unnoticed by most anthropologists,[31] this is an art form in which women in many parts of the Middle East and North Africa have a long, skillful tradition, using it on public occasions as well as to express private emotions. Aisheh Shamlawi sings a dirgelike song as she relates how her land was confiscated. Salima Kumsiyya composes poem-songs to celebrate her son's release from prison:

I sat in bed . . . whispering the songs I was going to sing for Walid the next day. It is customary to sing on these occasions a combination of traditional songs and others one makes up for the event.

Mrs. Kumsiyya sings these songs for the relatives and neighbors who flock to their home to congratulate the reunited family and share in their joy.

Psychologically, such celebrations in which whole neighborhoods join and in which women lead the singing and dancing, help to relieve the bitterness of the occupation.

Arising from their exclusion from literacy, oral poetry used to be widespread among rural Palestinian women. Women in Bourj Barajneh camp (Lebanon) could produce impromptu verses satirizing neighbors or eulogizing martyrs. In camps, women known for their voices and song repertoires are still often invited to perform at mourning ceremonies. Granqvist's studies in Artas (near Jerusalem), carried out in the twenties and thirties, are unusual in their careful recording of women's songs. These were many, marking each phase of marriage, as well as other life-cycle transitions such as circumcision and death. Closely linked to poetry recitation, song and dance are arts that women in camps still practice.

Several international exhibitions have recently drawn attention to the art of embroidery practiced by peasant women in Palestine. Though drawing on motifs from Syria, Iran, and Cyprus, traditional Palestinian embroidery is a unique art form, with no close parallel in neighboring regions. Peasant women usually embroidered the ceremonial and ordinary dresses that formed their *jihaz* (trousseau), though centers such as Bethlehem and Ramallah produced them for sale. Colors, material, and designs of dresses expressed regional and village belonging, as well as family status and individual skill.[32] Embroidering onto dresses was never repetitive or mechanical, but required aesthetic taste and an almost architectural ability to fill space with lively yet harmonious combinations of color and pattern. After 1948, peasant embroidery was revived through women's efforts and associations. Other handicrafts such as pottery and straw and rug weaving used to be practiced by women in rural areas.

The Family: Change without Rupture

Inevitably the women whose life stories are collected here talk about their families, offering valuable insights into changing Palestinian family relations from early Mandate times until today. The use of terms such as "evolution" or "traditional/modern" would only obscure the complexity and unevenness of what is happening. Two main points seem to emerge: families remain the basic framework of everyone's life, and of women's in a special way; yet conformity to norms of control over women has been breaking down since early in the century under numerous pressures, among them women's own struggles. Israeli occupation seems to have weakened the patriarchal dimensions of the family, for example through land confiscation and forced labor migration, while at the same time reinforcing its necessity as a vehicle of economic and psychological survival, of nationalism and resistance.

Within the family's cushioning role are contradictory implications. Kinship ties help people survive under prolonged occupation. A man faced with an unpayable court fine is helped out by brothers; a family whose home is demolished is taken in by kin. Has kinship also helped to diffuse anger, delaying its explosion against the occupation? For women too there are contradictions: their role in sustaining their families becomes politicized, charged with national meaning; still honor as "heroic mothers" does not lead to empowerment.

Control of women in the historic Palestinian Arab family took different forms depending on their marital status. Daughters were carefully guarded after the onset of puberty and married at an early age in parentally arranged unions that reproduced clan, class, and sectarian ties. Such control was justified by the language of honor, making a girl's "purity" an issue that concerned not only her close and extended family but also the community at large. Women's behavior after marriage was also a matter for public concern, but to a lesser degree. In this phase the responsibilities of mothering were the main means of control, though pressures against women living independently, outside the guardianship of a man, also played a part. This dual control system is still in place in many sectors of Palestinian society. One of the values of the life histories in this volume is that they offer an inside view of family life in all its structural and personal variety, in the process of change.

Class, sect, and region appear to be critical factors influencing family attitudes towards its female members, with middle-class Christians of the coastal cities among the first to adopt liberal practices, and with conservatism appearing most resistant in the rural hinterland, provincial towns, and among lower middle social strata. Implicit in the degree of independence that women win from their families is their acceptance of certain limits and a strategic sense of which struggles can be won, and of when and how to wage them. Social changes adopted as part of national struggle are the main legitimating context for women's individual struggles.

A striking change in women's lives has been the opening up of the phase of adolescence, filling this formerly brief period with activities, experiences, and contacts beyond the family. Education was the earliest and most legitimate of such activities; already one can see its effects in the life of Mary Shehadeh who begins writing for women's magazines while still a schoolgirl, and who meets the man she eventually marries through her writing. Several leaders of the Mandate period, for example Sadej Nassar and Ruqeyya Huri, took up nationalist activities as adolescents and continued them after marriage. Samiha Khalil made her first nationalist speech while still in school (a common theme in recollections), and though hers was an arranged marriage, her husband shared her nationalist outlook and did not oppose her public work. Marriage did not lose its compulsory moral character, but at least in the urban middle classes what women did before marriage began to affect its timing, the choice of spouse, and the conjugal relationship.

Unlike Mary Shehadeh, the older women in this collection come from inland towns and villages where social customs and culture changed more slowly than in the coastal cities. Umm Ayyash's marriage at the age of twelve years is a reminder of the peasant practice of betrothing girls at the onset of puberty or even before.[33] The age of girls at first marriage rose only gradually among camp populations; married in 1952, Umm Ibrahim was only fourteen when she was "asked for" by another refugee family from her village of Beit Jibreen. The research of Najah Manasrah as well as the histories of two much younger women, Fadwa Hussein and Samar Suleiman, demonstrate that in West Bank villages today marriage pressures still begin in early adolescence. Samar explains:

> A girl's reputation is only safe once she is married, so our mother had to agree to our marrying young. It was our father who had the authority to choose our husbands, although he had neglected us for so long.

Fadwa's story shows that land inheritance still plays a role in marriage making. Because her father had left her some land, one of her paternal uncles, to keep it in the family, pressured her to marry his son. Fadwa managed to avoid this particular marriage, but the lack of job opportunities in her village meant that her only escape was into another one. In conservative milieus such as villages and camps, girls may be able to reject specific matches proposed by their families, but they cannot for long reject marriage itself. The strength of family ties and the lack of alternative bases of economic and social independence means that for girls at this class level, rupture with their families is not a real option. Even young women who can easily find employment seldom carry conflict to the point of leaving home.

Even widows are not immune from marriage pressures. Umm Ayyash complains:

> A woman living alone is never left in peace. . . . I had to actively fight the notion that I was available. I wore black for seven years . . . but many were not daunted.

The force of social pressure for marriage in small communities means that families sometimes, as in Samar's first marriage, accept unsuitable husbands for their daughters. Most parents take great pains to investigate the background and character of prospective spouses, but the old argument that parents choose more wisely than inexperienced girls often proves fallacious. However, families that pressure their daughters to marry their candidates also accept responsibility for the marriage's success. In case of conflict or bad treatment, they intervene; if the marriage breaks down, they help out financially.

After 1948 increased access to university education led more Palestinian women into professional work, and both education and professional work seem to introduce types of revision in the marriage institution. All the women introduced in this volume who have gone through university or postsecondary training have either married men of their own.choosing or remained single. Apparently slight, the distinction between the right to *refuse* a spouse and the right to *choose* him is still a boundary between the acceptable and the unacceptable in many Palestinian milieus.

In arranged marriages, the main selection criteria was (and is) the reputation of the families involved and the similarity of their socioeconomic status.[34] As women gain in educational and occupational status, they begin to insist on compatibility of character and outlook. Siham Barghuti emphasizes this: "I was happy to have found someone who shared my outlook on life and was also committed to our people." Rita Giacaman says of her husband: "We initially got together because we had the same approach to medicine; both of us believed in primary health care."

Sociologists of the modernization school would doubtless find evidence in these histories that the traditional extended form of the Palestinian Arab family is being pushed out by the modern nuclear form based on "love marriage." But such a reading distorts a more complex and contradictory reality, obscuring such things as the continuing importance of kin ties in politics and the economy, the many kinds of exchange between parental and filial households, the continuation of marriages imposed on girls in certain milieus, or the fact that women who choose their own marriage partners still have to justify their choices in rational rather than emotional terms and obtain a family consensus. We are very far here from the love marriage and nuclear family unit of the family studies textbooks.

The reciprocal relation between women's actions in the community and their status in the family is well conveyed by Zahira Kamal's detailed and subtle portrait of her own family. After her father's death, as the eldest child and only wage earner, Zahira becomes the effective head of the household, installing a democratic regime and resisting marriage pressures for herself and for her younger sisters. Confined by town arrest, Zahira uses her home as a center from which to build the women's work committees, helped by her family. Eventually she is accepted in the role of household head by her larger kin group:

> When decisions need to be made, I am asked to represent my family just like my father would have been, and my opinions are given equal weight with those of all the male heads of the family.

In all these cases, the value of a woman's contribution to the community, whether through political or professional activity, changes her relations with her family and husband, strengthening her influence and creating grounds for a larger degree of independence. However, the line between pressing for legitimate, recognized rights and "going too far" is a delicate one among a people whom repression has made more attached than ever to their cultural roots and who are inherently inclined to pin on women the responsibility in symbolizing tradition. Women have to choose carefully the grounds and arguments for unconventional action.

Another contradiction: The spread of education and professional employment means that some women at least have other options besides marriage and motherhood. Yet the emphasis on mothering produced by historical and cultural factors has hardly weakened. On the contrary, human losses incurred through the national struggle have added a new argument in favor of large families.

The various ways Palestinian women act out their mothering roles are well displayed: Umm Ayyash, Umm Ibrahim, and Salima Kumsiyya are immediately recognizable as archetypal mothers. Women also extend their mothering into the community at large, in response to poverty and suffering—Amal Khreisheh feels guilty for spending time away from her two children, yet she is out there, asking for maternity leave rights for other women, supporting female strikers, and holding summer camps so that other mothers have some time off. But there is also criticism here of the way social pressures on women to fulfill the maternal ideal stifles their ambition and creativity. Wafa al-Baher Abu Ghosh points to this problem, one certainly not exclusive to Palestinian or Arab women, but experienced by them with particular intensity:

> People's expectations of females, that their primary purpose in life is to be wives and mothers, leaves a deep impression on women. It nips their ambition in the bud. They spend their teenage years, and even their university years, dreaming about marriage.

Wafa has rosy dreams for her children, but reacts with a courageous assertion of personal ambition: "I have to make something of myself. I would like to be somebody important in the future" (for example, minister of information in a Palestinian state), but now that she has had two children (both under the age of four), she admits that marriage and child rearing are harder than she had thought and modifies her ambition accordingly.

These life histories also call attention to the role friends and neighbors play in women's lives, and the importance of networking for society at large. This is useful since too many studies of Middle Eastern women have made assumptions about the closed boundaries of families and women's imprisonment within them. When Umm Ayyash's husband dies, she joins forces with another widow, who helps her with child care and selling her embroidery. We see friends and neighbors helping the Kumsiyyas rebuild their home. The close ties forged between women prisoners are used to build structures of individual and collective resistance.

There is an Arab saying, "Prison makes a man." Prison for women, with its implications of sexual exposure and assault, its total severance from family protection, produces a status transformation of a particularly intense kind. By now a high proportion of women in the Occupied Territories have passed through Israeli interrogation centers and prisons. Prison is a place where Palestinian women from different regions meet and where boundaries between more and less educated women are broken down. After such rigorous experiences, women cannot return to being the protected wards of their families.

The picture of the contemporary Palestinian family that emerges from these pages is of a highly flexible unit that remains in place partly because it has been able to absorb the many kinds of shocks to which it has been exposed, not least those related to its control over women. Earlier studies have tended to overdo the image of women as pawns of clan politics and prisoners of domesticity. Here they are observed in a wide range of actions—building associations and committees, joining the resistance, protesting prison conditions, criticizing neglect and archaism in school and health services—in other words, taking public action. Yet this radical departure in what women do is carried on from a firm base of family relations, rearranged to accommodate women's legitimate rights, yet retaining its own claims. Many political actions by women grow out of, and are sanctioned by, specific wife or mother ties; but family ties that draw women into political action can also be withdrawn. How to institutionalize the gains they have made through their work in the national struggle and how to prevent themselves being redomesticated, as British and American women were after World War II, are current topics of discussion among women.

Conclusion: When to Raise Women's Issues?

Only a few of the women whose life histories are presented here would call themselves feminists, yet their narratives reveal many implicit and explicit forms of struggle: for their own or their daughters' education; against arranged marriage; to bring up their own children; to enter a "man's" profession; to form or join a public body (committee, union, resistance group, etc.). Gains have been made. On the personal level, constraints on women's freedom and mobility have been loosened; on the collective level, a large part of Palestinian society admits that women are an "active force that cannot be ignored" (Mona Rishmawi). Yet these texts also suggest the individual, fragmented nature of women's struggles, as well as reticence towards articulating women's issues and raising public demands. Up to now, the most publicly acclaimed women's leaders, models for the rest, have been heroic women, those who challenge the occupation or take on national work without diminishing their care for husbands, children, and kin. Such women have not encouraged discussion of women's issues, nor have they called for change in gender relations, family law, or the division of household labor. The specificity of the Palestinian struggle has enforced its priority both theoretically and practically: by making discussion of women's issues appear premature; by overwhelming women with emergency nurturing tasks arising out of confrontation; and by dispersing women activists between different resistance factions.

Sensitivity to women's issues becomes more explicit among some of the younger women presented here, whose contacts with women at other class levels than their own has made them more aware of "engendered structures," ways in which women are systematically disadvantaged. As women's work committees spread to villages, they encounter cases of girls' schooling ending prematurely, overbearing natalist pressures, female disinheritance, high rates of female infant mortality and malnutrition, and women who bear twelve children in thirteen years of marriage. In urban areas girls work in sweatshop conditions arranged between parents and factory owners. Defining stands against such problems is a challenge for the women's movement as it moves into a stage of mass organization. A consensus already exists among the leaders of the four committees that women must organize around their own issues within the process of national struggle. The problem is to decide when and how to move on from this general position. Selecting key issues with a wide basis of popular support is an essential preliminary to the formation of a women's lobby that can present coherent demands to the national leadership.

The Intifada has had the effect of bringing nearer the prospect of a Palestinian state; already gender equality has been written into the state's declaration of principles (November 1988), without protest from the religious wing of the national movement. This is an indication of the legitimacy of the Palestinian women's movement, the fruit of a long struggle. Yet women such as Mona Rishmawi, a lawyer, are well aware that constitutional rights are meaningless without a strong women's lobby, rooted in a mass movement and armed with a carefully worked-out set of demands.

Working on a "feminist agenda" poses many difficulties and pitfalls. First is the problem of timing: paradoxically the Intifada involves women more deeply in caring for the victims of repression at the same time as it brings closer the time when women's issues must be raised. There are the dangers of splitting the women's movement into more and less feminist wings, and of alienating the support of parts of the national movement or public opinion. Further, as Mona Rishmawi points out, women's issues will have to be negotiated within the context of Palestinian factional conflict and coalition. She asks, "Where will women fit into this system?" Will women members of the various factions push women's issues or downplay them? How will the factions weigh their women members in the balance with a tactical need for alliance with the religious wing? Rishmawi sees hope in the awareness of women leaders that they need to plan for change but warns them:

. . . if women do not pressure politicians and do not get seriously involved in power politics early, their contribution will be forgotten.

O N E

Coping with the Loss of Palestine

In 1933, a Palestinian Christian woman delivered a prophetic speech from the pulpit of the Mosque of Omar in Jerusalem in which she said, "We see before us the shadow of our complete extermination as a nation, and eviction from the land on which we and our fathers and ancestors have lived for centuries" (Mogannam 1937: 98). What the speaker had predicted and feared came to pass. The establishment of the state of Israel led to the disruption of Palestinian society and the creation of a large refugee population.

The issue of refugees complicated the Israeli-Palestinian problem both because of the Palestinian attachment to the land they were forced to leave, and because of the enormous collective losses they had sustained. After the 1948 war, 880,000 acres of Arab-owned land was taken over by the Israeli Custodian of Absentee Property (Peretz, Spring 1954). Of the 370 new Jewish settlements established between 1948 and the beginning of 1953, 350 were on absentee property. Ten thousand shops, businesses, and stores were left in Jewish hands when Arabs left their towns and villages. Nearly 95 percent of Israel's olive groves were Arab owned, and the citrus fruit trees left behind accounted for 29 percent of Israel's earnings from export in 1951 (Peretz, Autumn 1954: 403, 404). Peretz confesses that "It would have been impossible to double the country's population during the first three years of its existence without utilizing abandoned Arab property" (Peretz, Autumn 1954: 405).

In contrast, living conditions for the Palestinians deprived of these assets were harsh. At the end of June 1953, there were 871,748 refugees depending on relief from the United Nations. The refugees formed a substantial addition to several countries ill equipped to handle their needs (Baster 1954: 55).

World Bank reports show that unemployment of the refugee population stood at more than 50 percent until 1954. The influx of unskilled laborers, former farmers, depressed the wage scales to half in some areas, and a third in others (Hazboun and al-Salihi, *al-Kateb*, June 1984: 24). As a result of these conditions, many Palestinian wage earners were forced to emigrate in search of work.

Population shifts in the area continued after 1967. In 1982, despite the high Arab birthrate, the West Bank had 110,000 fewer Palestinians than it had in 1967. The primary cause of population decline since 1967 has been Palestinians seeking refuge in the East Bank of Jordan or emigrating in search of work or to join relatives. A disproportionately large percentage of the emigrants between 1967 and 1980 were fifteen- to twenty-nine-year-old males (Peretz 1986: 89, 90).

Emigration affects the family in many ways. The vacuum created by the absence of the person traditionally considered head of the household is normally filled by the males of the family when important decisions have to be made, but Tamari (1981) found that in households where the husband was away—at work, in exile, or in prison—it was the woman who acted as the bearer of tradition in the family. Her role tended to have a conservative influence, based primarily on holding the family together (Graham-Brown 1983: 249).

If women live away from their in-laws, they have to be very careful about the reputation of their daughters. If the wives and their children live with their in-laws and are financially dependent on them, they have to account to the extended family for every move. No matter how long the man is absent, he still has the right to make major decisions affecting his children's lives, and he also has a say on whom his daughters marry. It appears that when men emigrate, or are absent for long periods of time, women and their female children pay for the emigration in one way or another, as the story of Samar Suleiman (and later Haniyyeh Ghazawneh) show.

The General Assembly of the United Nations Organization adopted a resolution on 11 December 1948, stating that all refugees be allowed to return to their homes and properties or be given compensation if they chose not to. That resolution was confirmed fifteen times between 1948 and 1967, but Israel refused to comply (Dakkak 1983: 67–68).

Today, 15 percent of the inhabitants of the West Bank are refugees, while 70 percent of Gaza's inhabitants live in refugee camps. There are over 5 million Palestinians living worldwide. Of those, 2.2 million now live in historic Palestine under Israeli control (Hajjar, Rabbani, and Beinin 1989: 105). But no matter where Palestinians went or what they did after 1948, they were essentially coping with the refugee experience: rejecting it, accepting it, allowing it to weigh them down or to inspire them.

Most of the women or the families of the women in this book had to leave Palestine as refugees; some lived in refugee camps for years, while others with professional credentials or privileged backgrounds were able to pull their families out of poverty. In this chapter, four women talk about how they coped or helped others cope with the psychological and economic effects of the disruption of Palestinian society.

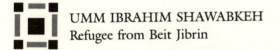 UMM IBRAHIM SHAWABKEH
Refugee from Beit Jibrin

Since the 1948 exodus, Umm Ibrahim has never been able to pull herself or her family out of the cycle of poverty. She describes the hardships she and her children endured in a refugee camp and explains how the 1967 occupation worsened her condition. Umm Ibrahim has some harsh words about the Palestinian upper classes, but sees her refugee status as a positive political contribution to the Palestinian struggle.

The village I was born in is called Beit Jibrin.* It is only a few kilometers west of here, just inside Israel. It doesn't exist anymore. The Israelis destroyed it after 1948 so there would be no possibility of our going back.

*Kitty Warnock interviewed Umm Ibrahim Shawabkeh in Arabic with an interpreter who knew Umm Ibrahim a little and had introduced her. The interviews were recorded and took place during three visits to her home, probably October–November 1984. Kitty translated her words herself as she transcribed the tape and edited the account for clarity and brevity.

Umm Ibrahim Shawabkeh in her refugee camp. Photo by Kitty Warnock

When I remember our life there it does not seem real—it is just like something you see on television.

I was twelve in 1948 when the Jews drove us out. We fled from our village when the soldiers came and started shooting people. My grandparents did not want to leave their home; they hid in a cave near the village and the soldiers found them and shot them. My father took my mother and me and my seven sisters into the hills. We hid for a month or so and then collected with people from other villages in a camp UNRWA set up, near where we are now. It was just tents all crowded together.[1]

At first we had nothing except the food UNRWA gave us. Then gradually, the men began to find work, mostly stonecutting. As there were no sons in my family, I had to go and work on the land for local people. Although we refugees were Palestinians, just like them, and came from villages just like theirs only a short distance away, some of the local people despised us and treated us very badly. Others were good, and though they were almost as poor as us, they paid us what they could—sometimes wheat, sometimes money.

In 1952 we met another family from our village [in Palestine], and they asked for me to marry their son. I went to live with them in their one room. My husband had a few sheep he had saved from the village. Sometimes he took them to graze in the land between the Israeli and Jordanian borders. It was forbidden land, and the Jordanian police put him in prison. Later he was put in prison for political reasons. The Jordanian army really did a lot of the Israelis' work for them! I was proud of my husband and didn't mind his leaving us, although it meant I had to work. I was proud to work; it's honorable to look after yourself, much better than begging. I worked at harvesting, or as a servant in the surrounding villages when there was no harvest.

When I was working, I had to leave the children alone in the house all day. None of my sisters or neighbors could look after them because they had children and enough problems of their own. We were refugees, and our families were scattered, and we were poor, so each family had to concentrate on itself, on God and on itself. I'd leave the house at 3:30 in the morning, come back in the evening, talk to the children for a bit and that's all. I never had the time to speak with anyone else, nobody did. There was no electricity or running water in the camp until a few years ago. We had to fetch water from a spring two or three kilometers away and carry it back on our heads. You might have to go six or ten times a day to get enough to do any washing with. It was impossible to keep the children clean.

At the time of the 1967 war, my husband was in prison and our eldest son, who was fourteen, was working in Amman. My husband was released and came home, but we didn't know whether our son Ibrahim was dead or alive. The Israelis came to the camp to take a census[2] and my husband thought, "I don't want to be counted here, in case they don't let me go over to Jordan, and I must look for Ibrahim who is all alone there." So he disappeared and hid in the hills.

After three months he came back and found a job, but eleven days later the Israelis found out about him and came to search for him. They drove around the camp announcing a curfew over their loudspeakers, then they rounded up all the men in the mosque to count them. That night they came here and threatened to blow up the house. I didn't believe they would because I knew they wouldn't dare damage UNRWA property. They just wanted to frighten us. They searched the place, and then took my husband away.

That was a desperate time for me. I have seven children, and with my husband away there would be nobody to bring them water to drink, and not even enough money for salt. I had to get my husband out of prison. I decided to go and ask at the military training camp near here. A neighbor pleaded with me not to go. He said that the Israeli author- ities had killed sixteen members of his family, and would kill me and my husband too. "Let them," I said. "I'm no better than other people they've killed." I put myself in Allah's hands and walked straight to the camp.

There was a celebration going on there. The guard was watching it and he didn't see me coming. When I touched his arm, he jumped round and stuck his gun against my chest. "How did you get here? You must have dropped out of the sky!"

"No, I came up the road. Why are you frightened of me?"

Other soldiers clustered around, all pointing their guns at me. Israelis, if they suspect a bird in the sky, they'll shoot it. One of the soldiers spoke Arabic, and after I explained that I wanted my husband, he asked, "The prisoner you are looking for, is he civil or political?"

"I don't know."

"Was it police or soldiers who came to get him?"

"Soldiers."

"Well, you have three choices. You go back home to your camp, or you can go and ask at the military headquarters in Hebron, or you can stay here and be killed."

Though it was dark and snowy, I walked to Hebron. When I arrived at the headquarters, I found that the training camp guards had been on the phone to them and that they were ready with a lot of questions for me. My husband hadn't admitted anything, and they wanted to trap me into saying that he was a fedai' (a commando). I was taken to Captain Itzak. He started off, "I was born in Jerusalem and grew up playing with Arab children, so I understand you. Tell me about your life from the begin- ning." I answered, "I ask for God's mercy, not yours. Release my hus- band, so that he can look after his children. You have got three choices: you can put his whole family in prison, or you can shoot us all, or you can let him out."

"Are you threatening me in my own office? Be careful!"

"Hush, you said you understand Arabic, so please listen. I'm just an ordinary person. I am not the Arab states. I didn't come here to make war on you. I came here because of my children. If you put them in prison, they will at least be fed; if you shoot them, they will be at peace after their difficult lives; if you release their father, he will look after them."

"Go away, and I swear to God that if you ever return to Hebron we'll never release him."

Three days later my husband came home. Half an hour after he'd been in the house, Israeli intelligence officers arrived and burst into the house.

"Who looked after the children while your husband was in prison?"

"We just survived on what our neighbors gave us and on the UNRWA rations."

"When the sweet-vendor came, who gave the kids money to buy sweets?"

"Some kind neighbors did."

"Why not tell us the truth? A man came down from the hills and gave you money. Arabs are famous for their generosity, aren't they? It would be shameful for them to let a woman and her children starve. Are you afraid of what the neighbors will think and say when they hear a strange man was coming to the house? Don't worry, we won't tell anyone."

I knew what they were trying to do. They wanted me to say that a fedai' had been helping the family, which would prove that my husband belonged to the resistance. Of course I didn't say any of the things they wanted, and they had to leave him free.

A month later my husband went to the hospital for an operation he needed on his back because of what Israeli investigators had done to him in prison. I went to Amman to fetch our son Ibrahim. I got permission from the Military Government for him to come back to the West Bank under the family reunion rules, because we needed him to support the family. I knew Jordan a little, because I had sometimes been there to work during the harvesting season, but I had no idea where Ibrahim was. I had to go around from one refugee camp to another, asking for him. When I found him he was living in a miserable state. We have no relatives there, so he had to live at his work, and eat whatever people gave him. He didn't know what had happened to us or whether he would ever see us again. He had joined the political part of the PLO, but when we explained that he was needed at home, they let him come back.

Those events took place eighteen years ago, but things haven't changed much since then. My husband is disabled and can't work. There are very few jobs anyway since the Lebanon war. Ibrahim gets what he can as a taxi and delivery driver. None of my children was able to travel to the Arabian [Persian] Gulf to earn money because they weren't educated.[3]

How could they concentrate on their studies at school? We were too poor. We couldn't buy any of the notebooks, rulers, and bags you need, and the children were ashamed of not having shoes in those early days. With so many difficulties at home they couldn't study well, though I tried to encourage them. We need education now that we haven't got our land.

My second son is serving a ten-year prison sentence. That has made me think a lot about our Palestinian society. I see him in prison and know about the torture and humiliation he suffers. He gave himself, I gave him, for the good of others, while his family hardly has enough to eat. If I saw the sons of blacksmiths, carpenters, and doctors, all working together side by side, I'd gladly join them. But as it is, the rich do nothing but sit comfortably in their houses, while the poor have to fight and pay. I give everything and the rich don't give me a crust of bread. They're in their luxurious glass-walled houses, and they don't care that I've been living with my twelve children in a two-room UNRWA hut for thirty years.

Look at this house—do you see how the mud washes down from the land into the room every time it rains? I look at the rich people in their beautiful clean houses sitting in the shade behind their curtains with their clean children; and I look at the poor, ill from having too many children, their feet all cracked because they haven't got shoes—look at my daughter's. Every time I walk past these big new buildings I pray to God, "Please help me build a nice house for my family, like you helped them." The Arab governments should help us, and the landowners, and rich people. We poor Palestinians haven't had help from anywhere, neither to live or to fight for our land. Rich people only think of themselves. A rich man here wouldn't even help his own brother. This is what has made us weak. We're free because we don't have a government; but we're free like sheep on a mountain without a shepherd. We find our food wherever we can, and no one looks after us.

As far as I can see, even the women's committee I belong to doesn't do much. I am a member of the prisoner's committee. Apart from me, all the members are educated women. They like to talk a lot and drink tea and seem important. But in the first four months I was a member, all we did was go to the home of one prisoner and wish his family well, and I had to pay for my own transport! I'd like to ask them, "Don't you see me? I'm a prisoner's mother, and so poor that I can't afford my bus fare—why don't you do something to help me?"

I have taken part in one useful thing. In the summer of 1984, my son was moved to a new prison, Jnaid. The prisoners went on a hunger strike, protesting their living conditions. A lot of women went to demonstrate in support of them. I was the only one from this refugee camp, but there were about a hundred and fifty altogether, and other women joined us during the day. We were Muslims, Christians, and Jews all together. It shows that it's not religion that divides people. I went without food for twelve days. The only time I felt ill was when one of the prisoners was released, because his sentence was finished, and he came and described what the conditions were like inside. It wasn't hard for me not to eat; all the time I kept thinking about the men inside. We have to feel with them—in our stomachs as well as in our minds.

There will never be a solution to our problem unless the PLO, or the Arab governments, and the Palestinians themselves can unite. I cry when I think of my children having a life like mine. I'm not interested in political events in Israel; I don't think they will make any difference to us. Israel is like a snake—it can shed one skin and grow another, but it's still the same snake, and a snake is never your friend.

Now the Israelis are talking about destroying the camps and resettling us. I'll refuse to move, whatever they offer me. As long as I am here, I hope to return to my home; but if they destroy the camps there will be no more hope. We'll lose the right to call ourselves refugees, we'll forget that we are Palestinian. We prefer to stay here, exposed to the sun and the wind, and keep the name "Palestinian," rather than live in a comfortable house somewhere else and lose our name.

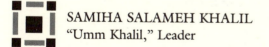

SAMIHA SALAMEH KHALIL
"Umm Khalil," Leader

Moved by the sight of refugees lining up in front of UNRWA to receive food rations, Khalil started a series of societies to help them. Her latest enterprise, In'ash al-Usra, became the largest of its kind on the West Bank. Mrs. Khalil talks about her childhood under British rule, her nationalist activities against British influence in Jordan in the 1950s, and the closure of the society by the Israelis in 1988. Khalil also comments on her impending trial for what Israelis call "incitement," and what she calls her struggle for freedom and independence.

I was born in 1923 in the village of Anabta.* My mother was a child at the end of the nineteenth century when Palestine was a part of the Ottoman Empire. My mother's uncle Basheer Bek was the governor of Nablus. When he walked through the streets of Nablus people stood up, and his permission was requested before any marriage was finalized. My maternal grandfather was a feudal landlord, a member of the Touqan family. In those days, only the upper class could afford education and they generally educated only their sons. My grandfather wanted to educate his daughter, but because of his status, he did not send her to the kuttab¹ with other children, but "summoned" a private tutor. Grandfather explained to the tutor that Mother should be taught "her religion and her duties." He stipulated that his daughter was to learn the Quran, arithmetic, hygiene, and good housekeeping—orally. Writing in those days was considered unnecessary, even dangerous for women; it could be used for writing love letters.

Mother's teacher was quite enterprising. She taught her spelling in a singsong manner. Each word had a tune, and long words were like songs. My mother could recite ten thousand verses of poetry by heart even when she did not know what the alphabet looked like. Mother taught herself to read when I was an adult. Some of my most cherished possessions were the letters she sent me in her own handwriting, congratulating me on the birth of each of my children. She used the Quran, which she knew by heart, to look up words she could not spell. As a result, some of the spelling was archaic, but she wrote lovely letters. When my oldest son Khalil was married, I made him a scrapbook of family mementos, including some of Mother's letters. The letters disappeared in 1974 when Khalil's luggage was lost on a trip between Amman and Algiers. I wince every time I think of that loss.

*This profile was compiled from a number of interview with Umm Khalil between March 1981 and June 1986 and one interview in August 1989. Mr. Khalil sent me several letters in 1990 to update the interviews. The main interview of 1986 was tape recorded, and Mrs. Khalil had the manuscript typed and returned it to me. I used that, my notes, the publications of the society, and Mrs. Khalil's writing to write her story. I asked her to tell me about her life. All the interviews were conducted in Arabic.

Mrs. Khalil gave me much more detailed information about the society than I was able to use because of space constraints. A very important part of Mrs. Khalil's contributions to the National Guidance Committee (NGC), as the only female in the twenty-two-member committee (formed to oppose the Camp David Accords), is not included because the committee, suppressed in early 1982, is still "illegal" to the Israeli authorities.

Samiha Salameh Khalil gave her first public speech in 1936 at age thirteen to protest British policies in Palestine. Here she is giving a speech to graduating vocational classes, 1985. Photo by Orayb Najjar

My mother, a city girl, was given in marriage to Yussef Mustafa al-Kubbaj, a "farmer" from the village of Anabta. Father was not really a farmer, but a landowner, and he was mayor for thirty-six years. His origin rankled Mother just the same. I used to hear her complain that fate had made her marry a farmer. Besides, Mother disliked the way girls were treated in villages. Anabta had no schools for girls, so she prevailed upon Father to let us stay with her sisters in Nablus, and they sent us to a convent school for kindergarten and first grade.

One day Father visited us in school and noticed that when we heard church bells, we folded our hands in preparation for Christian prayer. He took us out of school on the spot. Again, Mother insisted that we go to school and convinced my father to move from Anabta to Toulkarm. Toulkarm was only ten kilometers from Anabta, but it was considered shameful to leave the village of one's birth. My father never recovered from the move, which diminished his status. He complained that when he called "Mohammad!" in Anabta, thirty young men rushed to his side ready to serve him. In Toulkarm, he was respected, but it was not the same.

Mother flourished in her new surroundings. She joined the Toulkarm branch of the Arab Women's Union whose president was Wadia Khartabeel, originally from Lebanon. The union sewed clothes for the poor and collected donations for nationalist causes. I studied in a government-run school until the seventh grade.

The year was 1936, and those were troubled times in Palestinian history. One day, I heard that a demonstration was planned against the Balfour Declaration and the flow of Jewish immigrants into the country. What we chanted that day gives an indication of the state of mind we were in. We were under British occupation, yet we expected the British director of military operations and intelligence in the War Office, John Dill [1934–36], to solve our problems for us when we chanted:

Dabbirha ya Mr. Dill/ Yemkin a'a eedak bithill (Please fix it, Mr. Dill. Maybe it will be solved at your hands).[2]

Demonstrating women always ended up at the mosque. That day I gave my first public political speech at age thirteen, one I wrote with the help of my older brother the night before. I was used to giving speeches at school, but this was the first time I had spoken to the general community. No men heard me in that segregated demonstration, but I was very proud of myself, and that night I relived the events of the day with great satisfaction.

Despite the relative virtues of Toulkarm, it was no metropolis. There were no schools for girls beyond the seventh grade, so mother enrolled me as a boarder at the Friends Girls' School in Ramallah where I studied until the ninth grade. When my father learned that the tenth grade was coeducational he made me stay at home, and hired a private tutor to prepare me for the British Matriculation Exam (GCE).

One day I returned from a private lesson to find my family preparing for a huge dinner party. At first no one bothered to tell me why my mother looked so upset. Then my brother said, "For God's sake tell her, after all it concerns her." I learned that the feast was intended for the notables of our family, who were to be consulted on the suitability of the man my father had chosen for me to marry. I was sixteen and capable of dramatics. I sat on the floor and threw a fit—but it was useless to protest. To make matters worse, Father would not allow me to take the exam now that I was engaged.

While preparations for my engagement party were under way, I suggested to my father that the chairs be placed around the stand of the bride and groom, instead of facing them in rows. He was enraged that I could "presume to have an opinion" about my engagement party.

I was not to meet my future husband until my wedding day. We were married in 1940 in a traditional ceremony. My father handed me over to the notables of the groom's family, but his words were addressed to my future mother-in-law: "I am taking this jewel out of my heart and placing her in your hands. Please take care of her. I am giving her to you and not to your son. Please make sure that he takes care of her." My father spoke with tears streaming down his cheeks. I cried and so did everybody. It was right that he addressed his words to my future mother-in-law. In the old extended family, the mother-in-law was the real head of the household, and my groom, like me, was only a minor actor in the affair. The marriage was an alliance between two clans; we were lucky that our families had chosen well for us. Although I can see that arranged marriages can be oppressive to women, families often choose good partners for their children, and in the past used to make sure husbands treated their wives well.

A number of changes have taken place since my marriage. In the name of modernity, we are no longer practicing a number of traditions that were designed to protect women, but we have not replaced them with legal safeguards for women. Today, many women are defenseless, with no legal protection, and no brother or uncle with the authority to make sure a husband knows his place.

The Arab-Israeli war of 1948 turned our family life upside down and was a turning point for me as it was for other Palestinians. We were living in al-Majdal. Fighting broke out while we were visiting my husband's family in Taibeh, and we were unable to return home. We tried several routes and ended up in Gaza with relatives in a house that had to shelter thirty-one of us. The only driver we found in Gaza refused to take us back to al-Majdal because it was too dangerous. It was then that we realized the extent of our tragedy. We had lost our home and land. Twenty-six days after we arrived in Gaza, I gave birth to my son Samir, my fourth child.

I soon realized that there were people much worse off than us. Whereas we had our relatives, and had a roof over our heads, they had nowhere to go. I'd stand on the balcony and see women with a chicken or a goat or two stream past. Others who did not have these luxuries tried to sell their jewelry or their embroidered dresses for food. The most destitute women were trying to sell wood that was too green to burn, but there were no buyers. Palestine was in chaos. The whole structure of the government had collapsed and all the former employees of the British government of Palestine were now jobless.

Separation from our families was hard. Like other Palestinians, we sent notices to *al-Difa'a* paper "From Salamah Khalil to his brother Salim, how are you? Reassure us about your condition (taminuna ankum)."

In 1952 we decided that if we could not go back to al-Majdal, which had fallen into Jewish hands, we could go to Toulkarm, where my parents lived. I had not seen my parents for four years. My father, who was by then over seventy, was completely demoralized. He's been dead since 1959, but when I think of him, I remember him on the prayer rug, saying, "Please God, give strength to Abdul Nasser so that he will help us return to Palestine." He could never adjust to being landless. He said he could not believe we could lose all our land and just sit there, when in the past blood used to be spilled if anyone took even a foot of land that did not belong to him.

I tried to reassure my father that the situation was not entirely hopeless and that one day Arab armies would come to our rescue; and I believed it. My thinking about Palestinian refugees went through several changes.

I resented seeing them lining up in front of food distribution centers for meager rations. I felt that the United Nations was turning my people into beggars, instead of looking for a just political solution and helping them return to their former towns and villages.

In the 1950s, I came to realize that the Arab countries had many problems of their own, and that it was unrealistic to depend on them to help us regain our homeland. I read about this and other conflicts, and I came to the conclusion that no one gives another freedom on a silver platter. Freedom is always taken and not given. We needed a strong Palestinian leader. There I was full of energy and ready to follow such a person, but no one appeared. I thought, "Why wait for others? I am Palestinian too. I am not helpless. I can make a difference."

When I started talking about doing something to help refugees, people simply laughed at me. "Who do you think you are? The United Nations?" I established the first society "Jamiyyat al-Ittihad al-Nisai'i" in 1952, but asked Rudainah el-Barghouti to be president and I became vice-president because I did not want people to think I established it only to be president. A group of women who shared my ideas about self-help met on October 1, 1956, and we formed a society that came to be called "Ittihad al-Mara'a al-Arabiyyah" (The Union of Arab Women) of al-Bireh. I was elected its head and led it for three years. I appointed six assistants, each from a different clan to draw the whole community into the society by equal representation, and to facilitate the distribution of goods and services. Unemployment was high, and we needed to help women earn their living in an honorable way instead of begging. We gave women cloth and thread to embroider at home, we would then buy their finished product and sell it.

The first building we used as a union was a garage near my house. To entice women to come in winter, I brought in my own space heater. I told my children at home to jump up and down to keep warm. Our society got a shot in the arm when a disbanded women's organization donated its budget to us, and then some Arab-Americans gave us some money. We rented a two-room house with an open courtyard and enrolled twenty girls in a literacy course and twenty-five in a sewing class. We also opened a nursery.

While we were trying to help refugees, we still had to deal with family separations of our own. We had relatives across the border in what became Israel, and we spent a great deal of energy trying to arrange to see them through the "Mandelbaum Gate," separating Arab and Israeli Jerusalem. With good reason Palestinians called it "the Gate of Tears."

We were obsessed with returning to Palestine. We could not see how we could when the British, who promised the Jews a national home in Palestine in the Balfour Declaration [of 1917], still exercised strong influence in Jordan, and a British general led the Jordanian army. All nationalist forces in the West Bank united in their effort to remove Jordan from British direct and indirect rule.

We had our opportunity to affect the direction Jordan took in the 1950s when the government was considering joining the Baghdad Pact.³ People on both banks demonstrated against the pact, and in 1955, when high school student Raja Abu Ammasheh was shot in Jerusalem while she was lowering the British flag, I tried to comfort her mother, and read the eulogy at her funeral. After Raja was shot, twenty-seven demonstrations erupted all over the West Bank.

In 1956, the first demonstration in town started in al-Bireh from our society. Fifteen women left our building, and in front of them walked a hefty woman carrying a three-meter-high Palestinian flag supported on her stomach. It was an impressive sight. People saw us and walked behind us. When we walked past the schools, the teacher's training colleges, students poured out and joined us. Government-appointed officials tried to talk us out of demonstrating. One of them said to me, "Are you listening to the wife of Abdullah Rimawi?" (a Palestinian nationalist, journalist, and, briefly, a member of parliament). We continued walking, and our ranks kept swelling. By the time the procession reached the center of Ramallah, we had about five thousand demonstrators. Two days after the al-Bireh demonstration, Hasan al-Kateb, the district governor of Jerusalem, called me into his office. He was tall and had very long fingers. He took out a Jordanian dinar, spread it and said, "Where is this made?" He then answered himself. "In Britain." He added, "Look here, we do not want any trouble. Your husband is an educator, a respectable man. I want you to go and ask students to stop demonstrating." Demonstrations continued in towns and villages, and eventually, King Hussein asked the British commander of the Jordanian forces, Glubb, to leave the country. Jordan did not join the Baghdad Pact.

My husband was transferred to Amman from 1956 to 1960. I do not think the transfer was accidental. I was furious that I was taken away from the center of events. I had many plans for the society, and commuted to

Ramallah until 1958, but then had to admit that I could not run things well from a long distance and resigned from the society with regret.

In 1964, at the age of forty-one, I started feeling that there was something unfinished in my life. There I was preaching about the importance of education when I myself did not have a high school diploma. When I announced that I was going to sit for the Tawjihi high school exam with my son Saji, a few people encouraged me, but many did not see the point, my husband among them. He didn't say no, but he certainly made it difficult. He would come home and say, "We are having six people to dinner tomorrow." Instead of asking for simple dishes, he would ask for stuffed vine leaves, stuffed chicken, and ground wheat balls stuffed with meat (kibbeh).

I used to wake up very early in the morning to do all my chores and still have time to study without making my husband feel he was missing anything. When he came into the house I hid my books. He didn't like to see me study. I'd be anxious to get back to my reading, but he would purposely keep me talking all evening. When I finally sat down to read, I would start nodding and the book would fall from my hands. My daughter Saida would wipe my eyes with a piece of wet cotton and say, "Wake up, Mother. Please don't fail and embarrass me in front of my friends."

When I entered the exam room, all the high school girls stood up, mistaking me for a supervisor. I think my presence set a good example; in those days, older women simply did not study. When the results came out, my son's average was higher than mine, but I passed.[4]

The General Union of Palestinian Women (GUPW) was established in 1965. I remember my elation at seeing the word "Palestine" in use again for the first time since 1948. Hundreds of women delegates from different Arab countries attended our first conference. Mrs. 'Issam Abdul Hadi was elected president. I was elected general secretary, and we decided to start recruiting people on a mass basis. One day when we were waiting to board a shared taxi with a group of women, a man insisted that we go ahead of him and he said, "Make way for the ladies, they are going to liberate Palestine." There was excitement in the air. We all felt it was time for Palestinians to take their destiny into their own hands.

Also in 1965, we established the society of In'ash al-Usra, the society for "the Rehabilitation of the Family." From the beginning we rejected the ideology of "all or nothing." We started on a modest scale and expanded as our resources permitted.

In addition to day-to-day relief work, the society responded quickly to emergencies. On November 13, 1966, for instance, we responded to the Israeli attack against the village of Sammu'. We visited the wounded in hospitals, and we donated money to the families of victims. We also demonstrated and urged the Jordanian government to respond forcefully to Israeli raids on border villages. On January 1, 1967, we received an order from the Jordanian government closing the General Union of Palestinian Women, and the PLO moved the union to Cairo.

When the 1967 war broke out, a number of societies, with the help of the mayors of Ramallah and al-Bireh, organized twenty-three first-aid centers. I was in one of the centers when a man ran in shouting that the Israeli army had entered Ramallah. I was incredulous. I rushed outside and saw people piling up their belongings, ready to leave. I went from house to house urging families to stay: "This is your country! Don't you remember 1948? Do you want to become refugees again?" Some listened to me and stayed, but others were scared.

I had mixed feelings about serving as head of In'ash al-Usra under Israeli occupation. So I made a list of our furniture and handed it to the mayor of al-Bireh, Abdul Jawad Saleh, in preparation for folding the society. He convinced me to stay, pointing out it was not clear whether the occupation authorities would allow new societies to open, and so societies with licenses needed to stay open. The mayor lent us $250 of municipality money to replenish our depleted resources and we stayed in business.

Our services were in great demand after the war because of the new stream of refugees created by the occupation of the West Bank and Gaza. At least 10,000 were left homeless after the Israelis razed the border villages of Yalu, Emmaus, and Beit Nuba. I will never forget the sight of a woman who had made a crib for her newborn baby by digging a hole in the ground under a tree, and then making it soft by lining it with pieces of cloth and a crumpled old newspaper. The campaign we spearheaded raised the morale of the volunteers as well as the recipients.

We convinced teachers and professionals to give us a percentage of their incomes every month for two years. We stopped receiving regular donations, however, when the Israeli military governor informed us that, according to Jordanian law the Israelis claimed they were using, it was illegal to collect money more than twice a year, but he conveniently disregarded the text of the law which states that active societies are exempt from this restriction. We were and are one of the most active on the West Bank.

We refused to give up. We bought raw materials and employed women to make cheese, juices, vinegar, jam, and pickled olives. But making huge quantities of goods was far easier than selling them. I used to lie awake thinking, "What am I going to do with two thousand bottles of vinegar?"

Schools, hospitals, and institutions bought our products. Selling these items in shops, however, was a difficult proposition. We made marvellous fruit juice and cookies. Neither contained chemicals, and both tasted better than the Israeli product that flooded the market. But whereas theirs was professionally packaged and had a colorful label, ours came in recycled bottles with handwritten labels. Finally we asked the help of a university marketing professor and we came out with beautifully designed boxes. We followed his distribution and marketing strategies and started making a profit on the juice and the cookies. We got involved in a number of enterprises and our production centers took care of 85 percent of our expenses. In 1965 our budget was $500 a year; by 1989, our yearly expenses had reached 72,000 Jordanian dinars, or about $180,000.

When we started offering university students scholarships, we managed to convince eight rich people to support eight students. By 1987, we were able to give loans and scholarships to 360 students. But recently, the financial difficulties of the society forced us to reduce the number to sixty-two. We started with one paid employee and the number grew to 152. We started with twenty-five children in a one-room kindergarten. We now have 150 children. We also run a boarding home which houses 132 orphan girls ages four to sixteen. We run a sponsorship program where 1300 families receive $500 a year from donors; we also support 130 families who cannot work because of old age or sickness. Because of unforeseen events, we keep a fund to support families with one-time donations, and we support about 500 families a month. We have eighty-five doctors, each of whom treats ten of the patients we refer to them free of charge. Al-Makased Islamic Hospital treats people we refer to it for free.

For years now, our volunteers have knit 400 sweaters a year for political prisoners of the Ramallah area. We also provide prisoners with socks and underwear to spare their families the expense of these items.

Funding is a political issue. We are funded by a number of donors. In 1969, al-Bireh municipality gave us a piece of land on which to build our headquarters. Equipment for digging was donated for our use. Municipality engineers donated their services, and Palestinians from all walks of life took part in the work camp we held to dig the foundations. The new

In'ash el-Usra graduating class of 1985. The society graduates 200 students each year. Photo by Orayb Najjar

three-story building soon became too small for us, and the Islamic Conference bought us a piece of land next to it and paid for building the foundation of the new building. Then a Palestinian philanthropist Zein El Mayyasi donated $500,000. When money ran out, the Norwegian Agency for International Development (NORAD) gave us $220,350. The money enabled us to establish large classrooms to teach a variety of vocational skills and we graduate 200 students a year.

I have been approached by a number of American charitable organizations offering financial aid. I always ask where they get their money from. If it comes from the Congress of the United States, I reject it. I refuse to take money from the enemy of my people on principle. It is the same Congress that gives billions of dollars a year to Israel in military aid and for funding illegal settlements on stolen Palestinian land. It is the same Congress that looks the other way when Israel uses phosphorus bombs against Lebanese and Palestinian civilians, contrary to United States law which restricts their use to military areas. I am not against receiving money from peace-loving international organizations in Scandinavian countries and in Europe and the Netherlands. In our sponsorship program, the largest group of donors is the Association Medicale Franco-Palestinienne who by 1986 were sponsoring 300 children at $500 a year. The National Council of Churches (U.S.) has donated money to us, and a number of Arab-American organizations help. Our own people, of course, donate money as well as olives, oil and other crops as Zakaah.[5]

The development and expansion of our society would not have been possible without the help of our 100 members and the twelve-member governing board. We do not provide skills in a void, we are concerned with the overall development of women. Library hours are mandatory for our students, and so are extracurricular lectures. Our students also have a folklore troupe. Our society was the first institution in the Occupied Territories to hold public celebrations of Palestinian culture after occupation, and many of our activities are designed to guard cultural artifacts against falsification. In 1981, the Israeli airline, El Al, decided to dress its stewardesses in what *The Jerusalem Post* described as "the most beautiful national costumes, designed by the best Israeli fashion designers, to emphasize the Israeli character of our planes." We proved to the public that those designs were stolen from the national Palestinian dress. We protested to the Israeli authorities as well as to UNESCO, and the project was shelved.

In addition to preserving our national heritage, I also encourage women to have more children. I once advertised that the society will give away 200 prizes to people with the most number of children. I realize that having many children constitutes a burden on women, but we are in a battle for survival, and the Israeli concern with our birthrate is to be taken seriously. Israelis want our land without Palestinians on it.[6]

Our rapid growth has attracted the attention of new groups who invited me to speak about our organizational strategies. Israeli authorities ordered me not to give any public lectures. Although I protested that my lectures are not political, the Israeli authorities understand that, in reality, teaching women self-reliance is political; making products that compete with Israeli goods, even on a small scale, is political. Self-help is political. It means that we are a people seeking and deserving self-determination instead of occupation.

Israelis do their best to delay our work. For example, it took us a year and half to obtain a license for our school bus. In June 1985, we got orders from Amman for $15,000 worth of embroidery. The shipment was not allowed through until we paid $1000 in taxes. Even though charitable societies are exempt from taxes, we had no recourse but to pay because the embroidery project puts about 4500 women to work.

I was imprisoned for a total of six times for periods ranging from one to twenty-two days.[7] Anyone who has been imprisoned is condemned to continue her imprisonment in the borders of her country after she is released. I was also placed under town arrest between August 7, 1980, and December 20, 1982. My application for leaving the country to attend thirty international conferences, including the Nairobi Women's Conference, were denied.[8] Israeli officials did not allow me to leave the country to address the American Black Congressional Caucus in Washington, (September 25–28, 1985), the only American official body I accepted to talk to. During that period, the Israeli authorities prevented me from seeing my children. All my applications for family reunion, ten per child, were rejected. Amnesty International took up my case and worked for my release from town arrest.

The town arrest hampered my fund-raising work as it was intended to. Before 1979, my trip to the United States speaking mostly to Arab-American organizations netted $300,000 in donations, and my trip to Iraq, $60,000. Between 1979 and 1986, the society was forbidden from holding money-making annual bazaars. In 1984, we were not allowed to raise money by selling tickets to "frugal dinners" of lentils and rice. Our cupboards were full of embroidery, but we were having difficulties exporting it, and finally, we could not pay the salaries of our employees for three months, and stayed afloat only because employees agreed to wait to be paid.

We were saved by a group of enterprising women in Amman who formed the "Friends of In'ash al-Usra Society." The group sponsored twenty-three children and promised to take on the expenses of forty-five boarding students. Through them, we received $532,500 worth of free medicine for all those benefiting from the services of our society. Because the society made our work known to unions in Jordan, an old dream of ours, a small factory for ready-made clothing was established with two donations of $37,500 and $7,500 from the Union of Engineers and the Union of Agricultural Engineers in Jordan respectively. Once again, our people have helped us circumvent Israeli obstacles to our development.

My relationship with the Israeli occupation authorities has always been uneasy. That is the only way it can be. Their aim is to present the occupation to outsiders as a normal state of affairs and present any resistance to it as working outside the law. Our aim is to end the occupation and expose their practices. I see my role as encouraging people to have hope, and Israelis find that threatening.

On a personal level, I was lucky that the husband my family chose for me held nationalistic views like mine. Together, we raised five wonderful children, one girl and four boys, who are happily married to people of their own choice.

Our children are highly trained professionals, yet because of their self-lessness, they have nothing to their name and lead unsettled lives. My son Samir, a pediatrician, volunteered to work in the Palestine Red Crescent hospital during the Israeli invasion of Lebanon. He was paid $90 per month. His needs were few, but when he wanted to send a gift to his son in the Soviet Union where his wife was studying for a masters degree in journalism, he had to eat one meal a day for awhile to afford one. There are similar stories about the other four.

My husband passed away in 1982. Israelis refused me the permission to leave my town arrest to attend his funeral in Taibeh unless I personally asked the "civil administration" for a permit, an institution all nationalists were boycotting. We buried him in al-Bireh instead. At night, I have plenty of time to review my life and the way I have lived it. Sometimes I compare the careers of my children to those of the young people who graduated with them and are well established and financially secure, and I feel guilty for the way we raised them. But when I reason with myself, I conclude that somebody has to sacrifice so that Palestinians can live in dignity. And if we as a people do not make these sacrifices, we do not deserve to gain our independence.

Despite the disasters that have befallen our people, I remain optimistic, perhaps because of our experience in building In'ash al-Usra from nothing into a large institution. We Palestinians are capable of being industrious and working for our own progress and development, but we need self-determination like all people in the world.

People ask me, "What about peace?" I say that I believe in peace: peace with justice. Such a peace cannot be obtained by the force of arms, and Israel, the fourth largest military power in the world, should understand this after its Lebanese debacle. Israel entered Lebanon under the guise of security, but security does not come from the barrel of a gun. In the age of missiles that can cross continents, there are no real borders. Security is a state of mind. Israel can achieve such a state when it stops oppressing Palestinians and when it gives us our rights, chief among them the establishment of an independent Palestinian state on our own land led by our sole and legitimate representative, the PLO.

Update

On 20 June 1988, Israeli soldiers broke into the society during a curfew in the town of al-Bireh. They seized files, addresses of sponsors, manuscripts, cultural documents, audio tapes containing the oral history of women, and videotapes of folkloric celebrations, as well as of other subjects.[9] The soldiers then welded the main building shut, but left the preschool and the orphanage open (Source: Data Base Project of Palestinian Human Rights.)

In a charge sheet presented to the Ramallah Military Court on 19 October 1988, Samiha Khalil was accused by the military prosecutor of eleven "illegal acts." Interviewed in July 1989 in a makeshift office she was sharing with a number of employees with their typewriters and copying machines, Umm Khalil had this to say about the charges:

What the occupation authorities list as "incitement" is what I call demanding our independence. When Israeli authorities charge me with asking for a Palestinian state, I consider it a badge of honor. Of course I want my people to be free and independent, and I have been vocal about it to anyone who would listen. For years now I have been saying that the PLO represents us. In their press conference, Israeli authorities claimed that we diverted $40,000 to the families of people who were killed, wounded, or jailed in the uprising. That again is no charge. Our raison d'etre is to help families who lose their main supporter for any reason. Every year in our financial records, we list the amount of money we contribute to families, but the Israeli authorities presented the matter to the foreign press as if it were a big discovery. I have always been proud that we aid the families of prisoners, and we have not done so in secret.

The least one can say about those charges is that they are ridiculous. Israelis consider throwing stones "a call to violence," and yet they do not consider shooting unarmed children violent. They do not consider demolishing homes, deporting people, and separating families violent. They seem oblivious to the fact that depriving university students of their educations is a thoroughly violent act.

The Israeli authorities want to try me for incitement. This is one of their desperate and futile measures to end the Intifada because they do not understand what it is. The Israeli government makes a grave mistake when it believes that by imprisoning thousands, by trying me, by closing this or that institution, it will end the Intifada. The Intifada is not lurking in any given institution that soldiers can close down and then relax. The Intifada is a spirit, an attitude that the occupation forces cannot arrest or deport. The Intifada is a group of young men and women in Nablus, who, on hearing that the homes of nine families had been demolished, took a shell of a house, then, overnight, painted it, installed doors and windows, then moved the families in. The Intifada is the cars coming and going transporting donated furniture, a fridge, gas, carpets to those families. The Intifada is the people who fought about whose turn it was to feed those families. That is the Intifada. It is not me or him or her, it is all of us together, saying enough is enough. No more occupation! We will not be cowed by the occupation or the occupier.

Trying me will not change anything.[10]

SAMAR SULEIMAN
Kindergarten teacher, member wcsw

Samar, the daughter of an emigrant, lives in the village of Abu Falah, twenty-three kilometers from Ramallah. Grid electricity and piped water came to the village only in 1984. By age eighteen, Samar had developed considerable social and political consciousness despite her village's isolation. She has lived through more than many women twice her age. She has traveled halfway around the world to marry at age fifteen, and was divorced six months later, returned, opened a kindergarten, and became the family's main breadwinner. Samar remarried at age twenty-three. Her story shows how the absence of her father and the power males hold (even while absent) have affected every single aspect of her life.

Winter 1984

My father went away to Brazil when I was three, in 1970.* Later I started

*Kitty Warnick writes that she interviewed Samar on tape in Arabic "probably in March 1985." She had some help with translating and transcribing. Kitty did not know Samar before she interviewed her. She let Samar tell her story chronologically, but asked many questions during the taped interview, mainly to clarify details. Kitty wrote the chapter from transcripts

Samar Suleiman in 1985. Photo by Orayb Najjar

asking my mother, "Where is he? Why did he go?"

"He went to Brazil to earn money for us. He'll be back in a year or two."

But a year or two passed and he didn't come. I asked again.

"He'll be back after a while."

By the time I was fourteen and old enough to think for myself, I didn't believe her anymore. I'd written him letters, but he only wrote back to us three times in thirteen years, and once sent us two hundred dollars. People from our village who went to Brazil saw him and told him he should come back because my mother and we four daughters had no one to look after us. He didn't have a good job there, and could have found better work here, but I think he was ashamed to come home as poor as he had left. He knew how people would gossip and criticize him. Anyone who goes to America is supposed to come back rich and build himself a grand new house. People are criticizing him anyway. They say

of the tape. I later updated the story when I visited Samar in 1986 and 1989.

he's probably living badly, running after women all the time. When I finally met him, after I married, my heart didn't feel any warmth towards him. I saw that as long as he has enough money to buy three meals a day, he is content, and he never gives a thought to his wife and daughters. He hasn't done his duty by us. It's our mother who has worked all the time to raise and educate us.

We were very poor when I was a child. It's only since I started working in the kindergarten last year that we've had any extra money. I'm the one who has paid to renew our old kitchen, for all other improvements, for our television set, and for our water and electricity. There are houses headed by males here in the village who have been unable to provide for their families what my mother and I have provided for ourselves. In the past we had no furniture, just mattresses on the floor; no electricity, because we couldn't afford to buy it from the private generators; no well of our own, so we had to buy water from our neighbors' cisterns and carry it home on our heads. My mother grew vegetables on her three-quarters of an acre of land and made milk and yoghurt from her little flock of sheep. We became experts at gleaning after the harvest; my oldest sister was especially patient and famous for how much she could collect!

This mother of mine has raised four girls on embroidery. That is how she earned money, and we started to work at it as we grew up. I started when I was ten. In fact it was my mother who introduced embroidery to the village. The traditional dresses of Abu Falah were decorated with ribbons, not embroidery. After 1948, some refugees who had been driven out of their homes in what is now Israel came to live in Abu Falah. My mother used to watch as they embroidered the dresses of their home villages, and she insisted on learning what for her was a new art. Gradually the women of Abu Falah adopted the embroidered dresses, and now we have customers in plenty from among our neighbors and as far away as Jerusalem. It's not too difficult to make a living. For a dress that takes us a month to make, we get one hundred dollars.

My mother believes in education, but she had to take my sisters away from school when they were twelve because the fare they needed to travel to the secondary school in the neighboring village was more than she could afford. I was the only one who insisted on staying at school. One day after my mother had taken me out of school I was sitting by our door crying and clutching my money box, resolving, "I'm going to sew and earn enough money to pay my fare to school myself." The father of one of my friends passed by and asked me why I was crying. When I told him, he put ten shekels (about one dollar at that time) in my box. He was not the only person who helped me earn my school fare. When the school went on trips, I had to say I couldn't go because we didn't have enough money. My friends clubbed together and collected the five dollars to pay for me.

My mother thought of opening a shop to bring in more money, but it was impossible as we had no man in the family. The village would not accept it. People watch you and talk about everything that you do; life is hard for women without men. For instance, if a girl marries and her husband goes away to America leaving her here, she must not wear pretty clothes or henna on her hair or gold jewelry. If she does, people will say, "What's this? A woman should only make herself look good for her husband." It's unreasonable, and no one with any understanding should care how people talk, but some women can't bear to be gossiped about.

My mother didn't care how people gossiped at her own expense, but she had to be careful about the reputation of her daughters, or nobody would have married us. We lived on the edge of the village, out in the wilds. A lonely house full of unmarried girls without a man to protect them would be sure to attract malicious rumors. A girl's reputation is only safe once she is married, so our mother had to agree to our marrying young. It was our father who had the authority to choose our husbands, although he had neglected us for so long. My mother tried to protest whenever she did not like a prospective groom, but had to accept the men he and our uncles wanted, however strongly she disapproved of their choices.

I was married at the age of fifteen. My husband was from this village but was living in Brazil. He came here for a visit and asked his relatives to recommend a wife. "Samar is a beautiful girl," they said. So he telephoned my father in Brazil to ask his permission, then came to visit my uncles and my mother. She was against the marriage, but my uncles didn't listen to her, just as they hadn't when my sister married. She quarreled with them and almost refused to come to the engagement party. As for me, I was so young I hardly knew what marriage was, and anyway nobody would have listened to me if I objected. My uncles persuaded me to accept by saying, "You'll be living in Brazil, you'll be able to meet your father." Though my mother said, "What do you want to meet him for? He's never done anything for you," I felt I needed to see him, so I accepted the marriage.

After the engagement party, my fiancé returned to Brazil, and I prepared to follow. We were getting married at his home over there. My mother got herself a passport so that she could travel with me. When my uncles heard what she was planning they said, "If you go, we'll take possession of your house." She couldn't bear to lose the two-room house. We'd only just built it and it was the result of years of work and saving. So she decided she couldn't come with me. She had even bought her ticket, but I had to travel alone.

As soon as I got to Brazil, I found that my husband and I weren't compatible. He was thirty, and he only wanted a young wife so that he could have lots of children. There was no feeling between us at all. He was a bum. He was out running after women all the time, while I was stuck in the house like a servant, with no freedom. I was too young for the responsibility of looking after a house anyway. Life over there is just the same as it is here, at least for Arab girls. I visited my father and said I was unhappy, but he took no notice. I tried to telephone my mother, but my husband wouldn't let me. After six months, when I'd had time to think about what I was doing, I decided to come back here to my village. My husband didn't care at all, and when I told my father, he just said, "Well, go then, but don't ask me for anything." I didn't have to. I had money and gold of my own that I'd been given for the wedding, so I could sell it and buy my own ticket home.

I came back to the village, and everyone was talking about me, yak yak yak. They thought I should have stayed in Brazil; they think everything over there is wonderful. I wanted to go back to school, but my uncles have such old-fashioned ideas they wouldn't let me. Then the Youth Committee (Shabiba)[1] asked me to be the teacher of the kindergarten they were opening. Although I hadn't finished school I was the most suitable girl for the job. I like children, and I especially like doing arts and crafts and creative things with them. There are still only a few girls in the whole village who have finished school, and the first two to have gone to college started in 1984.

Of course people were shocked when I started traveling to al-Bireh every day to train at In'ash al-Usra Society, but now that I am working in the kindergarten, it's alright. I think that by traveling alone and working, I am setting an encouraging example to other girls in the village.

It was hard to prevent gossip at first. Young men, members of the Youth Committee who were sponsoring the kindergarten, had to come sometimes to discuss business with me. Whenever they did, they had to fetch my mother as a chaperone.

My training was simple. I spent every morning for a few months watching and helping the teachers in the kindergarten at the In'ash al-Usra Society in al-Bireh. Then the Youth Committee found a room to rent, and we were ready to start.

Sixty-two children came at first—far too many! We decided to exclude the younger ones and wait until we had more space and money. You see how much the women here need a kindergarten. It's not because they are going out to work. Hardly any of the village women do that; three or four work at home sewing, and that's all. It's because they know it is good for a child to learn a little reading and drawing, get used to playing with other children and the atmosphere of a class, before he or she goes to school. Besides, mothers need a rest from having all their children under their feet all day. They mostly have so many children here, one every year, seven or eight or even twelve sometimes.

At the moment the kindergarten is rather crowded. We only have one room, with about thirty pupils. Well-wishers outside the village have given us some toys and money to buy three bicycles and some books for the children to look at, but we need a lot more money so that we can rent a bigger place and buy things like colored pencils and more books. Once a month I go to East Jerusalem to the Federation of Charitable Societies to borrow books and toys from their library, and I read the children a story every day. We do a lot of practical things like planting beans and tomatoes and pickling olives; we make paper sun hats for the children to wear when we go for walks. The five year olds know their alphabet and a little arithmetic. Pupils who came to the kindergarten are now doing much better in their first grade at primary school than their classmates. I was very proud when the primary school teacher told me that. The fee for each pupil is two dinars ($5.00) per month. It's not cheap for some families, but many are prepared to pay. I am paid $100 a month.

I hope to have a meeting for the mothers once every three or four months. We'll discuss or listen to lectures on whatever subjects they want—health, nutrition, child development. They are eager for information. More than twenty came to the one meeting we've had so far. I won't have time to arrange them more often.

Samar Suleiman's kindergarten class exercises before starting the day, 1985.
Photo by Orayb Najjar

I never have time to sit down. The kindergarten is a full-time job, as after class I bake bread and prepare food for the next day. In addition I now have my work with the Women's Committee for Social Work (WCSW), which I established at the suggestion of the Youth Committee six months ago. I visited the branch in Ramallah to see what they do, then I called together all the women in the village who were interested by visiting houses and putting posters up in the two village shops. We had a meeting in the kindergarten room and two women from the Ramallah committee came to talk to us. At the first meeting, we enrolled twenty members, elected an executive committee, of which I am one, and decided on our first activity. We chose to begin with a sewing class and workshop, so that girls whose fathers don't allow them to leave the village can learn to sew and earn money. We have a room of our own now and three sewing machines that the Youth Committee brought us. My aunt is the teacher, and there are fifteen students.

One of our most enjoyable activities has been a trip to Jerusalem for the celebration that the Women's Committees for Social Work all over the West Bank held on International Women's Day. Seven girls from the village went together in a taxi. We had a wonderful time. It was a big step: it was the first time any of them except me had been to Jerusalem without their parents.

Our committee will grow quickly once people see how useful our work is, and once men see that we're not doing anything bad. We'll start more classes—in health and literacy; we'll organize cultural events; we'll establish more work projects. Ours is the only active women's committee in the village, and the need for it is tremendous. This is just the beginning.

Update, Summer 1989

Samar, now twenty-three, has remarried to a thirty-four-year-old driver of a bus she once took on a picnic. After his first wife died, he married a relative, but the marriage lasted only a few months. Samar's husband has five boys and one girl. Samar gets along well with them, especially the eldest boy age fourteen. But in addition to taking care of the children and her own nine-month-old child (she is also pregnant), Samar shares a two-bedroom house with a sitting room, a kitchen, and a corridor with her mother in-law, eighty-five, and the unmarried female cousin of her father-in-law, seventy-eight. Samar's mother-in-law appears to believe that the family has done Samar a favor by letting her marry their son. "We asked for her hand so that she will take care of the children," she explained.

Samar got married despite her mother's objections because her husband "is a good man, and he was very interested in me." Samar said that every time she had a suitor, the village gossip mill started. A rumor was circulating that Samar was barren because she did not conceive during her six-month-long marriage in Brazil. A number of men closer to her age wanted to marry her, but their families refused to let them, fearing that Samar will not conceive. Samar herself believed the rumors and said: "I could not marry any of them and *fail again*."

It appears that a woman in her situation is expected to be content with a widower with children, one a brand new bride may not accept. Samar related with satisfaction how surprised people were when she gave birth to her baby boy. It would be an understatement to say that Samar has no time to work outside the home.

NAJAH MANASRAH
Nurse, teacher, researcher

Raised in Dheisheh refugee camp the first twenty-two years of her life, Manasrah was the first woman in her camp to go to college. Manasrah, who has left the camp for the city of Bethlehem, has not forgotten her refugee origin and leads a busy life as a volunteer, teacher, and writer who is now researching early marriage for women during the Intifada. Given the contributions of women to the uprising, Manasrah says she "will not allow" the establishment of a Palestinian state which follows the Iranian model for women.

3 July and 27 July 1989

My family hails from the village of Zakaria, occupied in 1948.* I was born in 1960 in Dheisheh refugee camp where I spent the first twenty-two years of my life. All ten children and my mother lived on the salary of my father, a teacher in refugee schools, and we were barely making it. So starting in the seventh grade, my siblings and I worked about half the year, and all summer. We gathered fruit in the hot sun, or did repetitive boring work in Israeli factories to save money for the rest of the year. All of us went to school, but I had to fight hard to go to university.

In 1979, I was the first girl to go to university from Dheisheh refugee camp, population 12,000. My family was subjected to intense pressure for even *considering* letting me go. There was a general fear of coeducation. People said, "Sending her to Bethlehem University will open her eyes, and then, who can restrain her?" But my older sister, a nurse, sided with me. She had fought some battles herself, of the "Are boys better than we are?" variety; besides, no one could argue with a scholarship that paid for everything, including books. I was allowed to register, and since then, other refugee girls in our camp have gone on to university. I believe that I have paved the way for them by taking my studies seriously.

People were right about a university putting ideas into a woman's head, though. At the University of Bethlehem, I read a variety of books,

*I chose to interview Najah after reading two of her articles in *Al-Kateb*. I interviewed her in Arabic on 3 and 27 July 1989. I asked Najah to tell me about her life and then asked her to describe her research. I wrote the story from my notes. Because of space considerations, I edited out detailed descriptions of her medical work because similar descriptions appear in Rita Giacaman's chapter.

I met students from different political groups, and I became active in the Union of Palestinian Working Women's Committee (UPWWC), where I developed a special interest in gender issues.

During the Intifada, I noticed an increase in teenage marriages, so I decided to investigate. My suspicions were confirmed (Manasrah 1989). People in villages and refugee camps are now marrying their daughters earlier than they did before the Intifada. There is even a certain percentage of families in some city neighborhoods who have the characteristics of villages; they too marry their daughters while they are still in high school.

Marriage records in the Bethlehem area show that 49 percent of the marriages in the sample I examined took place when women were under eighteen. In the Fawwar refugee camp in the Hebron district, 70 percent of the marriages were of girls under eighteen. In the Dheisheh refugee camp, however, most marriages were above age eighteen, perhaps because of the proximity of the camp to Bethlehem. In the northern part of the West Bank in the village of Bala' in Toulkarm, most marriages were of women over eighteen, whereas in the village of Athana in Hebron, the figure was 90 percent.

Islamic courts that follow Jordanian legislation have set the marriage age for women at fifteen, and for men at sixteen (Christian Palestinian women are allowed to marry by their church at age eighteen, men at age twenty).[1] It used to be that some girls postponed marriage by insisting that they needed to finish school first; but some teenagers told me that the long-term closure of the schools by the Israeli military government deprived them of that excuse. Young women of that age cannot keep suitors at bay on their own when they are pressured to marry.

Various other factors account for the early marriage phenomenon. Parents are afraid of their daughters' missing the twenty-three to twenty-four ceiling after which a woman is considered too old if unmarried. Parents also fear disfigurement. The cases publicized in our media about the woman whose elbow was shattered, another who was paralyzed, several women who lost an eye each, makes parents pressure girls into staying at home, often unsuccessfully. In common with other societies, women here are valued for their looks, and once injured, become bad marriage prospects. In families where marriage is the only "job" available to women, having them remain unmarried is serious business.

Parents also fear sexual violence against women in prison. They have heard about the cases of rape by Israeli soldiers that we've had recently so

Women in Bethlehem run through the streets with a Palestinian flag, summer 1989. Photo by local photographer

families pressure their daughters to marry before anything happens to them. Fear of injury has also had an effect on demonstrations. You hear young men ordering girls to go behind them, both to protect girls and women from the foul language of soldiers, as well as from bullets. Boys say that girls need to be behind boys because once Israeli soldiers start shooting, girls do not run fast and may get caught. Some girls and women comply, but others reply indignantly, "You're no better than we are. We want to throw stones just like you!" In some villages of the North, I was told that conservatives have insisted on separate demonstrations for men and women, where men lead, and women follow, with some space between the sexes.

Many have grudgingly noted how active women were, especially in spontaneous street action. When a young man is about to be arrested or loaded into Jeeps, women descend on the soldiers and wrest the man away. Many have literally put their own lives in danger, and the whole community is grateful to them, and yet, some want to have their cake and eat it too. They want to have women save men, but still want to enforce old-fashioned values about mixed gatherings. They want women to demonstrate, yet they do not want them to be arrested. A number of women had serious fights with their families over the issue of participation. I even heard a mother shout at a ten-year-old girl, "Come in, the army will shoot you!" The girl replied, "If boys can die, why can't I?" The mother turned to me plaintively and said, "See how strong willed she is!"

There is no doubt that the mass involvement in the Intifada has touched every sector of society and has involved women who have never participated before. While working for the Union of Palestinian Working Women's Committee, it used to be hard to organize around a political program. In 1981, 1982, and up to 1984, when you said, "the aim of this committee is political discussion," some women used to run away; politics was not for them. But the Intifada has followed them right into their homes; tear gas shot in alleys and housing units does not distinguish between political and apathetic women, between the old or the newborn. Collective punishment and indiscriminate shooting by the Israeli army has politicized even the most uninvolved.

Take my personal life, for instance. Every single decision Mohammad and I had made since we met was affected by the occupation. I met Mohammad in college and learned that he sat for his Tawjihi high school exam in prison. We got engaged a year before graduation and got married in 1982. I went on to finish college, but his study was interrupted by his detention because, for a total of three and a half years, Mohammad was in some sort of town or house arrest. As a student, Mohammad supported himself as a house painter, and he also worked part-time at *al-Talia* weekly newspaper, where he now holds a full-time job. Because he could not get permanent employment, he stayed home and did the housework and the cooking.

Shortly after my marriage, I became the main wage earner in our family. I worked with the Catholic Relief Services in village health counseling, and I worked with the Caritas as a staff nurse in the night shift. I was on my two jobs for eighteen hours a day. I had to go to Nablus twice a week, so often I had time to sleep or eat only during that drive. I could take that punishing schedule only for six months, then I found a full-time job in 1983 in a mental health institute. It was one of those jobs where you are the whole staff, you are the director, the teacher, and the janitor. Only two other full-time teachers worked with me, and they taught and went home. I stayed on for a year and a half. Not only did I have to support the family, our social life was limited. I could not go anywhere without my husband who was not allowed out of the house after dark.

To diffuse the tension of our stressful lives, we resolved to talk matters over. I sometimes carried communication to an extreme when I used to wake Mohammad up and say, "I want to talk to you. There is a subject we did not really resolve." Mohammad did not appreciate being awakened, but I felt it was important not to ignore problems. Mohammad is not a traditional authoritarian male. He has confidence in himself and does not feel threatened by sharing housework, putting the apron on, cooking, or washing the dishes. Mohammad's friends tease him and say, "Your wife rules you," but he shrugs these remarks off. He believes in the equality of women, and he practices what he preaches, unlike others who are liberal only on paper.

Mohammad was a calming influence on me. I met him when I had radical ideas. I saw nothing wrong with staying out very late, with living alone. I had my chance to live alone when I did my graduate work in the United States. I realized how lonely it was to be alone, not just physically alone, but cut off from all family support. I realized that we are social beings, not simply a collection of individuals each doing his or her own thing. We are a *community*, with a certain degree of interdependency. Perhaps it is easier to be individualistic if you were raised in a society that values individualism like the United States, but we are a society of groups. We come from an area where we all know each other. In Bethlehem, we worry about what happens in Nablus.

I chose not to have children of my own. In this country, I am an anomaly. I got pregnant in 1982 and was not ready. I felt trapped and got an abortion. Without planning for it, I got pregnant again in 1986 and thought that since I had not heard from the different agencies I applied to for a scholarship to graduate school, I will let the pregnancy take its course, but I had a spontaneous abortion. Shortly after that, I learned that AMIDEAST awarded me a scholarship to the University of Illinois, and was relieved I was in a position to accept it.

It was hard to explain to anyone why a married woman wants to go abroad to study. People said I was crazy to leave my husband alone for years, that he would find another woman. My mother said that perhaps he will return to his first wife, a woman he divorced before we got married. Mohammad was pressured too. He was told, "If you love her, why let her go?" My father was very supportive. He said that my education will be good for our future, and advised us to put emotions aside and think ahead. That was the push we needed. My father has a special love of education. The first few years we were refugees, my then twenty-five-year-old father and his friends used to gather children in the mountains near a quarry, sit them on the rocks, and teach them to read. At that time, the refugee camp still had tents, and when it acquired permanent structures, he and his friends asked UNRWA for a school and got one built.

I graduated in March 1988 with a masters degree in psychiatric nursing (M.S.N.). When I returned from the United States, the question of children came up. By then, I had decided not to have any. "No married woman is without children!" I was told. "You are looking at one," I answered. "But children will take care of you in the future," they ventured. "Well here I am, my mother raised me for twenty-two years, and what have I done for her?" "You have a point there, but how about just *one* child?" they'd say. I see myself not wasting my energy on one child, but serving many young people with my teaching and volunteer work. Mohammad says that it is my body, and so it is my decision. I believe that the fact that he already has teenage children by his first marriage makes it easy for him to accept my decision.

Being free to work outside the home allows me to work for the Palestinian community. I was out of the country when the uprising started. Shortly after I returned in April 1988, there was a mass demonstration for Jamal al-Sha'er, nineteen, who was shot dead in a demonstration. About one thousand people took part in his funeral, and flags decorated a two-kilometer stretch of the road. Before we got to the cemetery, the army sprayed the demonstrators with rubber bullets. As a nurse, I was able to help. One young girl was shot in the abdomen and was very scared. I helped take her away. A plane threw pebbles on people's heads, many were injured in their heads or shoulders. People dispersed, one group took the martyr, and the other struggled with the army on the ground. In addition to our dead or wounded, we have had young men who were shot in other areas, like the Dheisheh refugee camp, smuggled into our area so that the army would not determine when and how they would be buried.

You could not remain unmoved in the Intifada. Even if you remained home, little kids knock at your door and want to hide from the troops. Many children in our neighborhood were shot and injured by bullets and by shrapnel, and one broke his arm as he slipped while escaping from soldiers. The uprising has sobered us up. I changed my behavior in a number of ways. I cut down my expenses, and I curbed spending on unnecessary luxuries, and paid my debts.

We live in a tense atmosphere. The Israeli authorities have systematically rounded up people from lists of Palestinians who had been previously arrested or had been placed under town arrest under the assumption that they are likely to be active. Because Mohammad fits into that category, he often does not sleep at home in anticipation of night raids for mass arrests. One night the army spread in the neighborhood and we were certain that Mohammad would be arrested. He considered slipping out but we decided against it, and it was quite tense from 9:30 to 12:15 P.M. I myself got tired of army terrorism and went to sleep at 11:30. I thought, "What the hell, let them do as they please!" What the Israeli soldiers did was ridiculous; they took a bicycle, and four of them mounted it and clowned around on it, laughing loudly, throwing stones at people's houses, and banging on doors. We refused to open.

By May 1988, I had volunteered my services for the physically and mentally handicapped. I also volunteered to work in the Bethlehem Union of Palestinian Medical Relief Committees. I conducted three first-aid workshops and lectured about first aid for tear gas inhalation, burns, and broken bones. We tried to prepare people for helping themselves in their own neighborhoods. Women were particularly interested in these lectures. Whenever my group of doctors and nurses heard that a place in our district was under curfew, we conducted medical days there as soon as the curfew was lifted, both to raise people's morale and because we were certain the area was in dire need of medical services. If we knew there was a demonstration somewhere, we knew there were injured who were afraid of going to hospitals where they could be arrested, and so we went to that location, for example to Battir and Husan. In addition to victims of the army, there are poor people who cannot afford to go to the hospitals, and so do not seek medical care, so we try to have doctors go to them.

In August 1988, I was employed as an instructor in the Arab College of Nursing. I teach mental health and psychiatry. I deal with post-traumatic stress disorder. I discuss it in class, but I also try to do something about it in our community. People suffering symptoms of stress do not seek help and do not even know it is available, so we have to identify them. We go to a village and ask if someone was especially traumatized by events, and one case leads to another. Some people, especially children, are terribly shaken when soldiers break into their homes at night. Others do not recover from seeing a loved one shot dead or badly injured.

In addition to medical issues, I like to involve the student nurses in discussions on social issues. I bring up the fact that women in Islam get half the inheritance of a male, and some students defend the practice on the grounds that men support women. Some defend wearing shari'a dress on the grounds that it protects a woman. The kind of women I fear most are women who defend their own enslavement. There is a rise in fundamentalism in the region, and there have been cases where women were pelted with eggs or threatened because of their dress. In some villages, pamphlets were distributed calling on women to wear that dress. In some cases, parents supported their daughters and quarreled with fundamentalists; in other cases, many have found it easier just to don that dress. In one case, I know a seventeen year old who was in a pair of jeans one week and in shari'a dress the next. It turns out that her uncle had been shot, and she heard some conservatives say that he was not a martyr because he was not a believer. She explained to me that she wore the shari'a dress because one can die anytime, and added, "I do not want to die a Fteeseh" (a carcass, a carrion). There are also a number of leftists who were not very religious who saw so much injury and death around them they started to wonder, "What if there is a God? What if there is heaven and hell?" It used to be that some would say, "I'll enjoy my life now, and when I get older I will repent." Now people are seeing hundreds of young people never get older, and they say, "What if I too will die tomorrow?"

Some people are alarmed by the great increase in women wearing conservative dress in the Occupied Territories, but I see it as a defensive mechanism of a society that feels threatened. I see it as a transitional period, like the problem of early marriage, and a return to all kinds of tradition—some good, some bad. For example, there is a noticeable increase in the "Awneh," where a whole village or neighborhood gets together to help families, just like old times.

Religion need not be oppressive. My father is religious—he prays and fasts, but he has never tried to pressure any of us into prayer. He used to say, "You know what is required, and it is up to you." Having grown up in this atmosphere, I have certain expectations for a Palestinian state. I hope that we will have a democratic Palestinian government. I think that women who have become leaders in neighborhood committees will not be ready to go back to taking orders. I believe that if we follow up on women's issues, we can effect changes. We can make sure, for instance, that no one is allowed to pull a young girl out of school so that she can walk behind the sheep her family owns.

When we build our new Palestinian state, we will need the skills of women. We also want them to be productive, but not just in child-bearing. Some people justify marriage to more than one woman at the same time on the grounds that the family will have more children. Women are not incubation machines; they are not chickens or rabbits. Sometimes, you hear people urging a woman whose fourteen year old was shot to give birth to another one. In theory, it is one to one. But in practice, that woman spent fourteen years of her life taking care of that special person, and there is no way one birth will make up for another, demographics notwithstanding.

We refuse to be as involved as we are in resisting Israeli occupation, and then end up like the women of the Iranian revolution. I do not think that will happen to us. I will not allow it! I refuse to hide, as if it is shameful to be seen, as if it is shameful to occupy our rightful place in society.

Update

Najah and Mohammad had a girl in 1990 and they called her "Quds," (Jerusalem).

The Land,
Two Farmers

Land has always been the most important issue in Palestinian-Israeli politics. In 1903, the Sixth Zionist Congress set up the Jewish National Fund (JNF) as a purchasing agency to acquire land in Palestine for Zionist settlement. By 1948, when the Jewish population of Palestine had already reached 31 percent of the total, the JNF had only purchased 6.6 percent of the land.

Using six laws enacted between 1945 and 1953 by the British and Israeli governments, Israel expropriated the land which had been left behind by the refugees who fled or were expelled. Most of the land was confiscated by the use of the Absentee Property Law of 1950, but it was possible to confiscate so much land because the Israeli definition of absentees included the 30,000 people who fled from one place to another *within* the newly formed state (Edge, *FE*, 16 October 1989: 8). Under that law, any person who left his or her usual place of residence between 29 November 1947, and 1 September 1948, was considered an absentee. Furthermore, the custodian was protected from being questioned about the information sources that led him to issue a decision by virtue of this law. And if someone was classified absent when he or she was present, the custodian was protected by the law which stated that "No deal concluded spontaneously between the Custodian and another person in connection with property which the Custodian believes to be absentee property at the moment the deal is concluded may be invalidated, but shall remain in force even if it is later proved that such property was not absentee property at that time" (Hirst 1977: 188, 189).

After 1967, the basis for Israeli land confiscation was Military Order No. 59. The order gives Israel the right to use land belonging to "the enemy." Under this order, any land used by the Jordanian government— for schools, hospitals, or offices—became eligible for confiscation. The order was reinforced by Military Order No. 364, which states that the mere proclamation that a particular piece of land is state land gives Israel the right to confiscate it. In 1979, a comprehensive survey of all land of the West Bank was undertaken by the Office of Absentee Property, after which authorities declared that most of the land of the West Bank was amirieh (state), matrukah (abandoned), or mawat (uncultivated) land not registered in the tabu (Turkish land registration documents). Sixty percent of West Bank land is not registered in the tabu (*FE*, 24 May 1987: 8, 9).

The occupation authorities amended the Jordanian Town and Village Planning Law of 1966 and thus the planning power of the district commissions was turned over to the Israeli Higher Planning Council. The advent of the Likud government caused further erosion in Arab planning power. Jewish regional councils on the West Bank have become "special planning commissions" (Peretz 1986: 66). Allowing Jewish settlers to plan for the use of Palestinian land has resulted in severe restrictions on where Palestinians could build, and has speeded up the expropriation of land. Says Don Peretz,

At present up to 70 percent of the land in the West Bank could be available for exclusive Jewish use under a variety of administrative and legal instruments used by Israeli authorities. These devices include outright expropriation, closure for security or military purposes, classification of land as protected natural areas, confiscation for public purposes, and outright purchase (1986: 59).

In 1982, a number of cases were uncovered where land had been obtained by fraudulent means. The courts failed to take action when evidence of forged signatures were brought to their attention (Shehadeh 1985: 41). Investigation proved that many of those schemes were undertaken by Israeli government officials like Avi Tzur and Claude Malka, both members of Herut Party's central committee (*FE*, 20 December 1985, 10).

While dealings with the Israeli court system leave a great deal to be desired, Palestinians have no recourse when they are set upon by armed settlers who defy court orders, work on land when they are not supposed to, and shoot at farmers.

In this chapter we find the stories of two farmers: "Umm Ayyash," who has lived a hard life but had the satisfaction of remaining on her land and tilling her daughter's field, and Aishah Shamlawi, whose family land was confiscated. The Shamlawi interview took place first in her home and then on the confiscated land. Since passion ran high in the family at the sight of the expropriated land, and many Shamlawis joined the conversation, the contributions of the rest of the family and a neighbor are included, both to present Mrs. Shamlawi's tale in context and because the defiant reactions of a young neighbor provide a sharp contrast to Mrs. Shamlawi's entreaties to "you High Court" and to the Arab governments for help. Although the events related below took place before the Intifada, the reaction of the young neighbor is a good example of the impatience the young feel with what their elders have put up with since 1948. Mrs. Shamlawi asks for mercy and pity, while the young man stresses rights and justice.

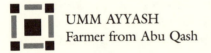 UMM AYYASH
Farmer from Abu Qash

"When I see a plowed field, I feel secure. I would feel lost without it. I see a plowed field and I know what my life is."

Life has not always been easy for Sara Qasem al Abed, "Umm Ayyash." But a combination of hard work on the land she farms, a deep faith in God, a long friendship, and a sunny disposition, has pulled her through.

Summer 1985

My mother is a Druze from Lebanon,* a strong free woman.[1] Her brother and my father were friends who served together in the Turkish army. When her brother died, Mother was left with no one to support her, so

---

*I met and took photos of Mrs. Ayyash in 1984. I was grumbling about the heat as I drove back from my work, while she was still in the hot sun, where I left her early in the morning, reaping wheat on her daughter's field. When we wanted to interview a farmer for the book, Umm Ayyash came to mind. I visited her in her home in the village of Abu Qash and interviewed her in Arabic. I asked her to tell me about her life.

Umm Ayyash reaping wheat in her daughter's field in Ramallah, 1985.
Photo by Orayb Najjar

my father, who was fascinated by her beauty, offered to marry her. He said, "Come with me, and I will feed you. Our country Palestine is beautiful, and you'll like it." Those were the days of hunger and locusts, and Father charmed her into accepting. You know how men are. He put her into a cart and brought her to the village of Abu Qash—another village, another world. I think he tricked her into accepting his proposal because she had no idea how far Palestine was from Lebanon on horseback.

Mother kept to herself. She did not visit many people and she did not gossip. She had twenty pregnancies, but only three of her children survived. When my father died, her independent spirit served her well. She took charge of the farm, plowed and harvested, even though she had never farmed before. She milked seven cows a day and sold the milk to Miss Nabiha Nasir (the woman who founded Birzeit School in 1924). We learned farming by watching her. For me farming has a special meaning. When I see a plowed field, I feel secure. I would feel lost without it. I see a plowed field and I know what my life is.

When I was growing up, farming was what everybody did. Villagers also raised cattle. The poorest among them had fifty sheep if not a hundred. Today things have changed. People now work outside the village for wages. I myself, however, continue to farm on a modest scale. Every year I harvest the land of my married daughter in Ramallah and get half the crop for myself. I have a thick vine that shades the east side of the house, and almond and lemon trees. I also grow my own vegetables. I wake up at dawn to pray, and then I putter in the garden before I touch anything else. Green land is a blessing from God. Last year, the lentil crop was so plentiful I sold some. This year it yielded next to nothing.

My life has not been easy, but I have managed to do my duty by God and by man. I was married when I was twelve years old. I had no idea what marriage was. I was delighted with the new clothes I was given as part of my trousseau. I snatched a colorful jacket and ran with it to the spring to admire it. The whole village found the incident amusing. After the wedding, whenever my husband came near me, I said I wanted my mother. He was twelve years older than me and knew how to be patient. He just smiled and let me go to my mother's house nearby. He waited until I fell asleep and then carried me home.[2]

We had three girls and one boy before he died in 1960, at the age of fifty, from an internal hemorrhage. I found myself a widow at the age of thirty-eight. My husband never made much money. His salary as a telephone operator was only $18 a month, and we were poor. But I was shocked to discover after he died that he owed people $450. To support the children, I took in washing. Every day when I was done, I sat on my wicker chair by the door and embroidered hats and dresses until dusk. I could not work indoors because we had no electricity, so natural light was not to be wasted. Like my mother I did not visit much, and besides there was no time left after I finished my chores. I did reasonably well at embroidery because I acquired a reputation for tidy work and had no trouble finding customers.

I believe my reputation spread largely due to the efforts of my dear friend Miladeh Rabia. Wherever she went she talked about my embroidery and brought me customers from this and from other villages. As a result of her efforts, I made about $50 a month. I put my money in my chest [saved] and paid our debt in three years.

Miladeh was a widow living on her own with six children. We rented a small house together. She and her children lived upstairs, and her children and mine became like brothers and sisters. I owe Miladeh a great deal. She taught me how to buy all the year's supply of food to save money, and she taught me how to make my own soap. So together we cut down on living expenses since we grew most of our food and collected herbs from the surrounding hills. But we still needed cash to buy clothes and school supplies for the children.

The best thing about having Miladeh there was that she was my friend. We always carried our coffee to each other's houses and comforted each other when things got rough. I earned a little money working in people's houses. I once worked for an old lady who had to be fed and she preferred to be fed by me instead of her daughters because I told her stories about the old days, the days of hunger, and that made her eat. In another household, an educated woman I worked for did not know about house-keeping. She had never learned how to cook. She'd enter the kitchen and say, "I am totally useless." She was right. There is a time for everything— a time to learn from books and a time to do housework.

But all this work in homes was irregular. I needed a permanent job that offered retirement benefits, and a lady I once helped pick grapes got me a job as a kitchen worker in the Lutheran school in East Jerusalem. Work at the school was scheduled in shifts. One week I worked from 6:00 to 10:00 A.M. and traveled back to Abu Qash to be with my children, and the next week I worked from 10:00 A.M. to 7:00 P.M. and stayed away for a whole week because there was no transportation back to my village at that hour. I left my young son with his older sister, and Miladeh kept an eye on them and fed them with her children.

A woman living alone is never left in peace. Everyone tries to marry her off. I was rather good looking in my younger days and several people said, "Your husband was a good man, but life goes on, and you need to think of yourself." But all I wanted was to earn enough to give my chil-dren a good life. My husband was poor. Had he been "happy" [rich], I might have viewed remarriage differently. But I could not see how the people who were interested in me would be able to support all of us. So I said I had no intention of remarrying, but no one took me seriously, and I had to actively fight the notion that I was available. I wore black for seven years to discourage attention towards myself, but many were not daunted.

A man who lived nearby used to stand on the verandah and say he could smell my lovely cooking. He asked if he could "pour his oil over my flour" [share/marry], but I wanted none of it. I had forgotten that there were things that gladden the heart. I had forgotten what living with a man was in my struggle to get by.

Once, an old man came to talk to me about marriage on behalf of an acquaintance. When I realized what he wanted, I said, "Haj, you'd better leave. I think I hear someone calling you." I did not even offer him any coffee, and in Arab culture, that is unforgivable. He left in a huff and said to people, "She pulled the chair out from under me. This is no woman, this is a witch, and no one should marry her." I was satisfied that the message was finally getting across. I needed that reputation for self-protection. I needed to be left in peace to raise my children. After a hard day's work, I had no energy left to think of myself, of companionship, or of living with a man. To catch the two buses I needed to go to Jerusalem, I had to wake up very early. I would get dressed and glance at the little pieces of flesh lying there needing me, and my heart would break for them. The image of my little son hanging on the rails of the bus crying for me haunted me at work. When I sent my daughter to an orphanage in Jerusalem, I worried about how she was adapting, but I wanted her to have a good education. She later became a kindergarten teacher, and her salary helped us.

Work at the school was not without its problems. In my day, workers had no unions to look after their affairs; every person was for himself. The first confrontation I had with my employers was over lunchtime. I never miss a prayer. We were given half an hour for lunch. Instead of eating with the other employees, I washed and prayed. Some people complained. They said, "When does she eat? Does she steal her food outside lunch hours?" Our Swedish boss came for a visit, and my problem was reported to him. He asked me for an explanation, and I said, "God has rights over us, and I need to pray." He was very sympathetic. He extended the lunch hour for all employees from half an hour to a full hour and he said I should keep the keys to the kitchen storeroom because he believed I was an honest woman. I took on the job and watched the supplies like a hawk.

I worked at that school for eleven years. Standing in the kitchen for hours was hard on my varicose veins. I would stand on one leg, and lift the other to rest it, but finally I had to see a doctor. We could see a doctor free of charge, but he prescribed special socks for $25. To my surprise, those were deducted from my wages. When my daughter was due to give birth, I took an eight-day leave to visit her in Amman to help her. At the end of the month, I discovered that the eight days were subtracted from my salary. I felt that it was unfair because it was an emergency situation; I was needed elsewhere. My immediate supervisor was not afraid of God. He did not understand that if you are merciful to those on earth, heaven will be merciful to you. He claimed that he had paid someone to replace me in my absence. I resigned in a fit of anger but soon discovered that once you resign voluntarily, you lose all benefits. I am illiterate, and no one told me that before I resigned, so I hired a lawyer who discovered that my employer had not in fact paid anyone else to replace me, and my benefits were restored.

God watches over people, and He is just. Bad things happened to my employer. His eighteen-year-old son committed suicide. The man said, "I have been unfair to this woman. Bring her to me, I want to make amends. I want to ask her forgiveness." He apologized to me and even gave the $25 he had deducted for the socks.

I felt sorry for his poor wife losing a child like that. The relationship between a mother and her children is very special. A mother is a school for children. Take the relationship between my mother and myself. I have been taking care of my invalid mother for years now because my sister and brother live abroad.

My mother lives close by. I visit her every day and take care of her needs. She has lost control of her bladder and so she needs changing constantly. This morning after I washed her and changed her clothes she grabbed my hand and kissed it. "Thank you, please forgive me for the trouble I am giving you," she said. I was very touched and tears came to my eyes to think of her being so alert and worrying about me. I said, "Oh no, Mother. I am the one who has to apologize to you. You bore us, nursed us, and worked hard for us," and I kissed her hand.

I told my friend Miladeh what had happened when I visited her to congratulate her on the marriage of her sixth child. We have known each other for over twenty-one years now and like to talk about old times. She moved away after we built our own two-room house. She urged me to stay and visit with her that day, but I said I had to take care of my mother. The way she acted that morning affected me. I told Miladeh that I will visit her soon, but if I do not it is because of my mother's health.[3]

With regard to my own children, God has been kind to us. My work has paid off; they are all settled. My three daughters are now married. My son worked in the Arabian Gulf and now he is back here working for an air-conditioning company. He lights up the house. I would like to see him happily married and then I can rest.

Update

Mrs. Ayyash's son married his cousin. Mrs. Ayyash now lives with her daughter Nijmeh (Star) in the town of Ramallah, and works in her daughter's land "to the best of her ability." Mrs. Ayyash was hurt when she was hit by a car driven by an Israeli settler. She has sued for damages.[4]

■■■
■□■ AISHEH SHAMLAWI
■■■ Farmer from Hares

"Our land was gold. . . . Lentils it fed us, olives it fed us, wheat it fed us. That is where we got our food and drink, from the land." This is how Mrs. Shamlawi describes her family land in the village of Hares. When the land was confiscated, the Shamlawis became ridden with debt. Here, she, her family, and a neighbor relate how the confiscation came about.

Summer 1986

Mrs. Aisheh Shamlawi: It all started in the seventh month of 1982.* We went to the fields to pick figs and found surveyors on our land. We asked them what they were doing, and they claimed they did not know. "Go ask the government," they said. My son and stepson went to Israeli officials in the city of Toulkarm, the officials sent them to the city of Qalqelia, in Qalqelia they said, "No, go to Toulkarm." The men then returned to Toulkarm and were told that the police would come to our land the next day to investigate, but the police never did.

Two days later we found surveyors on our land again and tried to prevent them from surveying the land. Shortly after that the police came. Instead of talking to us, the Israeli policemen asked the Israeli surveyors, "Who stood in your way?" The surveyors said, "The owners of the land

---

*I interviewed Aisheh Shamlawi in her home in Arabic and took notes while she spoke. I asked her to tell me about the confiscation of the family land. I had read about it in the press. I deliberately did not record my conversation in her home to give her a chance to relax. When she and several other members of the family took me over to the confiscated land, I tape recorded their reactions. I chose to include other family members and a neighbor in this story in order to preserve the context because it was not a monologue like other accounts. It was also important to show the differences between attitudes of the young and the old; Mrs. Shamlawi talks about fear of God, and asks for mercy on the basis of need, while the neighbor, nineteen, talks about rights and asks for justice. He is of the Intifada generation. My most important concern in this story was to preserve the lyrical language most members of the family used. I worked from the tape, and attempted to preserve the order and the rhythm of words in my translation. Repetition and the sentence structure below occurred frequently: "Stepson, sixty-three: We are farmers. When it is plowing time, *we plow*, when it is planting season, *we plant*." Parallel structure: "*Sometimes*, we work for others for half the crop. *Sometimes* we work as laborers." Word order: "Whatever it takes to feed the family, *we do*." In my reconstruction of the conversation, I moved some information from the end of the transcript to the beginning, because that move helped readers understand the chronological sequence of events. If two people repeated the same information, I used only one of them.

did not allow us to work on it." We said, "Of course we would not allow them to work on it. This is our land, our olives, our almonds, our figs. Why are these people here?" "We don't know," said the police, and took their names down, then told us that the surveyors will not be back.

A week later, the surveyors were back.

Mrs. Shamlawi's son, twenty-six: We came upon another surveyor on our land. He claimed that he was surveying the land for an electricity pole, "No," I said, "you are doing nothing of the sort." The surveyor said, "Look, I am just an employee, and here is the address of the company I work for in Tel Aviv." So I took the address and went to Tel Aviv. The company told me, "This is our land, we got it from the Custodian of Absentee Property." I said, "Look, this is ridiculous. Here I am, one of the owners of the land. We are not absentees, we never went anywhere."[1] But the man insisted that the land was confiscated by an ordinance in February 1981, along with the land of two other villages, and that the Arab owners were given thirty days to appeal.[2] That was the first I've heard of this ordinance. I insisted that we were not notified, and did not receive even one document that suggested that our land had been confiscated, and without papers, nothing doing.

Neighbor, nineteen: Even with papers, confiscation is unjust and illegal. This is your land, they have no right to take it.

Mrs. Shamlawi's stepson, sixty-three: For a few months we hesitated about hiring a lawyer, thinking we could clarify the matter simply by proving our presence on the land and ownership of it to the Custodian of Absentee Property, but we got no satisfaction moving from one Israeli official to the other, and felt the case was going nowhere. So [in October 1982], we went to the office of lawyer Felicia Langer who asked us to prepare documents to survey the land and prove our ownership of it. I was born in 1923. My brothers and I inherited the land from my father, and he got it from his father. We did not expect Israelis to believe us, so we produced inheritance papers and records that showed that we paid taxes on the land to the British and, above all, we said, "here is the land that we have planted all these years, look at the crops, look at the trees." An Israeli official tried to say that what they were confiscating is not agricultural land, so we took him there and he saw the olives. We also showed them that we owned a quarry.

Mrs. Shamlawi: Trucks with stone as big as a room used to be taken to Kuwait, Saudi Arabia, Abu Dhabi through Amman. When the Israelis occupied this land, we decided to stop cutting stone. It was hard to get permission to export anything, and the taxes Israelis levied were too high. We were always here, always plowed, always planted. My oldest stepson took care of his brothers when his father got old.

Stepson: The lawyer also asked that we survey the land, so we did, and paid a surveyor $250. Of course we had to pay the law firm before it took the case to the Military Court at Beit El. The lawyer Abed Asali, who works for Langer, got a court order to stop Israelis from surveying the land for two months, and [in May 1983] the Military Appeal Committee ruled that cultivated lands are not included in the confiscation order. We knew our land was agricultural land; it fed the nine of us, our wives and children. We considered the matter settled, but two years passed and [in April 1985] another surveyor showed up on our land. That winter, we again had trouble with surveyors on our land.

Mrs. Shamlawi: At 4:00 A.M. despite the pouring rain, we could see people in our land because our house overlooks the area. So the whole family rushed to the site and found about fifteen men, all armed, surrounding three bulldozers, uprooting our trees. They would approach one, fell it, scoop a lot of dirt, and then bury the tree under. Trees that took thirty years to grow fell, just like that. When they saw us running towards them, the Israelis called the police. We argued with them and we physically tried to prevent them from working on our land by standing in front of the bulldozers. I was one of the people they pushed to the ground into the mud. My sons and stepson were beaten and hand-cuffed and taken to the police station in Toulkarm. The rest of us were ordered back to our house. They were armed, so we had to comply. We stood outside our home, and watched from a distance as tractors uprooted our trees, one after the other, all day and into the afternoon. Shortly after the tractors stopped working the men were brought back from detention.

Stepson: At the police station, we tried to tell the police chief what had happened, but he refused to even listen to us. We were kept outside in the pouring rain while the settlers who arrested us went in and told their version of the story. We were outside the Toulkarm police station, shivering in the cold and rain like wet fish—and no one bothered to get us any food even though we were not released till 4:00 P.M. By then, Israeli bulldozers had uprooted 150 trees out of a total of 2,500.[3] The next day, the police chief came by in a car and told us not to ob-struct the uprooting. He turned to the men in the bulldozers and said, "If they obstruct your path, just pick them up in your bulldozer, or shoot them."

Mrs. Shamlawi: I don't understand it. How can the government let those settlers loose on us, like cows? They had guns and tractors. Who do we complain to?

Son: Settlers telephone the police and they appear immediately. In our case, if we call the police, not by phone, mind you, but in person, and repeatedly, they say, "O.K., O.K., we'll be there," but they do not come. It may take a week before they even deign to pay any attention to us. All Israelis have to do is call the Ariel settlement police and say, "We need you," and the police rush to the scene. Here is the situation: they trespass on our land, we call the police, they do not come. The settlers call the police, the police come and arrest *US*! There is a law, but it is for Israelis, not for us. These people are here to confuse my brain. It used to be that in the old days a person would stand and throw a stone and say, this is how far my land stretches. The whole village knew who the land belonged to, and who tilled and tended the land. I *know* this land. I do not need surveyors and maps to tell me where its boundaries are. I have tilled it, year after year. I ask by what right do Jews come from the United States, from the Soviet Union, from Syria, from Israel and take over our land? The Israeli government builds them factories over our land. They build roads, settlements, on our land. There is no justice. One person simply takes over the land of another.

Again we went to the authorities for help, and [in May 1985] we received a letter from a person who is in charge of government property. The letter again stated that agricultural land is excluded from confiscation. [In June 1985], the court of First Appeal in Nablus issued a restraining order against doing any kind of work in the land. Shortly after that [in July 1985], the Military Appeal Committee met at the request of the Custodian of Property [Custodian of Absentee Property] and decided to change the decision of May 1983 and to exclude from confiscation only those lands which were heavily planted with olive trees. In this new decision, they said that wheat or barley was not considered agricultural land, so we lost 150 dunums out of 215. The committee claimed that our land was excluded from confiscation earlier due to an error.

So [in August 1985], we appealed to the High Court of Justice against the change of the decision of the appeal committee. The court refused to rule on the case and let the decision stand,[4] but decreed that we pay court expenses as well in the amount of 2 million shekels [about $1250]. I once showed a piece of paper we got from the court to one of the Israelis and he said that all we were given is not land, but a street through the land.

Mrs. Shamlawi: These people are thieves. The money we paid them we had to borrow. We are poor (fukriyyeh, injibariyyeh). We lose, we

"Ya Allah!" (Oh God!) Aisheh Shamlawi, left, is agitated at the sight of her land.
Photo by Orayb Najjar

borrow. You know God, don't you? I am telling you the truth. Meat has not touched our lips for two months now. On top of that, they threaten to shoot us. We said: High Court, give us our rights so that our hearts can cool. We went to it for justice and we did not get any.

Son: They plowed the almonds under, they destroyed the retaining walls in order to claim that the land is not agricultural land, and now it is not, and they may take it all. We fix and they destroy, and when my brother protested, they beat him up.

Stepson: We are farmers. When it is plowing time, we plow, when it is planting season, we plant, when it is time to repair walls we repair them. Sometimes, we work for others for half the crop. Sometimes we work as laborers. Whatever it takes to feed the family, we do.

Mrs. Shamlawi: Allahu Akbar (God is great), the Arab countries do not protect us. We have served those trees all our lives.

Neighbor: The problem would be funny if it were not sad. Sad because the owners of the land, the ones who sweated over it for years, have to be hauled to court, where the judge is appointed by the government. If they call the police for protection, what they hear is: "What are you creating trouble for?" The persons who are defending their land are troublemakers, people who are trespassing and uprooting trees are now law-abiding citizens!

Stepson: With a tree, it is like you raise a child. You tend it, you watch over it.

Mrs. Shamlawi's daughter-in-law: I used to plow with a cow, so that we can live.

Stepson: I said, here, look, even though I do not think I need proof of ownership, after all, anyone can see I have been working on the land, I showed all the papers, I paid the lawyers, I went to court, and yet, they simply disregarded all evidence.

Mrs. Shamlawi: Lentils it fed us, olives it fed us, wheat it fed us. That is where we got our food and drink, from the land. I have four boys, and my husband has one boy, that makes five, I have two girls, and my husband has two from another wife and they and their children all live from the land. Who do we complain to? Allahu Akbar! What do they want with us? God turns things upside down. Oh God, where are you? Do not turn your eye away from the oppressor, oh God (ya, Allah!).

Neighbor: In the West, when they talk about us, foreigners sometimes talk about the land as if it is a desert, they say we do not take care of the land. They say we are terrorists. But why do they say that? Each person works within his capacity. I am poor. I have no tractor, I have no bull-dozer. I clear the land with my hands. I plow. I have a horse, a donkey. I just want to live. I say to them: "What do you want with me. Leave me alone! I want to plow in my own way, within my own limited means. If you cannot help me, and you are not helping me, at least do not harm me."

Mrs. Shamlawi: The land yielded thirty kuntars of wheat a year (1 kuntar=256.4 Kg.), this is not counting the barley and the lentils. Our land was gold. Many years we did not have to buy a single sack of flour or any of our food needs, and sometimes we had money left over. When the weather was bad, however, we were short of money and crops, and the men worked as laborers for cash. Even in between the work season, they worked as laborers in Israel. But now, how will we manage? Some of them have ten children. Look at my hands. Bony. From hunger. I swear to you during those past four years they have given us trouble, after we borrowed money to pay for the lawyers in two cases, and for land surveyors, no one was left to lend us any money. I swear to you that there were times we were so short of cash that all the children had to eat was fried tomatoes. And I myself. . . .

Son: Say it, don't be ashamed.

Mrs. Shamlawi: I am too old for people to hire me, and I want to help. I now sit in the streets of Nablus and beg. My daughter did not complete high school; we pulled her out of school. No funds. My son left school to work. Other people have someone working in Saudi Arabia and sending them money; we don't. We are peasants. Some people have daughters who are teachers, but we do not. One of my sons is in Amman, but he is sick and out of work. We have to send him money to support his family. We tried to have family reunion so his family can be here with us, but our application was rejected. You see, we are farmers. We have been farming all our lives, we have no graduates. Our land is all we have.

Neighbor: Assume that you have all the money in the world, that would be irrelevant to the issue. This is your land, and the Israelis have no right to it!

Mrs. Shamlawi: Oh God! We are holding onto you—have mercy on us. My God, where are you? Oh God, have pity on us. It is not right, for four years now they have brought us nothing but worry. One kills one or two, but a whole family? If they take all our land away that is what they will be doing, killing us. And where shall we go? To whom shall we complain? Hey, you High Court (ya Mihkama Ulya), you are supposed to be just, you have treated us unfairly. For God's sake, you High Court, you have melted our hearts. We have taken refuge with you (istagarna fiki),[5] but you have not responded. (Sings with a tune that sounds like a dirge) "You Arab countries, you have not helped us."

Neighbor: Where are we living? In South Africa? This is racism. This man used to live comfortably. He had money. Now he has been turned into a daily laborer to pay for the debt they incurred when he borrowed money to pay the surveyors, the lawyers and for transport—and, he has lost his land!

Mrs. Shamlawi: What I do is pray all day. My head hurts, here, here, my hands are bony, from want.

Son: We always had something in the land. We rotated crops to preserve moisture in the soil. One year we would plant the wheat here, the beans here, the lentils here, and then let the land rest and plant something else.

Neighbor: Israel has, indirectly, passed a death sentence on the family. I say indirectly, because in their law, they boast that they do not have a death sentence in Israel, but in fact, in a roundabout way they pass death sentences on people.

Mrs. Shamlawi: Tell people about us. . . . I don't know if it would do any good, though. We have had many journalists visit, even some from other countries. What is the name of that place? Where did that man come from, that man who came before? . . . Yes, Japan. We walk with them on our land, we show them the roots of uprooted trees . . . (uproots some barley from a clump of buried soil) here, look! Does this look like agriculture to you? Is this agricultural land? There was an oak tree here . . . we show visitors the roots that have been plowed under, they take photographs, but it does not change anything.

THREE

Encounters with the Occupation Authorities

Women started resisting the occupation shortly after the 1967 June war. In July 1967, women began compiling memoranda on torture, mass arrests, and administrative detention to send to foreign diplomats, the Vatican, and the International Red Cross. They felt at liberty to do so because at that time, women were not yet watched very closely, and could meet with foreigners and brief them, and lead strikes and demonstrations (Antonius 1980: 36).

Women in Palestinian society often act as guardians of tradition and protest changes that affect the moral fiber of society. In August 1968, for instance, they sent a petition to the head of the Israeli government protesting the deteriorating conditions in the old city of Jerusalem, the opening of night clubs, and the resulting noise, the gambling, prostitution, and drug use (*Palestinian Yearbook* 1968: 554).

Palestinian women are often entrusted with the position of supplicant to occupation authorities. They presented petitions to the British in 1929, and to the Israelis during the early years of the occupation. The letter women sent to Israeli premier Levi Eshkol to protest the Israeli military parade in Jerusalem in 1968 said the event was "evidence of an ugly picture of provocation and the disregard for the feelings of thousands of Arabs in the city." The women added that they expected "a message of peace and justice, not the buzz of Jets and the roar of heavy machines of destruction" (*Palestinian Yearbook* 1986: 560). In February 1969, Moslem and Christian women staged a hunger strike in the Church of the Holy Sepulchre in Jerusalem to protest the murder in Gaza of three women and the wounding of thirteen others (Karmi 1976: 6).

The women's movement as well as independent women were affected by developments in the PLO. Between 1965 and the early 1970s, the PLO stressed armed struggle for the liberation of Palestine (thus the recruitment of women commandos). Between 1971 and 1979, at least 1,229 women were arrested (Antonius 1980); few, however, were arrested for armed struggle like Rawda Basiir, whose story is told in this chapter.

Commenting on the reality of women's involvement in armed struggle, one female activist in Lebanon said,

Of course we have female commandos and of course we have training camps for women. But when their training is completed, they are sent home again. Because of all this our women don't trust themselves when it comes to military action (Bendt and Downing 1980: 100).

Women, however, were always active in demonstrations and sit-ins. The activist role of women has not escaped the Israeli media. Israel Television reporter Rafik Halabi writes,

I have seen women and children in the Amari refugee camp burn tires into flaming barricades. I have seen girls building roadblocks out of stones as other girls . . . have rained rocks on Israeli soldiers (Halabi 1981: 105).

Describing a demonstration at a girl's high school in Ramallah, he says,

An officer raised his gun and sent a warning shot into the air but they were not deterred. Then the officer aimed his rifle straight at them menacingly, and one of the students shrieked, "Go on, make me a Muntaha Hourani!"–a reference to a girl killed during a demonstration in Jenin in 1974 (Halabi 1981: 106).

Women actively joined the 1976 and 1981 uprisings, but they joined in even larger numbers in the 1987 Intifada. Israeli soldiers have killed women as well as men during the Intifada. Rita Giacaman and Penny Johnson caution, however, that death statistics do not reflect the extent of women's activism. Of the *first* 204 Palestinians killed in the West Bank, fifteen were girls or women. By 1 September 1988, forty-nine women had been killed, and by December 1990, the number reached seventy. An estimated 300 women have been detained for longer than a day when the number of males had reached 20,000. Thirteen women were placed under administrative detention in contrast to 3,000 to 4,000 men. "Since these indicators are also used by Palestinian society to measure activism, it is unclear how visible or valued women's activities are in the collective assessment of society" (Giacaman and Johnson 1989: 162; Tawfiq, *FE*, 24 December 1990: 8).

So despite women's occasional involvement in commando activity, especially in the early years, and despite female casualties in the Intifada, most activism by women is of a nonmilitary nature. In fact, there appears to be a division of labor between Palestinian women and men, where it is more acceptable for women than for men to ask for peace. "We want peace in the land of peace," read one banner women carried in a demonstration against Israel's plan to hold a military parade in occupied Arab Jerusalem in 1968 (Karmi 1976: 6). That division of labor can also be seen within the PLO outside the Occupied Territories. "In Palestinian symbolism the women usually fight for peace and the men for justice" (Bendt and Downing 1980: 31).

With the Palestinian move to accept a two-state solution in the early 1970s, stress shifted from the idea of "return," by the barrel of the gun if necessary, to staying on the land and building institutions that would enable the population to resist various Israeli pressures. Volunteer work flourished in the West Bank, and every single group seeking legitimacy made public service its cornerstone. The women's movement was no exception. In addition to taking part in public protest against the occupation, women continued to be active in their societies, and Israeli authorities were not kind to activists. But nonactivist women could not escape the pressures of the occupation and had to live with the imprisonment of husbands, sons, and brothers, and had to endure the loss of incomes, the imposition of curfews, and collective punishment.

Between 1967 and 1982, Israeli authorities demolished 1,265 houses (*Ha'aretz* on 20 October 1988 in *al-Talia*, 27 October 1988, 8). Ronny

Talmor, a researcher of the newly formed Israel Information Center for Human Rights in the Occupied Territories, B'Tselem, revealed that during the Palestinian uprising, since December 1987, at least 334 houses were destroyed or sealed in the West Bank and Gaza. About 4000 people (mostly extended families) were left homeless after the demolitions under study. In many cases, neighboring houses also were damaged. Talmor concluded that in only 1 percent of the 173 house demolitions in the West Bank had the suspect been convicted before demolition took place. The figure was only 10 percent in Gaza (Salome 1989: 36A).

Dedi Zucker of the Citizens Rights Movement, described house demolition as "vandalism carried out by a state," a form of dual punishment, where a suspect has his house demolished by the military and then stands trial and gets punished in court (*FE*, 31 July 1988, 4). Few Israelis, however, realize how radicalizing each house demolition is to the families involved, as the story of Salima Kumsiyya shows.

The stories in this chapter describe several encounters women had with the occupation authorities, as Israelis searched their homes or demolished them, imprisoned them or their relatives. We also see how women and their families and neighbors coped with these pressures: disbelief and indirect resistance in the case of Na'imah al-As'ad, her daughter Shurouk, and Salima Kumsiyya; direct resistance in the case of Rawda Basiir; and inadvertent martyrdom in the case of Haniyyeh Ghazawneh. Each of these accounts tells us about how the occupation has disrupted the daily fabric of women's lives and explains why women are more active in the uprising than they have ever been in Palestinian history.

RAWDA BASIIR
One of the leaders of the prison movement

Born in Jerusalem in 1952, Rawda grew up in a village near Ramallah. After two years of college, she studied in Italy for a year, majoring in the education of the deaf. She then worked in an institution for the deaf in Bethlehem for five years, until she was arrested and sentenced to eight years in prison for membership in an illegal group and for carrying explosives. Her meeting with the first generation of Palestinian female prisoners taught Rawda that the struggle for Palestinian human rights and self-determination has to continue even in prison. The realiza-

tion made her lead a nine-month prisoner's strike to establish the right of women to be treated as political prisoners.

My father, a schoolteacher, used to listen to the news every day and talk about it.* At the age of four, I knew the names of countries involved in the Suez crisis of 1956. Father taught us to be ambitious. I saw too the lives of women in our village, where the only idea is that a woman should marry and have a family. I resolved not to end up like them and put all my energy into studying.

As I grew up, I began to feel that we could do something to help ourselves—but it was the civil war in Lebanon in 1976 that finally shocked me into action; seeing how Palestinians were under attack wherever they were led me to join a group of young men and women in our village in doing volunteer work. My parents supported me. Villagers could see that we girls were working for the sake of the work, not because we wanted the chance to chat with men. When we went from house to house collecting money, everybody gave us whatever we asked for, even the poorest. In addition to cleaning the streets and building a bus shelter, we read and discussed books about politics, literature, and the Palestinian cause. We didn't have any definite ideology as a group. We just wanted to work and take part in the great struggle that our people were engaged in. I was dreaming of guns and fedayiin (guerrillas) and what we would achieve.

One of our group, a PLO member, suggested that we move into armed struggle. We were a little afraid, but ready. We carried out some successful operations, then one evening, we were in my family's empty house in Jerusalem, preparing a bomb to put on a train bringing Israeli soldiers back to their camps after the weekend. The bomb exploded as our leader was assembling it. He was killed, and three of us were badly injured.

The army took me to hospital, where my wounded hand was X-rayed. I was left to bleed until the second night after my arrest, then, at another hospital, they put some dressing on my hand. The next day I was taken to

*Kitty Warnock taped six hours of conversations with Rawda in English on 20 December 1985 at her home in the village of Taibeh. She then transcribed and edited the tape. Kitty was introduced to Rawda by her friends and colleagues in the Palestinian Union of Women's Work Committees (PUWWC). Kitty sent me a long version of this article as well as the original transcript to facilitate editing. In addition to shortening sentences here and there, I deleted a section about Nasserist influence on Rawda because other women in the book talked about that period. I deleted a poem because it lost its power in translation, as Rawda herself commented it would. I inserted more information about the first prisoners who had a formative influence on Rawda, added information about her breaking off her engagement, and inserted Rawda's refusal to accept chocolates from the warden.

Muscobiyya interrogation center. For the first few days I was put in an underground cell, the notorious Cell Number Ten. It's the size of a bed, the toilet a hole in the corner blocked up with filth, a blanket crawling with lice, not a crack for air or light. You wouldn't think you could survive in such a place, but I was so weak from loss of blood when I arrived that I hardly noticed where I was and fell asleep immediately.

At night, they filled the cell with noise. It came in through a ventilator shaft in the ceiling, terrible sounds of voices shrieking and groaning. Most likely it was a tape recording intended to demoralize me. I lay there too weak to move but my mind was working: "I can bear a lot, but this terrible noise may affect me. It may come back into my mind and haunt me in the future. I must struggle against it." So I told myself over and over again, "This noise is nothing, it's not real, it's just a trick my enemy is trying to use to destroy me. He will do worse than this, but I must overcome everything. I am a representative of my people, and I have to be strong for their sakes."

Ten days into my thirty-five-day interrogation, I realized that my hand needed attention. It was swollen and all blue and brown, and very painful. I complained to the prison doctor, and I was taken to a Jerusalem hospital. The doctor there said, "Your arm is broken in several places, and the bones in your left hand are completely crushed. Why didn't you come to us earlier? A day or two more, and we would have had to amputate it." I was lucky I complained when I did. During my interrogation, the officers used to hit me on the face and head and on my arm and hand and threaten to smash the plaster.

After I was sentenced to eight years, I was moved to the main women's prison, Neve Tirza, on December 15, 1977. For six and a half years, I shared a room with Therese Halaseh, the first woman to spend twelve years in prison. She was a strong woman with a leader's personality; we learned a lot from her. She and I were the leaders together. We often disagreed about issues and would shout at each other, but in the end, we always sat down and discussed and reached agreement. Therese became ill with abscesses all over her body; nobody knew why. She never let us see how much pain she was suffering. I bathed and dressed the abscesses; she would not let the guards come near her. One day, in October 1983, the guards walked into our room and said to her, "Pack up your things, you're leaving." I sat there with my face in my hands. When I lost Therese, I resolved that I would never let myself become so close to anyone again. You become too vulnerable.

You know how you meet one or two people in your lifetime who have a profound effect on you, who change the direction of your life? Aisha Odeh was one of those. She was the first woman the Israeli military imprisoned after 1967, and I had always known of her and her heroism. She had been in prison for nine years when I arrived, then I was with her for fifteen months until she was released. I was determined to draw strength from these revolutionary women and learn from their experience.

An important step towards liberation was our liberation from the fear of rape. By publicizing that Israeli interrogators had raped them with sticks, two of those first women prisoners arrested after 1967 asserted that it was one of the enemy's acts and not something they should personally be ashamed of; they gave all women the knowledge that they need not be defeated—the ability to rebel against the social customs that make rape such a powerful weapon against us.[1]

From all the other comrades, and from Aisha most of all, I learned how to stand up to the authorities, how to understand the tactics of struggle and wait for the correct time to act. I learned that the struggle we are waging outside doesn't end when you come to prison, but continues, though in a different way.

Struggle in prison eradicates everything weak in your personality. Aisha said, "Our growth in prison is like the movement of roots. You don't see roots, but they are there, reaching deep and building the base for new structures." All the experiences I had in prison contributed to my growth, even the sad ones. I saw my beloved Aisha ill, with blinding headaches, with stomach pains and abscesses all over her body. Those were the times when we were most powerless. We could not send her to the hospital, we couldn't bring her medicine beyond the few aspirins the prison authorities gave her. Another prisoner, Rasmiyyeh Odeh, once lost her sight all of a sudden, for fifteen days, and we just had to sit and watch.

On March 9, 1979, the first prisoner exchange took place. Aisha and most of the first-generation prisoners left. It was my turn and others' to take over the leadership, and we chose to strike on Israel's Independence Day. We refused to share in the special meal. How can they expect us to celebrate the fact that Israel took our land?

We didn't waste a minute of our time in prison. We read about imperialism, capitalism, economics, socialism, Marxist theory, history, psychology, and women's liberation. A great influence on me at this time was Brigit Schulz, a German woman who had been studying sociology at

Heidelberg University and was able to teach us a lot. I used to say that she was like Lenin, studying all the time.

Brigit was captured with a Palestinian group in Nairobi in 1975. She was tortured in Kenya and then handed over to the Mossad, the Israeli Secret Service. They were kept in dungeons with bags over their heads and were physically mistreated. For a year, the Israeli government denied knowing where they were. When Israeli authorities had to admit the group was in Israel, Brigit was brought to Neve Tirza prison. For three and a half years she was kept in solitary confinement. She shared a lawyer with Aisha, and he managed to transfer her to live with the rest of us.

It was two days before Christmas, 1978, that I saw her for the first time. She was so excited, she was speaking German, Hebrew, English, French, Arabic, all mixed up. I started crying; I thought she was confused because she had been alone so long, and I couldn't bear it if that had happened to her. In fact she was amazing. I never have imagined a person could be so strong. She impressed us all deeply by being so normal after three and a half years of isolation.

Brigit became one of those special people like Aisha and Therese. We studied a lot together. I taught her Arabic. She translated for us her German newspapers and magazines which the censors never bothered to check carefully. Our own were heavily censored. We also discussed all kinds of theoretical and feminist issues. I have lost touch with her now. I'd love to know what she's doing. I think she is involved in the Green Party.

My family was stunned by my imprisonment. They had not known anything about my work. For the first five years my mother used to weep all through her visits. I tried to encourage her gently—"I'm a human being, mother. If you weep, I'll start weeping too," and I said, "Look at me! Don't you see how well I am? I am stronger than I was at home." But my words didn't help, and eventually I said, "Look, if you don't stop crying now, I'm going back to my room and I will not see you anymore. I can't bear to see you in this state." She stopped at once, and she's never cried since.

Sometimes new ways of thinking and old ones struggle together like a boiling sea inside you. You want to change but you haven't the strength. My fault was that I had been too passive. My Christian upbringing taught me that I should love everybody. Now I started thinking, "No, I will like only those people who deserve to be liked." I also demanded respect from prison authorities. You walk a fine line all the time and try to determine how far you must adjust to circumstances in order to stay alive, how far you can refuse them in order to preserve your independence. Before you do anything in prison, you have to think, "Am I doing it merely because I have been ordered to?" I never obeyed any order without thinking about it. It comes naturally to me to invent things for myself, but many girls find it frightening because it is not something our school education teaches us here. If one of my comrades wanted to copy something nice I have made, I would say, "No, don't copy it. Never repeat something that has been done before, think about it and improve it every time you do it."

It made me sad to see how easily the Israeli prisoners gave up their individual, human personalities soon after arrival. They were afraid of losing their privileges. They would even betray their comrades sometimes, in return for small favors from the prison administration.

This sort of weakness never occurred among Palestinian prisoners. We were few, fifty-five during Aisha's time and around thirty after that. If one of us showed signs of weakening, the others gave her new strength. The prison authorities never succeeded in breaking our unity, by force or bribery or any other means. It is important for the whole Palestinian struggle that prisoners be strong and organized. People expect women to be weak, but when they see us in prison they realize that it's a good thing for women to be strong. Men like it especially—they like strong women in general, it's only as wives they are afraid of them! I think the position of women in society will improve as women themselves become strong. Why should men give up any of their privileges to women who are weak?

Israelis are taught to think they are superior to us. We prisoners had to show them that we were not inferior to them, that in spite of being in prison, and in spite of the brutality we had suffered at their hands, we were still strong, civilized, and human. Our presence did affect most of the Israeli prisoners. When the guards asked, "Why are you associating with those Palestinians who kill your children?" they answered, "They are our friends, they are good people." The guards didn't change. They were sadists who treated us like animals and had lost everything good and human in their characters.

The first generation of women prisoners imprisoned after 1967 struggled to force the authorities to recognize their Palestinian identity. For some of the guards, the very mention of the name Palestine was a provocation. If we said to them, "We are Palestinian," which for us was a simple natural statement, they regarded it as a hostile act. To please them, one would have to say, "We are Arabs." Of course I am an Arab, but in the context of prison this was irrelevant; the only identity that mattered was that I am Palestinian.

The first wave of Palestinian prisoners also demanded to be treated as human beings, to be given medical care during investigation, and to have their straw mattresses replaced by regular beds and sheets. Our struggle throughout my time in prison was to win recognition as political prisoners. We chose work as the locus of our struggle. In June 1983 we gave notice that while we had no objections to cooking and cleaning for ourselves, we would not clean and cook for our jailers. In September a new warden was appointed and she wanted to prove that her authority was absolute. One day in October, we heard scuffling noises from the direction of the dining room. We craned to look through our windows, and saw the guards stuffing our books into bags and dragging them away. We started to bang on our doors and shout for the return of the books. Soldiers wearing gas masks appeared in ten minutes and sprayed tear gas into our cells.

My friend Therese ran into the bathroom and put her head to the window gasping for air. Soldiers sprayed gas directly onto her face. She fell in a heap on the toilet hole. I was clinging to the window of our room with a blanket over my head. When I looked around and couldn't see Therese, I went into the bathroom and saw her unconscious on the ground, picked her up and dragged her to my place at the bedroom window. Then we realized that there was more gas than air coming in through the windows, so we tried to close them. When the soldiers started beating on them from the outside, my comrades yelled, "Get down, Rawda, in a second they will open it and spray gas straight into your face, get down!" I let go, the window burst open, and the room was filled with a new cloud of gas.

That gas hung in the air and clung to our bedclothes for a long time. The gas burned the paint off of the window frames, and traces of it were still visible burning in through several new coats of paint eighteen months later.

For a week after the attack the guards wore gas masks whenever they came into the block, so you can imagine what it was like for us who had to breathe it twenty-three hours a day with no protection. Some of the women went on vomiting for weeks. Many of them lost their voices and talked in a whisper. My skin fell off my scalp in great flakes, and another woman was burned all over her face. The weaker ones who had given up and thought they were going to die drew strength from those of us who were stronger. We endured nine months of punishment for our strike. were deprived of books, notebooks, sewing, and of the lectures we organized among ourselves. The authorities wanted to defeat us with boredom.

Nothing was going to make us give up our struggle. We all spontaneously boycotted the warden by refusing to speak to her. Our boycott was very effective tactic and a psychological weapon. She felt she had lost control. Whenever she came to our section, she would leave completely enraged. I watched her getting angrier and angrier. She needed to dominate us.

In the Occupied Territories and in Israel, Palestinian and Israeli women's organizations demonstrated and held public meetings of solidarity with us; the men's prisons were alerted to strike in sympathy with us. Various human rights organizations protested the use of tear gas in closed areas. When we began our hunger strike on March 7, the warden could hold out no longer. On March 8, the security officer of the prison told us that the warden was ready to speak to us. We said that we boycotted her because of the gas, and she brought the gas because of the library, so we will talk to her after she brings the library back. Two sacks of books were brought as a gesture of good will, and we went to see the warden. "Before we begin our dialogue you must say you will end your hunger strike." "No, we began our strike because we do not want to work for the guards. If you grant us that, we will end our strike at once." She accepted our conditions and then offered us some chocolates that were on her desk, but we refused them, saying, "No, thank you, we will all start eating together." We asked the warden if she realized that that day was March 8, International Women's Day. She did not because the prison authorities don't recognize it, thinking it is just for Communists. "No . . . you should know that it is a day of significance for all women, this day of our victory."

I was released in 1985. My mother is unhappy; she thinks that now that I am thirty-three it is too late for me to marry, and she wants to see me settled and wants grandchildren. But while in prison, I broke off my engagement with the man I was in love with since school. He is not interested in political activity and just wants a wife who will sit nicely at home.

I could not accept such a role. I don't need a man to give me strength. Sometimes I find myself giving strength to men, not taking it from them. My father has always understood me; we have been good friends since I was a child. He accepts that I am strong and know what I want. You never know when you will meet the right person. I may find someone with whom I share a common ideology, someone who is like me. That is what is important. I don't believe in the sort of romantic passion I longed for when I was younger.

Of course liberation struggle is hard and shows who is strong and who is weak. Some of our people now, faced with difficult economic circumstances and lack of opportunities for personal freedom and development, are opting out and trying to leave, it's true. I can understand them; especially if you have an education it is very difficult to accept that you cannot put your studies into practice. It was hard to accept when I came out of prison that I might not find work. I did not find quite what I wanted, and I accepted the offer of a post as head of a new school for the deaf, a Muslim charitable society. I am happy with the job and feel I have achieved a lot already in the two months I have been working. I always give everything I can to whatever the situation I find myself in—it's something I learned from my father.

When you come out of prison you want your life to go back to normal, you want to work and give of yourself after such long futility, so I can understand people's frustration. But I have confidence that if we understand our enemies' tactics, we will be able to defeat them.

Update:

Al-Fajr English language weekly newspaper of 3 September 1990 printed this news item about Rawda al-Basiir:

WOMAN DETAINED ON WAY TO GENEVA

The Jerusalem Magistrate's Court extended for another 24 hours the detention period of Rawda al-Baseer [sic], 41, of Nablus, who holds a Jerusalem identity card. Baseer was arrested at Lydda airport August 27 as she was preparing to fly to Geneva for a conference of nongovernmental organizations on the Palestinian question. Baseer, who is married to ex-prisoner Ibrahim Skeikheh, has been detained before.

NA'IMAH AL-AS'AD
Teacher, union activist

Na'imah, a teacher, thought she was going to spend her morning being interviewed about education and the teachers' union; instead, she spent it talking to a lawyer about her husband's arrest and receiving neighbors who want to help.

4 July 1989

An Israeli patrol passed by our house and spotted national Palestinian slogans on our garden wall.* "Wipe those slogans off," they ordered. We explained that we did not write them and so were not responsible for them. One soldier confiscated my identity card and told me that when he returns, he wants to see a blank wall. Shurouk, my fifteen-year-old daughter said, "Don't bother, we will not remove them." That made him quite angry, and he left in a huff.

When the three soldiers returned in their Jeep, we were working outside. Soldiers could see that our garage was full of books, and that my daughter was sorting them out. They wanted to know what the books were doing in the garage. We explained that we used to own a bookstore in downtown Ramallah (named "Shurouk," "sunrise," after our daughter), and when it was ordered closed, we moved its contents to the garage to protect the books. He could tell from the cover that some of the books were about resistance and got agitated.

"Get those slogans off the wall," they said. "When we give an order, the citizen is required to obey." Just then, my husband As'ad drove home, and one soldier went up to him, and spoke to him in a tone that suggested he was reporting an errant child, and that he had no doubt that my husband would side with him. "Look, I told your wife to remove the slogans on the wall, and she refused. If she does not paint them over, I will get a bulldozer and demolish your wall." "Go get the bulldozer," As'ad said calmly. "The inside of our house is our responsi-

*I interviewed Na'imah in Arabic on 4 July 1989. Originally we had planned to talk about her activities in the teacher's union and about schools, still closed by Israeli authorities, but when I arrived at the appointed time, she was talking to a lawyer about the arrest of her husband and the "search" of her house, and neighbors were streaming in to support her. So the topic was dictated by events. The story was written from the notes I took that day.

bility, but the outside of the wall that faces the street is your responsibility. Go bring a patrol, let it camp here, and nab people who write these slogans." And with that, and quite unceremoniously, As'ad took our two young daughters and put them in our car and drove away. The soldiers were so surprised that anyone would dare do that they were slow to react. As'ad knew what was coming, and wanted to spare the children the wrath of the soldiers. He was confident I could handle the situation.

The soldiers moved towards the front door, and just before entering, they kicked the flowerpots at the entrance of the house spilling their contents. "Bravo," I said. "You have won—against the flowerpots." My remark enraged them. Sarcasm makes you feel better, but will get you nowhere with soldiers. The three soldiers entered the house and looked around. You could tell one was surprised when he went into As'ad's office and saw wall-to-wall books. He started removing them from the shelf, and behind some books, he found a poster of a prisoner with his hands tied. "What is that?" "Oh, that is in Chile," I said, even though it was a Palestinian prisoner. "Chile?" he asked, and seemed satisfied with the answer, missing the comparison.

The soldier then proceeded to open all the cupboards. I think he was motivated partly by curiosity about what Palestinians keep in their homes and partly by a desire to irritate us. First, he went into the sitting room and snatched all the cushions off the sofas and threw them in the center of the room. Then he opened all the closets in the bedroom and threw their contents on the floor. I watched, as my dresses and my husband's clothes landed in a pile on the floor, on top of the sheets, the pillowcases, and the towels. I saw the contents of my drawers fly and land all over the room. It was so bizarre that I could almost remove myself from the scene and watch as if it were happening to someone else. I found myself explaining what was happening to myself, to better deal with the confusion: "Relax. All it means is few hours of tidying up. You should feel lucky you do not live in a village where they mix different kinds of grains with each other, and contaminate the olive oil." I looked up and caught a glimpse of a soldier placing his arm on the dresser as if he was about to sweep the perfume and other bottles off, but then he changed his mind, straightened up, and headed to my daughter's bedroom. On her wall, she had a line of poetry. "Read it!" he ordered. All the time, he was speaking to me in Arabic, but then I realized that he could not read the language. So I read in classical Arabic: "Itha ash'shaabu Yawman . . . " (If a people one day wants to live, destiny will respond). "Tell me what it means in English," he said. I translated: "It means that every people needs to have its own independence and its own state, and that no matter how long it takes, that will come to pass." Tension between us was rising. I said "Look, this is an old line of poetry and it is written under the logo of a newspaper published in East Jerusalem. You know that your censors examine papers every night, if you have any objections to the poem, go talk to the censors."

The soldier took one of our family albums and started looking at the photos. That was too much for me. Those photos were so private, and I felt that enough was enough, so I snatched the album from his hands.

"I will show you what I will do," he said, looking like a spiteful child. He strode to the vestibule between our house and the outside door. As I followed, he screamed at me, "STOP!"

I froze, and it was just as well because just as he slipped out of the iron door, he threw a concussion bomb on our staircase and it landed a few feet below my ankles. I do not know what the Israeli army manual instructs soldiers to use those bombs for, but I doubt that they are designed for indoor use for getting back at a woman and her daughter. The incident happened so quickly and so unexpectedly that it took me by surprise as the soldier had intended. The noise was so deafening that I felt a ring in my ear for fifteen minutes after they left. Throughout the "search" we were taking the whole thing in stride. But with the noise bomb, something snapped. My daughter Shurouk, who had been pretty composed while the soldiers were here, became hysterical. The sight of her in tears got to me and I began to feel the strain. Shurouk and two of her classmates had been through quite an ordeal for the last three months. They were arrested for forty-eight hours, and then detained for eight more days allegedly for throwing stones at an Israeli vehicle near their school in Jerusalem.

She was beaten during interrogation. The Israeli prosecutor wanted to imprison the teenagers but because of their ages, the court decided to exile them away from home and school to a convent for two months, after which they were placed under house arrest until the July 7, 1989, trial. The trial was postponed because the witnesses could not be brought to court, but the young women are still under house arrest—all this punishment and they have not been tried yet. I thought that Shurouk was handling the situation well, but that morning was too much for her. I was very thankful my husband took the younger children away.

We refused to remove the slogans. We felt that the people who wrote them were reclaiming their space, and there was a consensus in the Occupied Territories that you leave those slogans alone despite the penalties.

A few days after the incident, I woke up with an uneasy feeling at about 1:30 A.M. My husband and I looked out of our window, and at first nothing appeared unusual. Then we caught a glimpse of a silhouette of a man roaming around the house. I tell you neither of us had any inclination to find out who it was. All we knew is that the figure lurked around our house until about 3:30 A.M. Something was amiss.

At 7:00 A.M. a military patrol came and politely asked to speak to my husband. "I am going with them," he said, and left. When people are arrested, Israeli soldiers do not give them or their relatives any reason for the arrest. I was not sure whether he was arrested because he is the head of the Union of Palestinian Writers, because of the wave of arrests that week, or because of the wall graffiti incident.

After the news of As'ad's arrest spread, the slogans mysteriously disappeared. Someone in the neighborhood knew that it had now become a battle of wills, and to spare us further trouble, covered the slogans with a thin layer of cement from a nearby building site. We think it is a matter of time before the slogans reappear. In the past, Israelis were able to control the writing on the wall, so to speak. Not anymore. There is so much of it that all they can manage is the main streets. Flags are everywhere in all neighborhoods, drawn on buildings, hoisted on construction sites. On Folklore Day, youths even managed to draw a flag on a water tank in the middle of the town of Ramallah, right next to the spot where soldiers look down on the inhabitants during daytime hours. For a whole day, you could see the flag right behind the soldiers. You walk around in any neighborhood and you find huge three-dimensional victory signs with the colors of the flag, a rose with the colors of the flag. People fly balloons the colors of the flag. For the Israeli army, it's a lost battle—the occupation has to end. It is a pity that only a few Israelis know it.

Update

As'ad was kept in jail for three days and then released. In 1991, Shurouk was sentenced to a few months of social work.

HANIYYEH GHAZAWNEH
First female martyr of the uprising*

Haniyyeh, twenty-five, was the first woman to be shot dead in the Intifada.[1] Her life is re-created here from notes of interviews written by Wafa'a al-Baher-Abu Ghosh, Awni Abu Ghosh, and from several accounts they have collected from the Israeli and Palestinian press.

An Israeli journalist, Michal Kafra, had this to say about Haniyyeh Ghazawneh: At 12 noon, she died in al-Ram.[2] At two after midnight, she was buried. . . . The funeral arrangements took place hurriedly because the cold town was under curfew. Even the Israeli soldiers in the graveyard were shivering from the cold. The fifteen people who were allowed to attend the funeral with a permit from the military governor were standing around the grave; her father, mother, brother, uncle, and some relatives. At 2:30 A.M. they leave the grave. Haniyyeh is inside, and anger is bursting outside. The military governor declared that two shots fired from a distance of a few meters got Haniyyeh in her chest. The soldier ran away.

In the house of the martyr, women were sitting on mattresses on the floor, the mother was in the middle. The mother grabs my hand and says: "Why did you do that? . . . Why are you killing us?" I try to remove my hand but she holds it tightly and asks, "Why did you kill Haniyyeh, why?"

Lawziyyeh Ghazawneh (Haniyyeh's mother): On that day on 3 January 1988, a day I'll never forget, my daughter Haniyyeh, and my daughter-in-law, Amirah, removed our furniture to the courtyard and were helping me clean the house. And suddenly, we heard screams and shouts in the neighborhood. Haniyyeh ran to the balcony and then dashed downstairs.

---

*I wanted to interview the mother of a man or woman who was shot in the Intifada, but two appointments with other families fell through, one because the person who knew the family could not make it at the last moment, and in the second case because the family in question was afraid of Israeli reprisal. I left the Occupied Territories without an interview in the summer of 1989, but made arrangements with journalist Wafa al-Baher Abu-Ghosh and her husband Awni to interview a mother for me. I suggested some questions but left it up to them. I stressed that I needed word-for-word notes of what she says, in *colloquial* Arabic. That point was important because without it, it would be hard to hear the style of the woman in question. Both journalists did an excellent job and provided me with what I asked for, as well as with press accounts of the shooting death of Haniyyeh Ghazawneh. I used the interview with different members of the family to tell the story, intercutting between what each had to say, but preserving the chronological sequence of the story. I then used the newspaper accounts in the footnotes mainly to update the story.

I screamed after her, "Hey, girl, come back—the sons of the dirty one, the Israelis, are shooting." She did not listen to me and said, "I want to see who they are shooting at." I ran after her. Haniyyeh saw a soldier beating a boy all over. She could not bear to see the kid mistreated, so she tried to wrest him away from the soldier. The soldier got hysterical, threw the boy on the ground and stepped on his neck. Even though Haniyyeh was now only a couple of meters away from him, he gave it to her; two shots in the chest.

I heard the boy scream, "Ya khayyi, Ya bayyi, [Oh brother, Oh father] kill him, he has killed her." Then the kid screamed at the soldier, "Kill us! kill us! she's dead." Our neighbor hit the soldier in his chest and said, "You have shot the girl, and you want to take the boy too? Have pity!" The soldier let go of the boy who melted like salt and disappeared.

Haniyyeh was lying on the ground like a piled sack and her blood was flowing like a spring. It was unreal. It would have been easier for me to be stabbed with a knife than see what I had just seen. I gathered her in my arms. Her head was down. One eye was closed, the other open, as if she was saying good-bye. She said nothing, just sighed.

I beat my face, tore my clothes, and took the scarf off my head. Since that unlucky day, my tears have not dried. Shot, in front of my eyes, for no reason. She was not fighting with a stone or a bomb; all she did was try to rescue a child. Neighbors carried her outside to the street. A private car took us to the hospital with the car's horn going like a siren. Soldiers were waiting for us at the Ramallah hospital. Three young men helped us get Haniyyeh inside. The soldiers said nothing and just let us pass. Dr. Issa Salti examined her . . . I don't know; they said I'd better wait outside. Her blood was dripping under her like an open faucet. They put her in the morgue. I said, "Let her brother and father see her." When I saw my husband, I said, "Abu [father of] Haniyyeh, they have killed Haniyyeh." But by then, he had already heard the news and said, "She died for her country. She sacrificed herself for a young man."

It was not enough for the Israelis that we have lost our daughter, but the intelligence services came to the hospital and held a long investigation with us. I was told that soldiers returned to our house and searched our house thoroughly, even the drawers, looking for the boy!

Hamdeh (Haniyyeh's aunt): Our house is not too far from Haniyyeh's. I heard the sound of shots and rushed out. Someone said that my brother's daughter was shot in the leg. I put the hem of my long dress in

my mouth and ran to her house, but I missed the car that had transported her to the hospital. My husband followed them there. Soldiers
were surrounding the area. One of them tried to stop me but I pushed
him to the ground. He got up and ran after me and was about to hit me
with the butt of his rifle when another soldier stopped him and allowed us
in. My brother, Haniyyeh's father, said: "Don't scream, Haniyyeh is
dead." I kept the scream in my breast. The military governor came. He
was told how Haniyyeh died, but he did not believe our eyewitnesses. The
governor said he will investigate the incident himself, but he was scared to
go to the neighborhood. Despite the curfew he had declared, the whole
area was in an uproar.

You cannot believe the intensity of people's feelings. They rose up as if
they were one, as if Haniyyeh was their own daughter. Haniyyeh was the
first one shot in al-Ram. Since then, we have presented three martyrs.

Our family was detained in the police station until 10:00 P.M.; then we
were returned to the morgue. I will never forget the blood as long as
I live. Haniyyeh was bleeding profusely on the slab at the hospital. I
cannot take her out of my mind. Her mother and I washed her. We were
ordered to stay at the hospital until 2:00 A.M. That was the time
the military governor of Ramallah decided we were allowed to bury
Haniyyeh.

Lawziyyeh: Haniyyeh's aunt Hamdeh and I put her on the washing slab
in the hospital. We did not know how to turn her. No matter how we
moved her, blood still flowed. We were done at about 10:00 P.M. and
until two, people were waiting outside the hospital and outside our home
to take part in the funeral, but the military governor refused to allow anyone outside the family to attend the burial. Israelis were scared of
Haniyyeh's wedding. They were scared of her bridegroom, the earth that
was going to hold her. Soldiers surrounded the area, and we were ordered
to take the body first to the police station in Ramallah, and then, at 2:00
A.M., to the graveyard in al-Ram. About five military cars were there.
Israeli authorities said they did not want any "disturbances."

The burial of anyone cannot be described in words, but how can I
explain what it was like to bury our daughter, without a funeral, under
the cover of night, with guns trained to our heads? Despite all Israeli pre-
cautions, despite their despotism, Haniyyeh had a wedding, a wedding
given to her by all our people. The next day, you could see people all the
way from the front door of our house to the main street. Young men
carried empty coffins on their shoulders. Daily, people from all over the
Occupied Territories came to pay their last respects, and until today,
people have not stopped visiting to show their support for us. People's

appreciation for Haniyyeh has kept us going. The condolence ceremonies were beautiful, and she was a queen.

My anger has not subsided. Sometimes, I feel like tearing my hair out, tearing my clothes out. Some days rage overtakes me. I feel restless. I just feel like taking off and wandering into the mountains, away from the house that reminds me of my daughter. I feel I have enough strength and enough anger to break a soldier like a twig. Oh, if I had a chance, I would break one hundred of those bastards. Her death has spoiled even the things I enjoy. I have always enjoyed gardening, and I continue to grow vegetables and sell them in the neighborhood as a way of achieving self-reliance. But everything reminds me of Haniyyeh, the earth I dig, the continuing Intifada, the martyrs who are still falling daily. I think of how their mothers must feel, and I feel sad for us all. Peace? What kind of peace are they talking about? If it were up to me I would turn the world upside down. That thing called fear has left us. Victory awaits those who work for justice and defend it, and that makes us, despite all the martyrs, hold onto the land and to the rights of our people. . . . Haniyyeh is not a myth; she is just one of many in a long procession. But it is hard. I lie in bed at night, my eyes gazing straight up to heaven, and my tears fall from the side of my face to the pillow.

I have had a hard life, and just before Haniyyeh's death, I felt as if things were getting better. My husband left to the United States to find work and get a green card when Haniyyeh was two, Ni'meh was four, and Mohammad was nine months old. In twenty-three years, he returned only once. I raised the children alone. I hunched over the sewing machine for years. I raised them from the tiredness of days and nights, waiting for him to come home. Then, my husband returned for good, and I thought that we can finally be a family, but they shot her in front of my own eyes!

When the new year came, I said, "Haniyyeh, sew yourself a new dress. Wear something pretty, like other girls." Haniyyeh said, "I hope I die, I do not want a dress, why a new dress in these bad times?" It is as if the door of the sky was open.³ And suddenly, she was gone—left me here. They took her away from me, like they took our land. The price of Haniyyeh's blood was that Israelis have finally agreed to reunite the family, but even now, my husband has not yet been given his identity card.

I don't understand it. Israelis get upset when their glass is broken, but they destroy our homes on top of our heads. For the sake of a stone thrown at them, they imprison our children, deport or kill them, and every time we hear that a solution is under way, Israelis build more settlements. This is not their country. The country does not know them; they are mercenaries.

As the mother of the first female martyr of the uprising, I was invited to cut the ribbon for the exhibit featuring paintings and drawings of the martyrs.⁴ Israeli soldiers raided the exhibit hall and broke some of the paintings of the martyrs. Thank God the painting of Haniyyeh, painted by artist Abu Rasha in the colors of the Palestinian flag, has escaped their dirty hands. I feel better when I know that Haniyyeh is appreciated. Our unified leadership has called one of the streets near our house "Martyr Haniyyeh Street." That was the best present. The way Haniyyeh's death was commemorated was equivalent to the festivities of ten weddings. Visitors got to see the empty bullet shells that drained Haniyyeh's blood. She died while one was blinking an eye. She did not say "ach" or "oh"—she just sighed. I was right behind her. If she were in prison, I could at least see her. But after she was laid to rest with stones on top of her, how can I see her? I swear that a stone in the hands of a child is better than all the weapons of the Arab countries.

I prayed that the soldier's mother would burn for him like I burn for my lost child. I was told that the soldier who shot my daughter had an accident while training and that his hand was amputated. I call that divine justice. This is the punishment for someone who kills an innocent person.⁵

Haniyyeh's father: When I was in the United States, Haniyyeh used to write me and say: "Come back to us, we don't want money. We do not want anything. We want you." I returned three years ago. I did not know I was going to lose her; the three years passed like one day. I feel I have not spent enough time with her. I am a good Muslim. Heaven forbid that I should question God's design or her martyrdom. Everyone is honored she died the way she did, but I regret the days that passed without my seeing her. I am a believer, and a believer must be patient with calamity; acceptance is a characteristic of a true Muslim. It is fate. Her fate was written on her forehead before she was born. But it still hurts when someone close to you dies for no crime she has committed, except that she was the daughter of this earth.

Lawziyyeh: When my husband left to the States, I was afraid of gossip. I was afraid for the reputation of my daughters if they walked back and forth to school, what with no father to take care of them. I pulled Haniyyeh out of school after the fourth grade. I was afraid people would talk about us; these are bad times. It was better to keep the girls right under my gaze. I taught Haniyyeh to sew, she spent her time on the sewing machine. She baked, cooked, and helped me around the house, and she was devout. Everyone around us swore by the good breeding of Haniyyeh.

Amirah, twenty-six (Haniyyeh's sister-in-law): I have no sister in al-Ram, so Haniyyeh was like my sister. She loved children, even when we passed by Israeli children in Jerusalem, she would gently place her hand on their hair. My children love her. When we visit the cemetery, my young daughter says: "This is aunt Haniyyeh's house, when will aunt Haniyyeh visit us? Can we go visit her?"

Haniyyeh was planning to go on pilgrimage to Mecca the year she died. Visitors who came to pay their respects shook their heads in disbelief at how she died. Some members of my family live in Chicago. They led demonstrations on the forty-day anniversary of Haniyyeh's death. My mother took an Israeli flag with her and stepped on it in front of the Israeli consulate as Palestinians who carried Haniyyeh's photograph demonstrated. I wish we can all die the kind of death she died.

In Haniyyeh's house, Amirah shows visitors a number of national Palestinian dresses embroidered by Haniyyeh, and points to one dress, still incomplete, embroidered, but not yet assembled. Amirah explains, "I am not going to put it together. I will keep it in separate pieces, until liberation day. On that day, I will assemble that dress and wear it, because only then will Haniyyeh return to us."

SALIMA KUMSIYYA
Beit Sahur homemaker

In 1981, one could not by any stretch of the imagination have called Salima Kumsiyya "political." Her life was changed by the collective punishment imposed on her family for an incident she was not even aware of. While visiting her imprisoned teenager, she became aware of "injustices committed against other people's children." When Salima joined a hunger strike to protest the mistreatment of prisoners, she learned that she had leadership abilities others respected.

Overnight, she found herself in the limelight explaining to the foreign press not only what happened to her, but placing it in the national context. Here, Salima talks about collective punishment and the start of the tax revolt in Beit Sahur.

November 1981

My husband George and I had a dream: to retire in a house that we owned.* We realized that people like us could never afford to own the houses they lived in, and we knew that it wasn't going to be easy, but we started saving for the project in the 1950s.

We could not afford to hire help, so my husband, a stonecutter, did the work himself after his regular job every day. He cut the stone from the quarry, chiseled it, and transported it to the site. He was the cement mixer and the builder, and he often worked late into the night building it up stone by stone. By the time our savings ran out in 1961, George had built two rooms and a bathroom. Although the floor needed tiling and the walls needed painting, the nine of us decided to save rent money and move into the house, adding to it as funds became available.

The 1967 Israeli occupation slowed down building projects in our town of Beit Sahur, and my husband could not find regular employment. So to help out I cleaned the houses of three Israeli women in West Jerusalem. Office work it was not! Do you know what "spring cleaning" is? I spring cleaned three houses a day until my fingers bled so that our building could continue.

The ground floor was completed in 1972, the second in 1979. We occupied the second floor and rented out the first. Three of our children got married and moved out, and we were just starting to feel that our financial burden had eased when George's doctor ordered him not to engage in any heavy physical labor because of a liver ailment. I was left as the sole supporter of the family. We were managing relatively well until 15 November 1981.

That night we were awakened at 11:30 P.M. by loud banging at our door. We opened it and found ourselves looking at a number of Israeli soldiers. "Lead me to your son Walid's room," their captain ordered.

Our son Walid, who had turned sixteen the week before, had fallen asleep watching television. I had covered him with a quilt and left him on

---

*I heard Mrs. Kumsiyya's story in 1981 and asked for her permission to return with a tape recorder, which I did shortly before Christmas that year. I asked her to tell me about the demolition of her house. Her account was so lucid I did not need to ask many questions while she was telling the story. That account appeared in an article titled "The House that George and Salima Built," in *The Christian Century*, 2–9 February, 1983. I then returned to visit the family on 16 April 1985, 19 May 1985, and 2 August 1989. I took extensive notes during those visits. When I saw Mrs. Kumsiyyah in 1989, she was deeply affected by the death of a teenager in Beit Sahur, and she described events leading up to his death and the reaction of the town in detail. She also spent time on describing how children foil the army and hang Palestinian flags without being seen, but that information had to be deleted for brevity. All the interviews were conducted in Arabic.

the couch. George wanted to spare Walid the shock of being waked up by soldiers, but the captain insisted on waking Walid himself. The soldiers didn't find anything when they searched Walid's room, but they took him away for questioning. We were worried about him, but being convinced of his innocence, we expected him back soon.

On 16 November at 11:30 P.M., the military governor and his assistant and their men turned up. "We have an order to demolish your house and confiscate your land because your son has confessed to throwing a stone at an Israeli vehicle." My husband turned white. I thought the man was joking but a look at the soldiers' faces convinced me that he was serious. "You have half an hour to remove your belongings," he went on.

All telephone lines in our city were cut. We were not allowed to contact a lawyer, our mayor, or any Israeli official to ask him to reconsider the demolition of our house. We begged and pleaded to no avail. "Suppose he did throw a stone at you? Nobody was hurt. Besides, Walid did not build this house. His father and I did, and it took us twenty years." The soldiers muttered something about having to follow orders.

"Look at my hands," I shouted. "For fourteen years and two months I cleaned your houses to build this house. Is this my reward?" No one paid any attention to me. I remember my throat was so dry I had to keep going to the sink for water to be able to talk.

My husband was asked to sign the demolition order. He refused, saying, "Only an insane person signs a paper ordering the destruction of his own house." The military governor motioned to his men, who surrounded George and poked their guns at his neck, ribs, and back.

"Sign, sign, they are going to flatten it anyway," I said. He still refused, and the military governor forced his hand down on the paper and scribbled his name for him.

By then soldiers had started carrying some of our light furniture out. Some were kind enough to carry things out in one piece; some deliberately broke objects before tossing them out. My husband followed them around, shouting, "Less than twenty-four hours between an alleged confession and demolition. No trial! This is unheard of. This is the law of the jungle."

I felt I had nothing to lose, so I joined in. "You are always complaining about what the Nazis did to you. Look how you are treating other people." But the soldiers ignored us, and a few went around smashing chandeliers and bathroom fixtures. When my daughter asked why they were destroying objects, one soldier answered sheepishly, "It's going to be demolished in any case."

The remains of the Kumsiyyas' two-story house, November 1981. Photo by Orayb Najjar

When the house was ready for demolition, we refused to leave it and asked that we be buried in it so that we would not spend the rest of our lives bemoaning our loss. The soldiers had to carry us out bodily. Neighbors took us in, and shortly afterwards we heard an explosion. At 2:00 A.M. and at 4:00 A.M. we heard two more, and we later learned that a fourth house had been demolished in nearby Bethlehem.

Our tenants downstairs, Mr. Alfred Rock and his wife of eight months, were also evicted from their home, and lost most of their new furniture. Mr. Rock, a theology teacher, lost the notes of a book that he had been working on for ten years. When he protested about this collective punishment, he was told that, "A person who rents from a criminal is a criminal."

At dawn the next day, defying the curfew, we rushed to the site. Our two-story home was nothing but a pile of rubble. I could see parts of what used to be sturdy furniture, broken. Nearby lay a delicate lamp shade, intact. I picked it up and started crying, thinking of the number of times I had cleaned it carefully for fear it would break. George joined me, and we both cried so much that I don't think either of us is now capable of crying about anything.

The mayors of the towns of Bethlehem and Beit Sahur led the towns-people in a demonstration after the curfew had been lifted. Youths set fire to tires and chanted slogans denouncing the occupation. Christmas was approaching. The mayor of Beit Sahur, Hanna El Atrash, declared that since two of the four families whose houses were demolished were Christian, the town wanted to cancel public Christmas celebrations because "we have nothing to celebrate." Twenty out of twenty-two scout bands decided not to march in the annual Bethlehem parade. In the end, however, threats from the Israeli assistant military governor forced them to, but Walid's seventy-two-member band "forgot" to take their drums and marched with their flag furled.

The outpouring of support in the form of delegations from all over the Occupied Territories is what kept us going and raised our morale. We feel that the international outcry about the severity of the punishment, inflicted even before Walid was tried, has forced the Israeli authorities to release the plots of land (contrary to their usual practice) and allow us to rebuild. Palestinians here and abroad donated money, building materials, and their muscles to help us rebuild.

In April 1982, five of the young men arrested with Walid were tried, convicted, and given stiff sentences. But Walid's trial was delayed because, according to his attorney, the marks of physical abuse were still too visible for the Israeli authorities to risk letting him appear in the court-room.

He was finally tried on May 26. The charges: (1) throwing a stone at an Israeli vehicle; (2) twice raising a Palestinian flag; (3) taking part in a demonstration; (4) singing nationalist songs and shouting slogans; (5) distributing pamphlets; (6) membership in the PLO. Walid vehemently denied being a member of any organization; he insisted that he threw the stone because of his personal feelings against the occupation and not because anyone recruited him to. He also said that his conviction was based on his having signed, under torture, a document written in Hebrew and therefore incomprehensible to him.

Walid was sentenced to seven years in prison—half of which he would serve. Just before the sentence was handed down, Walid begged me not to cry in court no matter how severe his sentence: he asked me instead to let out a zaghrutah (trilling sound).

At the sentencing I was the only dry-eyed parent in the room. I kept my promise, and just before letting out my zaghrutah I shouted,

Salima Kumsiyya winces as she listens to her son Walid describing his torture during interrogation, 1985. Photo by Orayb Najjar

"Thank God I produced a young man that Israel is so afraid of that it has to sentence him for seven years!" That show of bravado was of course intended only to raise our son's morale. I cried nonstop for days after the trial.

We started cleaning up the rubble in December 1981. Volunteers came in busloads from all over the Occupied Territories to help us rebuild. Only one of the Israeli families I worked for came to hear my story. I decided to stop working for them all. A few Israelis who disapproved of their government's actions came and cleaned the rubble with us.

16 April 1985

While the house was being rebuilt, the volunteers lifted this and rebuilt that, but none of it touched me. Only one thing was on my mind–the boy. I'd go and visit him every two weeks and my anger would cool. So what if the house was destroyed? We did nothing shameful. It is not as if we stole or committed a crime. The matter is quite simple. This is our land, and this is our home and we are simply defending them. If we could mix the earth needed for rebuilding with our blood, we would do so.

One's country is quite dear, and we are proud of our son. Whenever I go to prison to visit him I am greeted with shouts from other prisoners: "Are you Umm Walid? Hello Umm Walid!" What more could I wish? Those young men have a mission: to endure the humiliation heaped upon them by their jailers. We parents have to bear their absence, and God will be merciful to everyone.

Walid has matured in prison. He's grown taller, thinner. He's no longer a kid. Lately, he has been concerned about us. He says, "Mother, you no longer work for the Israelis, and I know my father is ill. How do you manage?"

I told him not to worry his head about such things. But I confess that things are not easy. It has been three and a half years since I stopped working as a cleaning woman and using cleaning powders and bleach, but look at my hands: I have no fingerprints left—they have melted away. My finger tips are smooth, and what do I have to show for this labor? The old house is gone. I do not want to sound ungrateful to the volunteers who helped us rebuild. I realize that this house was built with the sweat of the Palestinian people, and we are thankful for that, but I have to confess that we still feel sentimental about our first home because we built it ourselves, stone by stone—it's different. Rebuilding has been expensive. Despite the donations we received, we are in debt to the bank. We live off the rent of the first floor of the house, I sell items I knit, and our children help out a bit. My greatest satisfaction comes from the thought that the Israelis who demolished our home can now pass by and see it rebuilt.

It's hard to describe what the absence of our youngest son has meant to us. Yet, we try to view the events of the last three and a half years as a learning experience. Because our son became a prisoner, we inhabited a different kind of world where we became aware of the injustices done to other people's children. We visit with parents of other prisoners, and we receive letters from their sons, who have come to regard us as their parents.

We became experts on prisons as we followed Walid from prison to prison for a total of six moves. We learned that Israeli prisons come in "models," some worse than others. We thought the Toulkarm prison was bad until Walid was transferred to Jnaid prison near Nablus on July 2, 1984.

Eighty-four days after the prison was officially opened the eight hundred inmates declared a hunger strike to protest prison conditions. Walid had complained to us on our first visit to Jnaid that prison guards beat and insulted him on arrival for no apparent reason, and that living conditions were subhuman.

After the strike was declared, we went to visit our sons but were turned back because, as part of the strike action, they refused to see us. Instead of returning home, the eleven buses full of relatives of prisoners from towns and villages all over the West Bank and Gaza turned around and made for the headquarters of the International Red Cross in Jerusalem.

We decided we were no better than our sons; if they go on a hunger strike, so will we, and we will break it only when they do. We developed a slogan for the occasion: "Yes to hunger, no to kneeling." We ate nothing for the first five days of our sit-in at the Red Cross. Not all the women could take it. Some fainted; some got sick and were transported to the hospital. I believe the main reason for their weakness was the fact they carried on so, beating their own heads and bodies and crying for their children. Village women gave us the most trouble. I felt it was wrong to show our weakness to the Israelis, and my voice got hoarse from repeating: "We are strong! Our spirits are high!" We finally decided that we should eat one meal a day to retain our members. I slept at the Red Cross for the duration of the twelve-day strike. The prison strike was called off by the prisoners on October 3, 1983, after they were granted most of their demands. I feel proud of our sit-in at the Red Cross. I never knew I had so much strength in me. I feel grateful to the inmates at other prisons and shopkeepers in East Jerusalem for going on strike for the sake of our sons. I appreciate the schools and institutions that supported us. We all banded together and we won.

19 May 1985

Walid was due to be released on May 16. The whole family was nervously waiting for the event all that week. I hummed while I did my housework. On the last night before his release, our eyes were on the clock, and we were counting down, twelve hours to go, eleven. . . . We knew that Walid's friends would be coming to welcome him at about lunchtime, so we decided to cook while we waited. We stuffed four and a half kilos of vine leaves, eighteen kilograms of zucchini, and nine kilos of eggplant with rice and meat. Relatives stayed behind the next morning and cooked the meal.

The rest of the family turned in at 1:00 A.M., but I felt wide awake. So I sat in bed, long after George fell asleep, whispering the songs I was going to sing for Walid the next day. It is customary to sing on these occasions a combination of traditional songs and others one makes up for the event. I must have got carried away, because George woke up. When I told him I was rehearsing my lines, he said in mock anger, "Are you sure you are O.K.? Please tell me if you need a psychiatrist." I told him that I have never felt better, "My son will be home tomorrow, and I simply cannot contain my happiness."

We arrived at Jnaid prison with friends who were also awaiting the release of their sons. We were all buzzing with excitement. But an Israeli soldier deflated our enthusiasm when he said, "If you make any commotion, we'll hold the boys for another week." Instead of letting us wait in the waiting areas as usual, he ordered us to go across the street from the prison. We were so desperate to see our sons we complied without a word.

The boys emerged at 10:45. After I had my fill of kissing Walid, his sisters and brother took their turns, and I broke into song.

Ayeeha!
Prison is no cyprus.[1]
It is not a snake that bites.
Only heroes go to prison
And there, even an illiterate learns.

هيه والسجن ماهو قـبرص
ولا فيه حيه بتقرص
السجن للأبطال والأمّي فيه بيـدرس

I also sang:

We planted sesame in the heat.
We were told that its stem will not be green, and thank God,
And thank God, it got green, thank God.

We planted sesame up high.
We were told its stem will not be trodden on.
And thank God it sprang forth and blossomed,
And made bells.

زرعنـا السـمسـم في الحر الحمدلله
وقالوا عيدانه ما يخضر والحمدلله
والحمدلله فرعن واخضر الحمدلله
زرعنـا السـمسـم في الراس
وقالوا عيدانه ما ينداس
والحمدلله فرعن وسـواله جراس

The night before, we had decorated the house on the inside, and we placed colored lights on the outside, so I sang this song:

Ayeeha!
We have decorated our house
In honor of our men.
This is the great happiness for Walid.
We hope that all our heroes will be released.

هيه زينـا دارنـا
هيه في عزرجالنـا
وهذي فرحه لوليـد
وعقبال جميع أبطالنا

I sang this song at the top of my voice for the benefit of the men still in prison. On our way home, we met eleven taxis full of Walid's friends. They turned and accompanied us to Beit Sahur. They had white flags which they put at the entrance of our house as a sign of joy. I am happy to say that not a single guest left our house without being fed.

I am not exaggerating when I say that three-quarters of the inhabitants of the town of Beit Sahur, both Christian and Muslim, came here to congratulate us, and we spent the next three days receiving well-wishers from all over Palestine. Out came chocolates, sweets, and juice for them. This is something wonderful about Arab culture, how people stand by each other.

Of course many relatives and acquaintances sang with me, as is the custom.

I have lots of plans for Walid. I want him to go to the University of Bethlehem, not far from us. For the time being, however, I want to concentrate on fattening him up. He spent his years from sixteen to nineteen in prison, eating a poor and insufficient diet for a growing boy, and it shows. He smokes heavily and hardly touches his food. He says, "Mother, don't push me. I am not used to eating much. I need time." I try to hold myself in check, but it's not easy, so I prepare him a nutritious soup every day and try to get him to eat the meat his body so badly needs.

It is so good to see him there. For me, having him with us is a unique kind of joy. I never felt so much happiness at my own wedding, the weddings of my children, or even after the birth of my children. And what makes the occasion so special is the fact that, in a few days, an exchange of prisoners will take place between the Palestinians and Israel and many men with long sentences will be released.

My voice is still hoarse. Two days ago it disappeared completely from singing and singing all the songs I had been humming for a week. I sang:

> Sing, Salima, sing
> Songs for the handsome one.
> We thank God of the Universe
> For Walid, with Kohl in his eyes.

غني سليمه غـــني
غناوي الـــزين
نستحمد رب العالمين
اللـــي روح وليــد
كحيل العين

My favorite song was:

> We have sliced open a watermelon,
> It was red and delicious.
> We have rebuilt our house,
> Our son has returned to us,
> And all the scoundrels got is scandal.
> (the verse rhymes in Arabic)

هيه شجحنا بطيخة
هيه طلعت حمرا ومليحه
اه والحمدلله بنينا الـدار
ورجعوا شبابنا
وما ناب الأنذال غيرالفضيحه

Our house was not the first to be demolished by the Israelis, nor will it be the last. Yet I believe that we caused Israeli authorities the most headaches. We contacted international organizations, religious figures, and even the pope, asking them to condemn this collective punishment. Whenever my husband talks about the demolition to pilgrims who stop by, he says, "Israelis claim that they are helping Christians against Muslims in Lebanon. We are Christian, and Christ was born up there on that hill. Look what the Israelis are doing to Christians in the land of Christ." Once an Israeli official came to our new house and suggested we remove mementos concerning the old home, like newspaper clippings framed on the wall, a photograph of George and me standing over the rubble, and a porcelain horse that we saved from the ruins, but we refused to. We keep these items for everyone to see. To us, the horse is a symbol of the Palestinian people. It survived the blowing up of our home. It emerged slightly damaged, but it is still standing firmly, raring to go.

2 August 1989

Israelis banned neighborhood committees in town and declared war on people who grew vegetables in their own gardens. There is a family whose

"To us, the horse is a symbol of the Palestinian people. It survived the blowing up of our home. It emerged slightly damaged, but it is still standing firmly, raring to go."–Salima Kumsiyya. Photo by Orayb Najjar

field was closer to their neighbors' house than to theirs, and they could not go out to water their plants or feed their rabbits and chickens. Luckily, their neighbors helped out. Then tax collectors started raiding the town regularly. We would see a bunch of soldiers–with very detailed maps of the town–conferring with each other. They started with the shops, and then went neighborhood by neigborhood. The day the contents of the pharmacy of Elias Rashmawi was raided, and about $120,000 of medicine was seized, we held a sit-in at the Orthodox church (June 28, 1989) and we decided to act in unision.

Economic conditions in the town were bad. This is a town that depends on tourists, and tourism was down, but Israelis wanted to collect taxes as if nothing had happened. The first few who refused to pay taxes had their identity cards confiscated. When we heard that some cards were confiscated (July 7, 1989), we returned our identity cards in solidarity with our friends by dropping the cards over the wall of the municipality. The Israeli officials were very worried. They knew they would be in real trouble if this idea spread. So they had the cards distributed to us to our homes.

The army decided to isolate us from each other by declaring long curfews. They had troops stationed on a four-story building where the soldiers could see anything that moved. But we refused to pay.

Every time you put your head out of the house, you cause a major crisis. Every morning George used to go out and open the water meter. When he got sick, I took on that job. All I needed to do was walk out into our own garden, and yet, that too was forbidden and I had a number of shouting matches with soldiers about it. Once George's condition worsened during curfew and I tried to go out and get a doctor but again I ran into obstacles. I got really angry and literally dragged the soldier into my house to where my husband was lying down. George's feet were swollen, and he looked quite sick. The soldier relented and we managed to get a doctor. George died on July 18, 1988. I would have liked for him to see Walid graduate from college, but that was not to be. When all West Bank universities closed, we sent Walid to the East Bank to the university. Enough years of Walid's life were wasted in prison, so we felt he needed a break.

Through the long curfews and troubles, we have found it difficult even to walk in our own neighborhoods without being accosted by soldiers. One day, my married son was visiting, and he and his friends wanted to leave the house and return to their homes. I said, "No, wait, let me check if the road is clear." You do not want to walk close to soldiers. They may be in a bad mood. Someone may have stoned them and they take it out on the first Arab they see.

It was a windy day last February, and it was getting dark. I opened the door and was startled to find an Israeli soldier leaning against it. He was scared too and made threatening gestures. I could see that he had come to the entrance of the house to be out of the cold because he was shivering, and he probably was not supposed to be here without other soldiers.

"What are you doing?" he screamed. I tried to be calm. "I am just opening the door of my own house." He was so young, barely nineteen, younger than my son Walid. Something came over me. I felt there was something I wanted to tell him. I used all the Hebrew words I remembered when I worked cleaning Israeli houses, and I also used sign language. I said,

"What are you doing here?"

"Guarding."

"What are you guarding?"

"I don't know."

"But these are our homes, and we do not need guards."

"But people throw stones at us."

"That is because you should not be here. We, the older generation, are more patient than kids, but they cannot abide your presence near their homes. They do not come to your areas, you come to theirs and chase them. Look at the abnormal situation we are in. I open the door of my own home, and you feel threatened. It is all Shamir's fault. He does not fear God. I bet that your mother is really worried about you. I bet she is now thinking, 'I wonder where he is, I wonder if he is warm, if he had a good meal. I wonder if he is safe.' I bet she would like to make you a cup of tea."

"Yes she would."

"What are you doing here? You are a young man, you should be enjoying life. I know that it is not your fault that you are here, it is the fault of all those generals. Look at all the young Palestinians killed every day. Your being here makes our life difficult and makes yours difficult."

I believe the soldier said, "They just dropped us up there on the hill and did not tell us anything. I don't know what I am doing here either."

Despite the language barrier, I know he understood me because he had tears in his eyes.

FOUR

Institution Building on the West Bank

New Forms of Organizing: The Women's Committees, Medical and Legal Services

Like all Palestinian institutions, the women's movement was affected by developments within the PLO. Between 1965 and the early 1970s, the PLO stressed armed struggle for the liberation of Palestine, and so some women were trained as commandos in Lebanon and Jordan and a few operated in the West Bank.

Meetings of the National Palestine Council in 1974 and 1977 committed the whole national community to the idea of accepting a Palestinian state in the West Bank and Gaza (Said 1980: 224). The Palestinian decision to opt for a political settlement to the conflict led to increased interest in institution building. Various communal volunteer activities which started spontaneously in the 1970s to fulfill various needs were officially encouraged by the PLO. Volunteer groups working in agriculture, education, and medical and legal aid provided badly needed services that helped Palestinians withstand various Israeli pressures ranging from land confiscation, to the jailing of wage earners, to the monopoly of the market, to the regular disruption of education. These efforts resulted in new forms of organizing that were encouraged by municipalities and universities, constituting a form of "institutional resistance" (Tamari 1989: 131).¹ Women were part of these efforts, but they also continued to be involved in charitable work.

Until 1978, two types of women's organizations operated in the Occupied Territories–charitable societies and several branches of the pre-1948 Arab Women's Union. The General Union of Palestinian Women (GUPW), founded by the PLO in 1965, is forbidden in the West Bank and Gaza, although several of its former important members remain active as members and heads of various other organizations.

A number of young women activists who participated in volunteer work at first tried to work within existing traditional societies but were dissatisfied with their top-down approach to social work because those societies did not have an

> organizational framework that would enable them to depend on the general women population. Most of the activities of these societies are located in cities,² hence deepening the schism between the city and the countryside and ignoring the needs of a large sector of women. Therefore, they are unable to bring about any qualitative change in the position of women. . . . This necessitated presenting other forms of organization for women from different social sectors, and organizing them in popular frames large enough to encompass tens of thousands of women who are ready to participate in the struggle for their rights and interests (PUWWC [1987]).

In March 1978, a meeting of about twenty women resulted in the establishment of the Palestinian Union of Women's Work Committee (PUWWC) (see Siham Barghuti and Zahira Kamal interviews). The committee's slogan was "towards a unified popular women's movement."³ Initially, the new committee consisted of women from different political streams as well as independent women. The group did not remain united for long, however, but split into four groups representing ideological divisions within the Palestinian movement, both because of their political differences and because each group felt the need to stress its own priorities for women.⁴ Women affiliated with the Communist party established the Union of Palestinian Working Women's Committees (UPWWC) in March 1980 because they felt that women's organizations, including the PUWWC, were not meeting the needs of workers and were not sufficiently stressing union affairs (see Amal Khreisheh interview).

The Palestinian Women's Committees (PWC) was established in March 1981. The PWC, which is sympathetic to the Popular Front for the Liberation of Palestine (PFLP), assigns relatively greater weight to gender issues than do other groups, explains one activist.

> We place the women's question before the national question. We focus all our activities on bringing the women out of their homes to make them more self-confident and independent. Once they believe in themselves, they will know that they can become leaders in any field they choose, including the military field. So if a woman first gains her own rights by breaking down her internal barriers, then in the house, and then in society at large, then after that she will also be able to deal with the occupation. It depends completely on the woman herself, not on her father or brothers. A woman cannot fight the occupation if she is not even convinced that she has rights, for example the right to leave her house, for whatever reason (Hiltermann 1988: 486–87).

In 1985, PWC membership ranged between 800 and 1,450 women working in forty centers, the lower figure excluding those who support the committees when necessary but are not formal members. The committees tend to be concentrated in the larger cities, and the percentage of uneducated and poor women in the PWC remains low (Hiltermann 1988: 445–46). PWC is trying to break out of that pattern by establishing innovative cooperatives in villages and by training women to take part in all phases of production, including marketing.

The Union of Women's Committees for Social Work (WCSW) started being active in 1982, even though some branches, for example, the Nablus branch, was operating with twenty members by 2 June 1981. The different committees united in 1983. An activist in the organization explained in the Summer of 1989 that women had been active before the formal constitution of the committee, but that they had operated through the "Shabiba" (youth) movement of Fateh. The group does not organize around a program but "those sympathetic to Fateh are drawn to us." The activist did not want to be identified because by then the Israeli government had declared the Shabiba movement an illegal organization.

In a 1983–84 publication, the WCSW admitted that in its early years members faced many difficulties because "the committees did not have set guidelines for their work and thus, initially, were unable to implement their goals." Since then, people working in different areas have started coordinating their activities, have given themselves a name, claimed 3,000 to 4,000 members in 1985, and in 1986 had thirty-six regional groups.

Although the group is the newest on the scene, wcsw has established twenty kindergartens with 654 children in 1986 (wcsw 1987: 7, 17–18). wcsw started with four literacy centers but ended up with only one because of its high drop-out rate.

wcsw has been working on establishing some internal guidelines to organize the committees. At present, the committees' structure is the most informal of all groups and so lends itself more to occasional mass gatherings than to sustained work by all members on a day-to-day basis.

Each of the four committees has tried to gain adherents by providing services.[5] Although activists stressed in the 1980s that their movement was primarily nationalist in nature, they found that they could not separate the rights of women from national activism and (to varying degrees) took a conscious decision to empower rural and refugee women by supporting their right to work for wages, by creating strong unions that safeguard women's rights, by encouraging illiterate women to join literacy classes, and by making sure health care is responsive to the needs of rural women.

While 1978 saw the establishment of the first of the four women's committees, 1979 saw the establishment of the Union of Palestinian Medical Relief Committees (UPMRC), one of several volunteer medical groups now operating in the Occupied Territories. Approximately 370 physicians are now members of UPMRC, 32 percent of them female (in contrast, 8 percent of the physicians in the West Bank and Gaza are women). The UPMRC now has a constituency of almost 800 physicians, nurses, laboratory technicians, village health workers, and other health professionals, and 52 percent of them are women (UPMRC 1989).

In addition to female volunteers who work in the health field, all medical committees work through women's and other groups to reach the Palestinian population. In January and February 1988, for instance, the UPWWC helped the UPMRC classify the blood type of people all over the Occupied Territories so that prospective donors can be contacted to help people shot by the Israeli army. "These activities are useful to the community in general, but they also provide us with a way to organize people," says Lina Mass'ad, who worked on the blood drive classification scheme. UPWWC volunteers clean hospitals, wash the linens, and help a regular staff that is overwhelmed by the continuous state of emergency.

What distinguishes these medical volunteers is not only the services they perform, but their interest in empowering people through health care. This philosophy of health care is shared by researcher Dr. Rita Giacaman, who is responsible for expanding health services in the villages around Birzeit University, and for conducting village profile studies that are being used for development planning (see Giacaman interview).

Another woman who has contributed to institution building in the West Bank is lawyer Mona Rishmawi. Rishmawi has defended political prisoners, but has also had an active and leading role in Law in the Service of Man (now called al-Haq), an organization that was established in 1979 to "promote the rule of law in Israeli occupied territories" and to document Israeli abuses whenever they occur.

Below are interviews with Rishmawi, Giacaman, and three founding members of two of the four women's committees. The accounts of these women chronicle their contributions to institution building on the West Bank and explain how their approach differs from older more traditional ways of helping people. The accounts also describe the Israeli reaction to their efforts and, in some cases, the personal price some of them have paid for resisting the occupation.

SIHAM BARGHUTI
Math teacher, accountant, and leader

Siham Barghuti, one of the founders of the Palestinian Women's Work Committees, now the largest women's group, describes how the committees were founded in 1978. She also relates how a series of town arrest orders, her imprisonment, and the imprisonment and subsequent deportation of her trade unionist husband have made it difficult for the couple to lead a normal married life.

6 June 1986

My family was not overjoyed by my arrival when I was born in 1948.* When I tease my mother about it, she guiltily explains that it was not the

*I interviewed Siham in Arabic in her house in Ramallah in 1985 and wrote her story from the notes I took. I asked her to tell me about her life and about the committees she helped found.

fact that I was the ninth girl that made it hard on them, but that my timing was a bit off. Palestine was in turmoil, Palestinians were being driven from their homes, and we had just moved because our house had burned down. So even though my parents' last attempt produced "the boy," my position as the youngest girl had a beneficial effect on me. I struggled in order not to get lost in the crowd. I was constantly trying to be heard, so I had to have something worthwhile to say. In retrospect, this was good training for my later life.

My father died when I was four. We were all influenced by the strong personality of our mother, who valued education; seven out of her ten children earned college degrees. I was conscious of living in a Palestinian environment even under the Jordanian regime. I remember hearing my older sisters in the 1950s classifying teachers by saying "this is a nationalist teacher, this is not." We were taught about Palestine in school, and we heard about it on the radio, but what we heard was pure demagoguery. Internal political conditions under Jordanian rule in the 1950s and early 1960s were not conducive to the liberation of Palestine. We resented having to stand up when the Jordanian national anthem was played before the start of every movie. The anthem said "long live the King," and we felt we had more weighty things on our minds than saluting King Hussein.

Political parties were banned in 1957 in Jordan. Even as a child, I was aware of the Jordanian intelligence placing people in the West Bank under surveillance because of their party affiliations. The Jordanian authorities were hard on Communists especially in the fifties and many of our relatives and friends were watched or arrested in those days.

My interest in feminism started when I was in the twelfth grade. Our Arabic teacher asked us to write an essay about "Women's Liberation." From my own observations, and from the excellent models of women I had around me, I was convinced that nothing warranted discrimination against women, and so taking up their cause was natural to me. I also was aware of the writings of Kassim Amin.[1] My composition stressed the importance of educating women, encouraging them to develop their personalities, and fostering their independence. My teacher asked me to read the essay to the class and that encouraged me to think and write about that subject.

The Algerian struggle for independence also affected me. I saw an Egyptian film about the life of Jamilah Bouhreid. I was impressed by the fact that an Algerian Arab woman took part in the resistance to free her homeland from foreign domination, was imprisoned and tortured by the French, and came to be considered a heroine. The turning point in my life, however, was the 1967 occupation of the West Bank and Gaza.

That year, the Israeli authorities conducted a census, and anybody who was out of the West Bank was considered a nonresident, creating yet another diaspora for Palestinians who happened to be studying or working abroad. At that time, I was a university student in Egypt. Israeli authorities refused me reentry to the Occupied Territories in the summer of 1968. The fear of being kept out forever was so great that when I heard that my mother had applied for a family reunion I fainted for joy, but my application was denied. Three more attempts failed, so I entered my own country on a "visitors' visa" every summer. The fear of permanent exile left an imprint on me. If I was serious before the occupation, I became doubly so after it. I felt deeply for the thousands of Palestinians who were kept out. I felt that, as Palestinians with a cause, we could not afford to waste our time on frivolous matters, that we should study and not bother with fashion or with dating. While waiting for a permit, I read Marxist literature that I happened to come across and it was instrumental in shaping my outlook.

I could not change my status into a permanent resident of the West Bank until 1971, a year after I graduated with a B.S. in mathematics. The worst part of getting a permit was that Israeli officials made you feel as if they were doing you a favor "allowing" you to live where you were born and raised. That was the ultimate rudeness and arrogance. On my return, I was appointed as a teacher of mathematics and science at a high school. Through my contact with students and by talking to other professionals, I began to sense that there was a void that needed to be filled. The occupation had stunned the population. It was as if people were holding their breath and waiting for occupation to end before resuming their lives. My sister Suheir and I joined a group that formed "al-Ghadd" (Tomorrow) club at the YWCA in Jerusalem.

In 1974 and 1975 we held poetry readings and read and discussed the work of Egyptian feminist Nawal al-Sa'adawi. My friends and I felt that as educated people, we had a role to play in reactivating the cultural life in the Occupied Territories and in helping raise people's morale. One of our members, Munir Fasheh, then a mathematics professor at Birzeit College, suggested that instead of confining ourselves to theoretical discussions, we should start doing volunteer work as soon as possible.[2] We moved our activities to Ramallah and al-Bireh because most of the people who were interested in the project were from those areas. The mayors of Ramallah and al-Bireh encouraged us to use the public libraries and facilities of their municipalities for our activities. Since most of us were teachers, we volunteered to help students prepare for their Tawjihi high school exams especially in subjects like math, science, and English. After the Tawjihi results were out, students held a party to thank us and it was then that someone suggested that we not confine ourselves to the academic field. The whole country was suffering from neglect; volunteer work in refugee camps and villages would be appropriate. Also, we were aware that by doing physical labor we were making a statement that all work, including manual labor, is valuable.

Our first project was fixing the playground of al-Ama'ari Refugee Camp School run by UNRWA. My sister Suheir and I were the only women involved in that project, and we received some ribbing on that account. Some men thought we looked "too bourgeois" and could not do heavy work, but we wielded shovels and shared the work equally, and, eventually, other women joined us. The work itself was satisfying, but I felt that it wasn't accumulative. I longed for work that would leave a lasting impression on society. Then, of course, there was the problem of women's involvement in volunteer work. The few who did join were mostly middle-class women from the city, and even after four or five years of voluntary work of that type, we had failed to attract women from the sites we worked in. It was *us* working for *them*.[3] In short, we were a bunch of naive leftists, feeling adventurous and feeling pleased with ourselves. But the truth was we had failed to penetrate the walls erected around women. We began to suspect that we were following the wrong approach by having mixed work parties, and that we needed to work only with women. So we tried to work with existing women's organizations like "An-Nahda al-Nisaiyya" and "In'ash al-Usra." We applied to the latter and joined it, but we felt uneasy about the way traditional women's societies function. For the most part, they consist of well-meaning, enthusiastic, dedicated members who administer services to needy women and to the families of imprisoned or martyred men. And while we recognized the need for such services in the absence of a Palestinian state, we felt that there was an urgent need for a more broad-based women's organization, with no age limit, one in which decisions were not formulated from the top down, but one which encouraged the participation of rural and refugee women in the decision-making process.

We published an open letter inviting women to join us. Between fifteen to twenty women responded on March 8, 1978, and the Women's Work Committee [Committees, later, when women in other locations formed committees] was born. As we talked and tried to formulate our goals, we realized that the field was wide open because so many areas of women's lives needed attention. At first, we decided to concentrate on women working outside the home. Experience made us realize that the union issue was important, but very narrow. Women work briefly before marriage and quit right after it. Without housewives, our pool of women consisted only of those who were between the ages of eighteen and twenty-five, the widowed or the divorcees, so we changed our tactics. We are still concerned about women being represented in unions and some of our members are active in the leadership of women's unions, but we have concentrated on women everywhere.

Our efforts at organizing were experimental, and we were flexible about changing strategies that did not work. Experience showed that we were more effective going into neighborhoods than inviting women to attend activities elsewhere. Slowly, we began to absorb the limitations we were suffering from and began to define "progress" in a different way. In conservative areas, we felt it was an achievement if we were instrumental merely in getting a family to allow a young woman out of the *house*. It became clear we needed to change social relations; we needed to work on several levels to help women fight triple oppression at home, in the workplace, and under occupation.

Our early activities were not well planned. We opened a literacy center here, presented a slide show about health there, but we did not have the desired impact. We started becoming effective when we worked at the neighborhood level. We recruited women cadres bound by common interests (i.e., a desire to improve a neighborhood) and encouraged them to make decisions on issues affecting their lives and those of their communities. We decentralized our organization and began listening to the women in refugee camps and villages and asking *them* about their needs. Some decided that a kindergarten for their children was a priority. Others said that they needed money-making projects. Others asked for literacy classes. We then formulated our general policies according to those needs. In 1978 we had twenty women; by 1986 we had 5,000.

Israeli authorities have raided our offices repeatedly, have investigated or imprisoned many of us, but they have not dampened our enthusiasm for organizing. I have held several positions in our organization and have also been quite busy doing volunteer work while holding a full-time job, first as a teacher, and then as an accountant in a West Bank women's cooperative called "Metin." So my "social life" was rather limited. I met my husband, trade unionist Ali Abu Hilal, while we were both doing volunteer work in 1981.+ I was happy that I had found someone who shared my outlook and was also committed to our people. We planned to get married in 1982, but I was imprisoned for two and a half years until August 23, 1984, because I disobeyed an Israeli order that confined me to my town.

I remember the first time I was called to the police station I thought that the Israeli authorities had decided to compensate us for the damage done to our cars in May; instead, I was told that I was confined to Ramallah for six months starting June 1, 1980. I asked the Israeli official who gave me the order why I was being placed under town arrest, and he said, "I don't have to tell you, maybe next time." And there was a next time; in fact, the order was renewed every six months four times until I was caught breaking it on February 26, 1982.

I had been under town arrest for one year and nine months and saw no end was in sight, so I took a chance and traveled. I was stopped on my way to the city of Nablus, outside the area I was restricted to. I am not sure whether I was caught in a routine check of identity cards or whether the Israeli authorities were looking for specific people, but I was taken to a police station and placed under arrest. At one point the head of the intelligence services in Ramallah asked why I was smiling. I said that I had no reason to be unhappy because I was just exercising my right to travel in my country. "I am going to really make you laugh," he said. I was interrogated for forty days without access to a lawyer. A judge "tried" me, again without a lawyer, and sentenced me to two and a half years in prison for breaking the terms of my town arrest and for allegedly belonging to the Democratic Front for the Liberation of Palestine. I had no chance to defend myself.

Trying to nurture my relationship with Ali was hard. Prison visits are usually confined to one's immediate family, but we were surprised when we managed to get a permit for Ali to visit me. All the women prisoners shared my excitement at his visit. The appointed day came and went with no sign of Ali. Only later did I learn that Ali had been arrested on December 5, 1982, the night before the scheduled visit. So for two and a half years I did not see him. Even when he was released in November 1983, he was placed under town arrest in Abu Dis, so he could not travel to where I was. What happened next is like the timing of Greek tragedies. I was released on August 23, 1984, and he was arrested on August 24 for breaking his town arrest order and trying to travel to Nablus that day. It was lucky that he had sneaked over to our house for five minutes the night before or else our separation would have been even longer. I spent the next few days receiving scores of well-wishers, but my thoughts were with Ali and other prisoners both male and female. Ali and I finally had a chance to get married eighteen days after his release on October 10, 1985. Next came the problem of finding work.

Ali was restricted to Abu Dis, a small village with no work opportunities. We asked that his town arrest order be moved to the city of Ramallah so that he could look for a job. The Israeli authorities promised to study the matter but let it sit until the end of his town arrest period. In July, the Israeli legal consultant told Ali that he could live in Ramallah. When his written order came, however, it stated that he was restricted to Abu Dis. Someone was playing games with us and so Ali refused to pick up the order and moved in with me in Ramallah.

On October 23, 1985, thirteen days after Ali and I managed to get married, the Israeli authorities came to our house at 4:00 A.M. I remember thinking, "I know that one cannot have a honeymoon under occupation but this is absurd!" It was easier for me to be arrested myself than to have Ali taken away, but I tried not to betray any emotion in order not to give the Israeli soldiers the satisfaction of seeing me upset. I also wanted to raise Ali's morale and said good-bye to him as if I expected to see him soon. Little did I know that he and others were picked up for deportation to Jordan.

After Ali was taken away, I was filled with rage. I paced up and down the empty house. I made myself some coffee. Worried as I was, I still did not suspect that this was anything other than a "regular" arrest, a normal event in the lives of people under occupation. We had recently moved to our apartment and did not know our neighbors well. I decided to wait till dawn before using their phone to call a lawyer. I tried to read but could not concentrate. My doorbell rang, and when I saw the brother of Dr. Azmi Shu'aibi, my sister Suheir's husband, I knew that Azmi had been arrested as well.[5]

My sister and I shared wonderful experiences over the years. As it turned out, we also had to share some unpleasant ones. Both our husbands were threatened with deportation at the same time. The men threatened with deportation at first petitioned the Israeli High Court against deportation on January 30, 1986. When it became clear that the court would not allow arguments based on international law to be introduced, and would not allow them or their lawyer to examine the evidence against them, they dropped their appeal because they knew that they could not have a fair trial. They were expelled the next day, and we were not even allowed to say good-bye to them.

While we adults can rationalize inhuman treatment, the deportation without good-bye was hard on my sister's three children. They knew that their father had been sick and that the original deportation order was delayed for forty-five days to allow for medical treatment, so they were extremely worried about him. My sister decided to follow her husband to Jordan right away. Israeli authorities told me that I was welcome to join Ali, provided I signed a paper saying that I will not return to the West Bank for three years. So here I am feeling like I did while waiting for a family reunion as a college student, only this time, I am being asked to choose between my husband and my country. All I can think of is: OCCUPATION MUST END! It is time we have our human and national rights recognized.

It's lonely to be conducting a marriage by correspondence, but I refuse to feel sorry for myself. My case is not unique. Many family reunion cases are rejected by the Israeli authorities every year. When I feel discouraged, I remind myself that the period that I had feared would be the worst experience of my life, prison, turned out to be educational. I am proud to say that I took part in the nine-month strike staged by thirty-two women prisoners between June 1983 and March 9, 1984, to force prison officials to recognize the principle that we were political prisoners. We established that we cannot be humiliated with impunity inside or outside prison, and that we would always refuse to submit to any orders that are against our principles.

In prison I learned that even though in a figurative sense other Palestinian women in the diaspora and women in the West Bank and Gaza are in the same ditch together, in reality, the different Palestinian communities are quite isolated from each other because of the borders that separate them. We knew very little about Palestinian women in Lebanon and they knew next to nothing about us. It occurred to me when I met Arab women from different areas that an Israeli prison is the only place where all Palestinian women from different geographical and political zones can meet. We met four prisoners from Lebanon and were surprised at the absence of any women's organizational network in that area. We communicated our organizational strategies to them. What struck me in prison was that many of the women were caught not for initiating or planning operations but for executing them. We cooperated to build the confidence of women who were shaken by the experience of being incarcerated. We took part in teaching illiterate women to read or teaching others a foreign language. Because we used our time after work in reading and study, our ward was so quiet that pregnant Israeli women or women with babies were placed with us to protect them from the rowdiness and drug abuse of Israeli criminals.

The Occupied Territories are hermetically sealed. Occupation distorts our relations with women in Asia, Africa, and Latin America. By denying us travel permits, the Israeli authorities have isolated us from other women who are waging struggles of liberation. Six members of our committee, including me, were denied exit visas to prevent us from participating in the Nairobi Women's Conference in 1985.[6] Those of us who managed to go found contacts with African, Asian, and Latin American women with experiences like ours exhilarating. We have resolved to exchange literature and learn from each other.

I often wonder how long it will be before I meet my husband again. I am insisting on my right to stay in my country. Each of us is in a different world. But I tell myself that we are together in spirit, we both have a cause, and we refuse to be defeated. I also think of what Winnie Mandela has had to go through. Her face on TV, emanating strength, has convinced me that we are fighting the same war; thinking of her raises my spirits.

Update

The Palestinian Union of Women's Work Committees wrote the following in its 5 June 1987 *Newsletter* under the headline, "Siham Barghouti: Forced into Exile":

> This spring Siham was even denied a 72-hour "pass" to see her mother who had fallen ill while on a family visit in Jordan. In April Siham's mother died of cancer in Amman separated from her youngest daughter, Siham. Two months later Siham made the difficult decision to live in exile with her . . . family. She joined her sister, Suheir, and brother-in-law, Dr. Azmi Shu'aibi, who was expelled at the same time as Ali Abu Hilal (PUWWC 1987).

On 13 September 1991, Israeli authorities allowed Ali Abu Hilal, Siham's husband, to return to his hometown of Abu Dis in the occupied West Bank. The return was made possible when the Democratic Front for the Liberation of Palestine made a deal with Israeli authorities whereby it would return the remains of an Israeli soldier it had to Israel and Abu Hilal would be repatriated (*FE* 16 September 1991, 2). It is not clear at this point whether Siham will be allowed to return to the Occupied Territories to live with her husband.

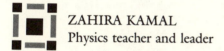

ZAHIRA KAMAL
Physics teacher and leader

Zahira Kamal, member of the Executive office of the Palestinian Federation of Women's Action Committees (PFWAC) (formerly called PUWWC), faced "preventative imprisonment," administrative detention without trial, and the longest town arrest imposed on any woman. In 1984, her case was taken up by Amnesty International. During and after her town arrest, Kamal has insisted on her right to ask for self-determination for Palestinians. Kamal continues to organize and remains confident that, because of grassroots character, the women's committees she helped found can withstand the onslaughts of the Israeli authorities.

25 June 1986

I was placed under town arrest from June 1980 until March 1986.* I was confined to my house one hour after sunset until one hour before sunrise. In winter, it starts getting dark at 4:30 P.M. so my time outdoors was short. The town arrest order meant that I had to sign my name in the registry of the Moscobia police station in West Jerusalem at 7:00 A.M. and 1:30 P.M. I was also not allowed to travel outside the city of Jerusalem where I live, but due to the efforts of UNRWA, I was given permission to travel from my house to UNRWA's Teacher Training Center for Women, where I work, a distance of twenty-five kilometers.

*I interviewed Zahira in Arabic in Jerusalem in early 1985, in Ramallah on 25 June 1986, and in Jerusalem on 1 August 1989. I asked her to tell me about her life and work and wrote her story from the notes I took.

Zahira Kamal, executive director of Palestinian Federation of Women's Action
Committees (PFWAC), 1986. Photo by Orayb Najjar

The order came two years after the establishment of the Palestinian Union of Women's Work Committees (PUWWC) in 1978, and just as it was expanding rapidly in villages, refugee camps, and towns of the Occupied Territories. My harassment began in 1979. I was interrogated by the police, but no evidence was found against me and I was released. A few days later, my house was raided and searched and some of my books and papers were confiscated. Still no evidence was produced, but that did not prevent the authorities from keeping me in Ramleh prison under "administrative detention" for six months. During that period I expected to be charged or tried, but no charges were lodged against me and there was no court hearing. After my release, however, I was slapped with a six-month town arrest order which was renewed every six months for six years. That was the longest town arrest order for any woman in the Occupied Territories, and Amnesty International took on my case in 1984.

When I received my first order, I took the time to analyze the situation objectively. Since 1974, I had been active in volunteer work. I was one of the women who established the PUWWC, the first women's organization that attempted *mass* recruitment of women. It was obvious that I had done nothing illegal that I could be tried for in a court of law or else I would have been tried and convicted. I figured that the Israeli authorities were threatened by our successful recruitment activities, and that their aim was to isolate me and to prevent me from organizing women into a force to be reckoned with. Once I reached that conclusion, my primary objective became the efficient organization of my time. I did all my reading and writing at night, and I used daylight hours for visits, albeit in a limited geographical area. Because our committees stressed power distribution among women from different districts, my absence did not hamper our recruitment drive, and in any case, people who needed to see me came to my house. My family played a very supportive role that alleviated the harshness of the town arrest. Despite my pleas, my mother, brothers, and sisters refused to take any outing outside the geographical area I was confined to and refused to accept any evening invitations I could not go to. But a strange thing began to happen. It was as if relatives and friends had decided that if Zahira cannot go to a party, then the party will go to Zahira. Relatives held engagement ceremonies in the early afternoons, or if that time was not convenient, held them at night at our house. Friends also took my "hours" into account. So collectively we had decided not to let the Israeli restrictions work in their favor.

Structure of the Palestinian Federation of Women's Action Committees in the Occupied Territories

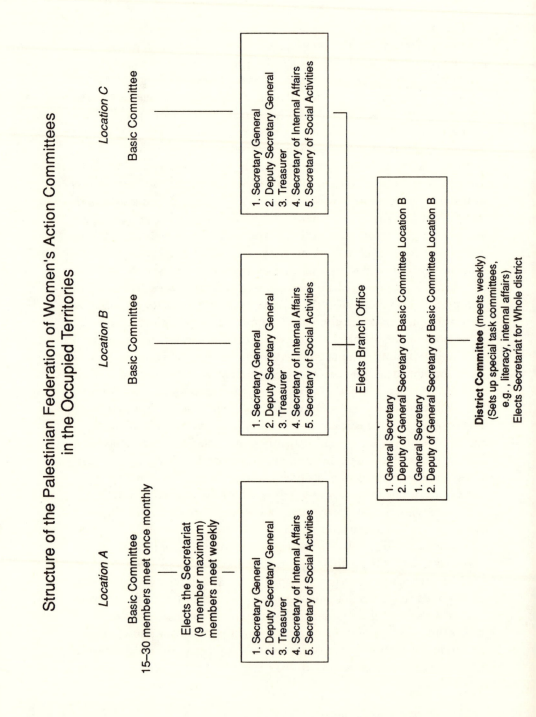

Location A

Basic Committee
15–30 members meet once monthly

Elects the Secretariat
(9 member maximum)
members meet weekly

1. Secretary General
2. Deputy Secretary General
3. Treasurer
4. Secretary of Internal Affairs
5. Secretary of Social Activities

Location B

Basic Committee

1. Secretary General
2. Deputy Secretary General
3. Treasurer
4. Secretary of Internal Affairs
5. Secretary of Social Activities

Elects Branch Office

1. General Secretary
2. Deputy of General Secretary of Basic Committee Location B
1. General Secretary
2. Deputy of General Secretary of Basic Committee Location B

District Committee (meets weekly)
(Sets up special task committees,
e.g., literacy, internal affairs)
Elects Secretariat for Whole district

Location C

Basic Committee

1. Secretary General
2. Deputy Secretary General
3. Treasurer
4. Secretary of Internal Affairs
5. Secretary of Social Activities

Secretary General of Basic Committee A	Secretary General of Basic Committee B	Secretary General of Basic Committee C	Secretary General of Basic Committee D	Secretary General of Basic Committee E

The Higher Committee
(meets every 3 months)

Composed of the Secretariat of the District Committees

Secretariat of District Committee A	Secretariat of District Committee B	Secretariat of District Committee C	Secretariat of District Committee D	Secretariat of District Committee E
Members of Executive Office elected during the conference	Members of Executive Office elected during the conference	Members of Executive Office elected during the conference	Members of Executive Office elected during the conference	Members of Executive Office elected during the conference
Any members appointed by the Executive committee	Any members appointed by the Executive committee	Any members appointed by the Executive committee	Any members appointed by the Executive committee	Any members appointed by the Executive committee

Elect the Executive Office 15–19 members (meets biweekly)

Elects from among its members

Secretary General	Secretary of Internal Affairs	Secretary of Culture and Training	Secretary of Public Relations	Secretary of Publicity and Publications	Secretary of Youth Affairs	Other
Deputy Secretary General						
Treasurer						

The General Conference of the Federation
(Highest legal body—Composed of all the branch offices and other active members specified by the Executive Office. Meets annually to approve program and internal platform)

Prepared by Orayb Aref Najjar & Kitty Warnock

Yet despite the high spirits shown by the family, the almost nightly visits by the police to check on me were disturbing. My younger sisters had nightmares where they would hear a doorbell in their dreams, get up, and open the door to find no one there. Any doorbell at night came to be associated with the police. Once when the doorbell rang and my sister called out, "Zahira, it's the police," I opened the door to find our neighbor wanting to borrow something.

The town arrest order had a pronounced effect on the play activities of my nieces, who visit us almost daily. When my younger nieces, both preschoolers, played house together, they always designated a police station in the corner of the room. One would call on the play phone to invite the other somewhere, and she would answer: "O.K., but first I have to sign my name at the police station," or, "Sorry, I can't come, its getting dark and I have house restriction orders at night."

The third grade teacher of my older niece phoned us to say that she had asked her students during a grammar lesson to give an example of a "recurrent action" and my niece answered: "Signing your name at the police station every day." The teacher wanted to know more about the circumstances of my confinement because other children were curious about it. To dispel my niece's fears, I passed by her school one day and took her with me to the police station. At first she was afraid to enter. After we left she said, "Auntie, I think you come here so that you will not be afraid of Israelis."

So the restriction orders were certainly inconvenient but in a curious way, they helped our recruitment drive. I teach physics and my subject does not lend itself to political discussions. But the mere fact that I was under town arrest sparked interest in our organization, and some students joined our committees.

My overall evaluation of the Israeli restrictions is that they failed to change my commitment to our cause or intimidate me into silence. I believe that Palestinians have the right to self-determination in an independent Palestinian state under the leadership of the PLO, our sole and legitimate representative. Our right to self-determination is recognized by the United Nations and by most nations of the world. My right to self-determination does not threaten anybody's security, so I am determined to exercise it despite Israeli penalties. Like many heads of organizations in the Occupied Territories, I was placed under "preventative arrest" for five days in 1982 when the elected Palestinian mayors of West Bank towns were dismissed by Israeli authorities. Israelis were under the illusion that our imprisonment would prevent demonstrations, but the whole West Bank erupted in demonstrations and strikes in which women took an active part. So if the occupation authorities want to crush the idea of Palestinian self-determination, they would have to jail every Palestinian. I get my license to make statements about our political future from a broad-based consensus of our people.

At present, there are numerous institutions in the West Bank attempting to provide badly needed social services to villages, so what is different about ours? We present many services presented by others, but our approach is more flexible and is constantly under review. Take the issue of literacy for example. The Union of Charitable Societies is working to eradicate illiteracy among women. The union will not hold classes in a village with less than ten learners and is very strict about attendance. We assign a teacher for as low as five learners. To prevent students from dropping out in midcourse, we try to be flexible about regular attendance. We realize that village life has a rhythm that we must respect. There are planting and reaping seasons, canning seasons, festivals, long preparations for marriages, time-consuming rituals for funerals. If a woman misses a class, we allow her to make it up. We figure that if a rural woman with ten children thinks she wants to learn to read despite her never-ending responsibilities, it is our *duty* to design a program that takes her needs into account.[1]

Palestinian society should stress women's education. Tension is bound to result in any marriage where men and women are not equal partners. The circumstances of my parents' marriage made me conscious of the importance of educating women. My mother was an orphan who lived with her uncle and was given in marriage to my father when she was seventeen and he was forty-five. The difference in educational levels between my parents strained their marriage. The last thing I saw before going to bed was my father with a book in his hands, and the first thing I saw every morning was my father reading. My mother had only an elementary education. Father's passion for books was a cause of friction between them, so it was with us that he shared that interest.

I myself had to struggle to get educated. I graduated at sixteen and was eager to go to college. My family reasoned that the three eldest girls would eventually get married and somebody would support them. My parents planned to spend their limited savings educating my two younger brothers so that the boys would support their sisters if the need arose, as is the custom here.

When I heard the news I went on a hunger strike until my father promised to register me at an Egyptian university. I had always wanted to study medicine but was not accepted at a medical school so I decided to be a vet. My family would not hear of it. My third choice was agriculture, but again they could not imagine me working with "peasants." I finally decided on a joint major of physics and research methods. Although I enjoyed what I ended up studying, the obstacles I faced made me sensitive to allowing women to choose their course of study and to live up to their potential. My younger sister Ghadir studied medicine and she helps examine the children in our kindergartens.

My education turned out to be a help to the whole family. When my father died, the responsibility of supporting the family rested on me. Because we lived on a limited income, we literally sat in council to decide how to spend our budget. One of us would say, yes I need a sweater, but my sister or brother needs this or that item more so I can do without. The democratic way of decision making carried over to my work in the women's committees when I was elected as a member of its Executive Office.[2] We do not have a leader with troops. We depend on discussion and consensus decision making.

Many see Arab women as homebound, or functioning mainly as housewives, but that is not the case. In addition to working inside the home, a large number of Palestinian women support large families, send male siblings to college, or support aged parents because many Palestinian men are out of the country or imprisoned. Some women are so overworked they become production machines sacrificing their personal needs for the sake of uninterrupted production. I am lucky in that I have succeeded in supporting my family without sacrificing personal fulfillment.

It is usual for our society to pressure women into marriage and I was subjected to similar pressures. No traditional marriage for me! When I was in my twenties, I took the unusual step of contacting a prospective groom to tell him not to officially ask for my hand to spare himself the embarrassment of a rejection. If I meet someone I am intellectually compatible with, someone who understands the pressures of my work and shares my political outlook, I will marry him even if he does not conform to my extended family's idea of a marriage partner. Yet I do not see marriage as an end in itself and feel pretty fulfilled because I am very much alive and productive on many levels.

One of my accomplishments on the family level is that I have stopped anyone from pressuring my sisters into marrying people they did not choose themselves. When decisions need to be made, I am asked to represent my family just like my father would have, and my opinions are given equal weight to the male heads of our extended family. So our society is not as rigid as some people believe; it responds to the changes brought about by the education of women. Our main problem now is to extend those advantages to *all* women in all social strata.

In most Asian and African countries, development is undertaken by governments. Since we are under occupation, we have to generate our own funds. Selling materials produced by women in bazaars is one way of making money to support our development activities. We are now trying to diversify into nontraditional areas for women's production. Our Issawiyyeh cooperative makes enamel hangings and brass frames. We are also experimenting with mass producing the baby food one of our specialists developed for low-income families. We also benefit from grants given by progressive international organizations interested in our development. For example, NOVIB, a Dutch organization, provides all our kindergartens with one hot meal a day. Terre Des Homme, a Swiss organization, supports health projects and health publications. The Welfare Fund Association, a Swiss organization, helps us with our literacy expenses. Oxfam also helps, and so do a number of international women's organizations. The United Nations sponsored an Australian kindergarten specialist who spent a year in the Occupied Territories and conducted workshops for our teacher trainees. The Norwegian Palestine Committee has been sending a dentist and a nurse to examine our preschool children since 1982. They have recently examined 898 children ages three to six. Our own dentists and doctors help us screen children for free and help check the spread of infectious diseases.

When we organize women, our main aim is to improve their lives by empowering them. We never establish a committee in any village unless the women of the village request it and are willing to run it. Although development plans are the responsibility of the central committee, they are based on the input of the districts where the centers are located. Leadership of every unit is local because people who live in a village can determine its needs better than outsiders, and each unit has no more than thirty members to facilitate direct involvement and democratic decision making.

Various committees use video tapes to initiate discussion of important issues. One function of showing videos about the struggle of women in other countries is to stress the point that women everywhere face the same problems, in Lebanon, in Chile, and in South Africa. There she is, sitting with her pregnant stomach in front of her, washing clothes outdoors in a pan. She has a dozen kids, she hangs up clothes, she cooks, she cleans. Her color and the color of her dress may be different from continent to continent, but her problems are the same. We use a tape like "No Consolation for Women" to stimulate discussion on the status of women. We play "Women Behind Bars," which includes a segment about Algerian resistance fighter Jamilah Bouhreid, to elicit discussion on female prisoners. Each committee decides what it wants to show, and the choice runs from child-rearing videos to material that stimulates discussion on national issues. A Gaza committee showed the two tapes mentioned above in its kindergarten building after regular hours. The Israeli authorities seized the videos (that were rented from regular stores) and wanted to close the kindergarten. A member of the committee, Lubna Uleyyan, refused to receive the closure order. Lubna argued that the kindergarten is public property, and so the women refused to close it with their own hands. She also told the officer that he had to shut down the kindergarten, by force, in front of the whole community. Lubna was placed in administrative detention herself, but the kindergarten remained open. Her story illustrates the importance of having local committees who make their own decisions and determine which risks are worth taking.

We like to make all women, whether they are of rural or urban origin, feel valuable in Palestinian society. We have resisted sending city teachers to villages. Teachers who come from more developed areas may not be sensitive to conditions in villages. For example, teachers may not understand that children have dirty feet because the cheap flimsy plastic shoes their parents can afford do not protect their feet like good shoes and socks do. Furthermore, one cannot expect children from homes without running water to be as clean as children where running water is available. In our kindergartens, children take off their shoes outside, clean their feet if necessary, and then move onto the carpeted areas. The mothers of many of the children marry young and have no experience raising kids. We help mothers organize into mothers' committees. Through the committees, mothers are exposed to progressive child-rearing ideas in the form of video tapes and lectures.

Training someone within each locale keeps the work force stable and gives village women opportunities to work. It is amazing how much talent one can find in rural areas. For example, the seven-year-old Hizma village kindergarten has become a model kindergarten because of its experienced and creative teachers. We now send aspiring kindergarten trainees from the city to the village for practical training. This type of reverse flow from a town to a village has done wonders for the morale of village teachers.

We are careful on how we present ourselves on the village level because social acceptance is important to us; we are of our people and not alien to them and we do not want to isolate members from their communities. But even under a traditional society, we have a leeway for action. Under Muslim law, or Shari'a, for instance, a woman has the right to half the inheritance of a male. Yet to prevent the fragmentation of land, social customs force a woman to sign away her inheritance to her brother and to then depend on him for support. If the brother is conscientious all is well, but if he turns out to be greedy, his sister is powerless when she need not be by law. So we see our role as informing women of their rights, urging them to keep land in their own names, and supporting them to withstand family pressure once they decide to do so.

We do not act as a consciousness-raising group in the Western sense; we just provide the atmosphere where a woman with problems can discuss them with others. Women discover after talking that what they have always regarded as personal problems are in fact social or national problems that only collective solutions will help alleviate. An intelligent woman who is pulled out of school for her "own protection" at puberty mistakenly believes she has a problem with an authoritarian father, but her problem is with a patriarchal society where there is unequal distribution of wealth between urban and rural areas. Often, to get to the nearest high school in town, a rural student has to take a couple of buses at great expense, or walk several kilometers (which many parents find unacceptable for teenage girls).[3] We cannot build schools in villages, but we can persuade a bus company to run buses to some villages at schooltime, as we have in the village of Jaba'.

Wherever we go, our attention is directed to cases where women are victimized. In Jenin, for instance, we found a sixteen-year-old girl who was being dragged from one quack doctor to another and from one fortune teller to another because she failed to conceive after six months of marriage. I would not be surprised that, if allowed to continue, such emotional and mental strain on that teenager would drive her crazy. We have women in their twenties who escaped into madness because they were pulled out of schools they excelled in and forced into marriages against their wills. We have women who were refused divorces but were sent home to live with their parents while their husbands remarried. We have women who have the "choice" of either staying in unhappy marriages or getting divorced and losing their children. We do not think that such women should be left to face these societal problems alone.

Despite the fact that we are increasingly getting involved in social issues, we do not view ourselves as being simply a feminist organization that is agitating for equality between the sexes. Some women wanted us to take on that role when we were discussing the direction we should take in the early years. We like to stress that the women's movement is part of the national movement. We believe that both personal and national liberation go hand in hand. When both sexes are deprived of their freedom and national dignity by the Israelis, it would be inappropriate for us to deal only with sexual inequalities. On the other hand, we will fail both women and our cause if we do not understand that liberating women from discrimination will better equip them for waging a successful national struggle.

Here I do not want to suggest that we are perfect. We are working with disadvantaged women, and they are the ones who run the centers and follow up on activities. Our programs are as good as the training we provide and they differ in quality from place to place and are still inadequate in many areas. But we are working to close those gaps, and I am very optimistic about our organization because we have the right approach to development. We are a genuine grassroots movement. That is why I believe we are the wave of the future.

Update: 1 August 1989

The uprising is the Palestinian answer to the inequities inflicted by Israeli rule. For the first time since 1967, Israel has started to realize that there are moral and financial costs to the occupation. At first, the Israeli army believed that all it needed was more time and more instruments of repression to crush the uprising, but the army failed because the Intifada is fighting the occupation on many different levels, none of which force can affect.

The Palestinian leadership has asked people to unite and women were first to respond. Women's committees started cooperating even before the Intifada. On March 4, 1987, we held our first-ever unified celebration for International Women's Day and pledged to get together on an anti-reactionary and antiimperialist basis. In 1988, we established the Higher Council of Women.

We felt that women's participation during the uprising has earned them a great deal of respect, but that we needed to institutionalize that

The religious movement is gaining ground in the West Bank and Gaza. Even the newly made doll in the center is now wearing Shari'a dress. The women are teacher trainees attending a workshop in East Jerusalem run by the Birzeit University Literacy Center. Photo by Orayb Najjar

respect; otherwise, women's gains will dissipate at the onset of the slightest social tremor. The example of what happened to women's rights in Algeria is not far from our minds. Algerian women joined the revolution but their status has not improved much after liberation. We want to make sure that we do not suffer the same fate.

For women to be part of the political decision-making process, they have to be part of the decision-making process at home. It is easier, however, to start by teaching women to make decisions about their own communities in the women's communities, and then hope that each will apply what she has learned to her own situation at home.

We have 5,000 members in our committees. There is a total of 25,000 organized women in all groups, and even though this is a large number compared to 1978 when we started, the number constitutes only 3 percent of women available for recruitment, so we need to work harder and recruit housewives and older women. We plan to better coordinate our activities with charitable societies and leave all service activities we often do to them. We need to concentrate instead on developing the social, educational, and political role of women. We would like to see a certain percentage of women represented in Palestinian institutions in a Palestinian state, not one or two token women, but a reasonable percentage that we can work to increase. Representation alone is not enough, however. It would not help if we have women leaders while the bulk of women are led like sheep. We realize that many women have not had as much experience in public affairs as men. In fact there are some women who are very talented and have native ability combined with practical experience in the struggle but lack the ability to conduct a theoretical analysis of our situation. We see our role as providing such women with the educational opportunities that would prepare them to occupy positions in public life. Eventually, we will be in a position to ask for equal representation.

I believe that any man or woman earns the right to political inclusion through participation. I have earned it through the slow process of being involved in all the developments that took place in the Occupied Territories since the early years of the occupation, so it is natural that I join in political discussions that have a bearing on our future.[4]

We are also taking a strong position against the intimidation of women in any way, especially through sex. First, we are trying to spread the notion that a man's honor is in his defense of the land and not in the sexuality of his female relatives, the mode of thinking prevalent in 1948 and beyond. Members of the women's committees are forcefully resisting the efforts of some conservatives to require women to wear conservative dress. There have been a number of incidents in the summer of 1989 when some women had eggs or tomatoes thrown at them for not wearing conservative dress. One woman caught up with her assailant and hit him. As a crowd gathered, the embarrassed man protested that it was the first time he'd ever bothered a woman over her dress. "I just want to make sure this will also be your last," she countered. In Islam, we say, "La Ikraha fid-din," "no coercion in religion." Each woman has a relationship with God and need not be coerced into any mode of belief or dress. My younger married sister recently chose to start wearing Shari'a clothes. Our relationship is as close as it ever was. I have not said a word about it; it is her choice. No one is against choice. No one, however, has the right to force others to follow suit, because dress is one of our personal freedoms.

There have been a few rapes and a few attempted rapes of Palestinian women by Israeli soldiers. Under the pretext of searches, some soldiers corner women and molest them. We moved to act when we noticed that; although women were beaten on all parts of their bodies, they were often pinched or bitten on their breasts and beaten on their sexual organs. In one case, we have asked lawyer Leah Tsemel to sue soldiers who molested and beat several women, one pregnant. Instead of letting the women hide in shame, we intend to shame the offenders, not the victims. Israeli women are cooperating with us in this matter through the Organization for Women Political Prisoners.

Israeli women made overtures to us in 1980. A group came to show its disapproval of town arrest against a number of Palestinians, including me. While there is an official Palestinian position against meeting with Israeli leaders,[5] we have nothing against meeting Israelis who respect our right for self-determination. We feel that many Israelis see us in a stereotypical manner, yet they need to know what we think. I feel that we know much more about them than they know about us. On the Palestinian side, most of us see the need for a two-state solution. On the Israeli side, they are split on this issue. The majority still believe in the continuation of the occupation.

We say that the PLO is our sole and legitimate representative, but many Israelis want to choose our leaders for us. This is ridiculous—the issue of who represents us is not negotiable, and some Israelis are acting as if it is, as if we are still at square one.

We have also been working hard at solidifying our links with international women's groups. After my town arrest order was lifted in 1986, I traveled to Moscow, Berlin, Budapest, Copenhagen, and New York, and I have made contacts with active women in all these places.

We are optimistic because the declaration of Palestinian independence of November 15, 1988, gave women equal rights. It is now up to us to define what "equal" rights mean. Most of the lawyers who write legislation are men, so it is important that the women's movement take part in conceptualizing what equality means and suggesting matters that need to be taken into consideration when laws are promulgated for the new state.

To succeed in activating women, we stress leadership training for women. In one session, we brought together sixty-five women for a four-day workshop where the women spent three nights in East Jerusalem away from home. Women could bring nursing babies and younger children with them. On the third day one husband came asking for his wife and said to me, "Why did you take her away? She has left the children at home." I told him that she was there by her own free will, but that he's free to talk to her. The minute she saw her husband, the woman placed her hands on her hips and said, "Our youngest kid who gives most trouble is here with me, so what do you want?" The husband complained that it was hard to cope without her. "Well, you coped when I gave birth," she said. "But that was different," he protested. "Well just pretend I am giving birth," she said emphatically, and with that she turned her back to him and went in. I followed her and said, "You know, you *are* giving birth, to yourself." I felt that she would not have responded to her husband with such indignation had she not felt that there was something in our program that spoke to her needs.

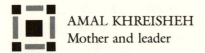

AMAL KHREISHEH
Mother and leader

Feeling that women are "the working class of men" and that the division of labor between the sexes is like the division between the capitalist owner of production and the worker, Khreisheh joined other women in establishing the Union of Palestinian Working Women's Committees (UPWWC) in 1981. The group stresses women's rights in the workplace and conducts unionizing workshops. Like many women, Khreisheh has been introduced to gender issues through her nationalist activities. She is now convinced that, while the occupation is the most pressing issue facing women, more time needs to be spent on ameliorating · factors that hold back women's development, foremost among them is all forms of discrimination in the workplace.

July 1989

I think my main problem is lack of time.* I share with activists the feeling that there aren't enough hours in a day to do what we need to do. I work in the women's movement, and I have two children. I feel guilty for not spending enough time with my children. I had no problems with raising the first child because my husband was under town arrest and so he

*I interviewed Amal Khreisheh in Arabic in Jerusalem in July 1989. I asked her to tell me about her life and work with the committees she heads. I wrote her story from the notes I took.

helped with the housework and with our child, but by the time the second child was born, the arrest order had expired. My husband helps whenever he can, but I now have much more to do. On the positive side, this experience of combining child care with activism has made me sensitive to the importance of providing women with services that would free them from housework and child care so that they can join public life in greater numbers. There are now proposals for opening cheap public restaurants, launderettes, extensive child care for young children, and clubs for older children. We ourselves are quite active in providing summer camps for older children, and we always have children's drawings in our bazaars.

Initially, I joined public life not because of my awareness of injustice against women, but for nationalist reasons. My first experience in working with organized women's groups came when I joined the General Union of Jordanian Women in Amman where I went to college. Through visiting refugee camps, my consciousness was raised. I saw a clear example of the oppression of women at Schneller Refugee Camp. A man beat his wife because she had been delayed at work and so had not prepared dinner. I began to absorb the equation. Here she was helping augment the family income, and she still had to do all the housework and could be attacked with impunity because of the social prerogatives the male had.

I returned to the West Bank and got a job as a social worker with the Union of Seamstresses in Nablus. I also became a member of the board of the Red Crescent Society in Toulkarm. The Israeli Ministry of Social Affairs controlled every detail of our work. You could not show a film without a permit, and their employees also interfered in election results. It became clear to me that we needed to create a mass-based framework, one that could impose itself on the occupation.

In 1980, union activists in five main cities formed special women's committees for working women. On March 8, 1981, fifty-five female delegates met and formed the Union of Palestinian Working Women's Committees (UPWWC). The purpose of forming our committees was to fill a void. At that time, other groups concentrated on students and already politicized women, and we felt that the interests of female workers were not being taken care of either by the male unions or by existing women's groups. At first, unions found our move threatening and tried to resist it, but the unions realized that because of conservative social customs, we were in a better position to help women. All representatives to the unions were male and had no access to women; they could not recruit them because women could not talk to males not related to them without inviting gossip and family sanctions.

We aggressively tackled the problems of women in the workplace in the West Bank. The weakness of the industrial sector and its dependence on small factories run by the owners have contributed to the concentration of women's work in the service sectors, in traditional "women's work." Women's work outside the home is an extension of what they do at home, raising children, care giving, nursing, and secretarial work. Women also do light repetitive factory work in the pharmaceutical industries, sewing factories, and in foodstuff production. In factories, there is an unwitting conspiracy between the employer and a worker's family. The employers oppress women by making them work long hours for low wages because they know that women are discriminated against in the home and that women or their families are not likely to complain. Sometimes, we have to fight so that workers get their wages on time, or in the appropriate currency. To "protect" the female employees, some bosses or labor contractors convince fathers that they are their daughters' guardians, and so would not allow young women out of the factory or allow them to talk to anyone from outside it. That of course keeps union representatives out. The factories, Arab and Israeli, often pick women up in buses from stations near their homes and then return them there. Often, a woman's salary goes straight to her father. When we started organizing, owners prevented us from entering factories and often threatened to call the police. To recruit, we visited women individually in their homes, and that was a much slower process than meeting with groups.

Women who work inside Israel work in what Israelis call "black work," jobs few Israelis want. Palestinian women are also heavily represented in seasonal work in agriculture and in cleaning hospitals and institutions. Because these jobs are mostly unskilled, women are treated as interchangeable parts of a machine and can be fired without notice. Employers can get away with hiring women without written contracts and can set any terms they like as they go along. Sometimes, women work nine to twelve hours without overtime. Palestinian women are paid about half the salaries of Israeli women doing the same job. Arab women must pay for maternity benefits, but because a baby must be born inside Israel for the mother to receive maternity benefits, women in the West Bank (with the exception of Arab Jerusalem) are deprived of those benefits. Women also do not receive unemployment insurance and family allowances even though 30 percent of their wages are deducted for "benefits." We are fighting for wage equality in the workplace both between Israeli and Palestinian women and between women and men. Palestinian women in government jobs get only forty days of maternity leave. In factories, pregnant women often get fired. We defend women's right to paid maternity leave. We encourage women to join unions and demand the recognition of women in unions. We believe this fight is crucial because women are the working class of men, and the division of labor between them is like the division between the capitalist and the worker. It is men who own the means of production, who run work, and who take value surplus in production. The disadvantages women labor under are indicators of the present economic system.

We must avoid romanticizing the reasons for which women go to work outside the home. Among the poorer segments of the population, women's entry into the work force has been through force of circumstances and cannot be looked at as creative self-expression of any given woman's talent. Women are treated like work reserve, and their income is still the secondary source of income. Poverty forces women to accept any working conditions they find.[1]

We encourage workers to demand a holiday on the first of May as well as on International Women's Day on March 8. We have called for the recognition of March 8 as a paid holiday and, in fact, deliberately founded our committee on that day. Our members have gone from factory to factory and managed to talk 100 employers into granting them March 8 as a paid holiday in 1982. Our success made women flock to the union, and we had to elect local and district leaderships, like Samar Hawwash. By 1989, we had 156 signatures of employers or institutions accepting March 8 as a paid holiday.[2] Before 1981, men talked about March 8 and tried to honor it. I myself attended a celebration at the Union of Workers in Toulkarm in 1981, and it was attended by about 150 workers. Nablus was under curfew, so I reached Ramallah with difficulty and was amazed that more than 1,500 women were in the street and had gathered in the al-Bireh Municipal Gardens. We started dreaming of really turning International Women's Day into a day of mass celebration, not just an occasion for intellectuals. We wanted that day, where blood was spilt for union affairs, to be an occasion to gather our potential and fight for equality in the workplace.

We celebrate International Women's Day also because of our internationalist perspective. We see the Palestinian women's movement as part of the international movement. We believe that solidarity among women's groups strengthens them and allows them to exchange experiences. We are especially interested in links with groups fighting national, class, and social oppressions in Africa, Asia, and Latin America. We are against apartheid in South Africa, fight for the release of political prisoners in South African jails, and are in solidarity with the struggle of Latin American countries fighting dictatorship of rightist regimes. We stress the news of those regions in our publications because we feel we are waging the same struggle.

We have hosted members of the Women's International Democratic Federation, which has 136 women's organizations from 118 countries (August 25–27, 1986). We have contacts with women of various countries in Eastern Europe and the Soviet Union. In 1988, we were pleased to work with a group of about sixty Italian unionist and activist women. Palestinian women from different groups shared a day-long conference. The Italian group also demonstrated with us against the occupation.

We do volunteer work. Community work uncovers people with leadership potential, but we often face the problem of finding ways to involve people who need to join but come from conservative families. In Beit Wazan in the Nablus district, we met a very active seamstress who cooperated with us during working hours, but could not stay for meetings after work. To win members of her family over, we paid them a social call. A week later, fourteen women met to help a poor family in town harvest its crop, so we passed by and picked her and her sister up. She worked harder than the young men who joined us. Her family trusts us, and now she is a full member and can even travel to other villages to organize other women.

We try to be aware of social customs. When one of our committee members in a village gets married, we make a point of visiting her. A visit in Arab culture has social significance: it helps legitimize us to the woman's family, it helps legitimize her relationship with the committee, and it also brings the woman some social prestige. Here is a group of women "from the city," including one female M.D., who are interested in her, visit with her family, and even go with her shopping for her trousseau.

Men can often be won over and become supportive of our committees. In the village of Abu Kash, a man of forty-eight, married to a woman of thirty-nine, just could not absorb the fact that her activities with us necessitated that she be so mobile – traveling between town and village. He was not sure how the village would react to her mobility; after all she was a married woman with children. We went and visited him. He was a logical man and we convinced him that his wife is talented and has a role to play in society. This woman was a natural leader, and when her husband saw how much others respected her, he started supporting her.

Yet one needs to admit that women's political consciousness far exceeds their feminist consciousness. We now have a real fear, a well-founded fear about the position of women after political liberation. We have a situation where women are leaders in the streets, but followers in their own homes. We are not discouraged though. Involvement in public affairs will make women conscious of gender issues. Involvement in national affairs becomes a prelude to the liberation of women if only because it enlarges their world as it did mine.

I was born in 1957. I owe my involvement in public affairs to teachers who encouraged us to read. We had a student union and a wall newspaper, and in 1974, I was called into the Israeli intelligence service for the first time when I was in the tenth grade in Toulkarm. Israeli officials wanted to know if I was a member of any political organization. "Do you have any contacts with boys?" they asked. At that time, I did not even look out of the window. They let me know they thought that wall newspapers were dangerous and that such behavior "was not suitable for an Arab girl." I was young and brash, so I said, "Show me something written that shows that it is forbidden to have a wall newspaper." Then the intelligence officer threatened me and called in my father and "advised" him not to let me get involved in politics.

We now use wall newspapers in our different centers. Centers exchange the information on those newspapers. There is no paper now on the board because in March 1989, Israeli soldiers raided this center here in East Jerusalem and broke one sewing machine and a few chairs. Instead of written materials, we now concentrate on "the Oral ['heard'] magazine," where oral bulletins are exchanged between committees and discussion ensues.

The Intifada has increased women's participation in neighborhood committees and all kinds of committees. Women's familiarity and close ties with each other in neighborhoods gives them special flexibility. Women meet in each others' homes. When a woman gets arrested, or when a committee is closed, women simply change the name of their organization and go right on working. So we have "Banat al-Reef Committee" (Daughters of the Countryside), the "Committee of Social Service," the "Committee of Housewives," and so on.

The Intifada, by default in some cases, has made it possible for some women to take up roles previously reserved for males. There was at least

Audience of a lecture on women, delivered by Islah Jad at the Union of
Palestinian Working Women's Committee's center in East Jerusalem, 7 July 1989.
Photo by Orayb Najjar

one case where the army surrounded the graveyard as a martyr was being buried and the men had to escape; a woman read the eulogy for him, unheard of before. Women now are more courageous about speaking up in mixed gatherings. At a seminar in the Hebrew University someone asked, "Is there a woman among the leadership of the uprising?" The mere fact that someone asked that question points to the importance of the contributions of women and the expectations others now have of them.

In our publications, we encourage women to take part in writing about women's contributions to the Intifada.[3] The Unified Leadership of the Intifada in its leaflets has asked parents not to ask for high dowries and not to have ostentatious weddings because of high unemployment. To encourage compliance, we run stories about women who describe how simple their weddings were, how they borrowed a wedding dress or did not wear a special dress. We stress how the families did not sing in order to show their respect for people who are mourning relatives shot by the Israeli army.

We see our activities as the expression of a new form of organizing that shuns philanthropic-style work and concentrates instead on creating a mass movement. We employ union organizing that adopts the issue of women as a nationalist and social issue and ties them in a dialectical manner.

There is a rise in the ideological and cultural influence of the women's movement in the struggle against old customs. During the Intifada, we have become concerned with the early marriage of a number of women. We met with fifty women last week in Kufr Ein in the Ramallah district. Discussions revealed that most of the males of those families who marry their daughters early are mostly workers and daily laborers who are finding difficulty supporting their families. To remove women from the dependency cycle, we have to offer them less talk and more alternatives. That is why we are moving in the direction of opening cooperatives to allow women access to independent sources of income in economically depressed areas. In our centers in villages, we introduce the idea of treating both sexes the same way. Initially we are greeted with some surprise — it is a new idea — but you see some response from people who never considered the issue before. We also discuss the rise of domestic violence.

Because of the general strike where shops are open only from nine to twelve, many men are at home starting at midday. Women do not have the outlet of visiting neighbors the way they do when the men are away. Long curfews imprison families with six to twelve children in a two-room house for days on end. There you have a man who has been humiliated by the occupier, and he goes home full of anger and takes it out on his family. It is hard for a woman to complain about her husband in a public meeting, but at least we bring the subject up and women feel they are not alone. A number of ideas are floating around now on the subject, among them the establishment of a battered women's center.

We have a patriarchal society; our representatives in the general unions are all male. Although almost half of the students and teachers are female, the students' and teachers' unions are represented by males; the writers' union has a male as its head. Changes need to be made in the structure of Palestinian institutions. Making women conscious of their rights under the prevailing social system creates an internal struggle within them. We explain to women the importance of their role and its connection to the structural changes we need to make in Palestinian society. That way, we solve the conflict women feel by placing the struggle in its proper path of social and economic liberation of women.

Because we realize that many women have limited experience in union-izing, we sponsor training workshops in which we talk about the history of the union movement and the importance of working for workers' rights. We also offer practical suggestions for strategies women can use in the workplace. We have to be careful because employers fire activist women as soon as they spot them, but one way to avoid unjust firing is by making employers sign group contracts with the women working for them. Then women can unite and ask for their rights. We have supported a number of strikes women staged to improve their working conditions.[4] We believe that the economic liberation of any woman is an important step in her social liberation and that both are tied to her liberation from occupation.

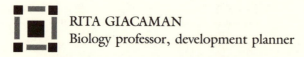

RITA GIACAMAN
Biology professor, development planner

Although Rita Giacaman started out as a self-involved westernized teenager, her experience as a college student changed her. Her experience as a medical profes-

sional in the Palestinian countryside has led her to discard the biomedical or "engineering" approach to medicine. She now advocates building a health infrastructure compatible with people's needs, taking factors like education, class, gender, and environment into account. After discussing health planning before the uprising, Giacaman describes how its mass-based infrastructure has enabled the Palestinian volunteer medical professionals to deal with the high casualties of the uprising. Dr. Giacaman also describes her newest project: planning for the needs of the growing disabled population, "not as charity cases, but as Palestinian citizens who deserve respect in the progressive state Palestinians are building."

19 July 1986

I share a great deal with a number of educated and westernized Palestinian women.* We all led politically sheltered lives before 1967, became politicized after the 1967 war, and adopted a progressive framework for thinking about social and political issues by the late seventies. It took the 1967 defeat to make us realize that we needed to be more in tune with the needs of our society and to use our advantaged position as educated women to serve it. The loss of the West Bank and Gaza to Israeli occupation has led many of us to become not only nationalists but also leftists and feminists. In my case, my new consciousness saved me from the fate of the female friends and relatives I went to school with. They married early, became well to do, and are now leading very boring lives.[1]

I went to St. Joseph, a French private school where teaching was done mainly by French nuns, or Arab nuns who had absorbed their colleagues' prejudices and pretensions. I will never forget my first day in kindergarten when one nun said to another, "Poor girl, she's so dark and takes after her mothers' rather than her fathers' family." I was traumatized by that remark. I felt unattractive because of my color way into my twenties. What happened was a mutilation of my view of myself to conform to some other norm of beauty which has been imposed on us and which we have absorbed, i.e., the whiter the better.

---

*When I interviewed Rita on 19 July 1986, I asked her to speak in English. In the conversation we taped, she used English but sometimes used Arabic. I also tape recorded a presentation she gave on the same day to journalism students attending a writing workshop. She talked about coverage of public health issues. I interviewed Rita again on 15 July 1989, to update my information about health care during the Intifada. She introduced the issue of taking care of the disabled. In this part, I depended on my notes.

When I was in my teens, I played the role of the Western teenager to the hilt. I listened to record albums and had crushes on Western singers and movie stars. I led a life that was removed from anything political; such a life of comfort makes you ambitious, but it restricts your ambition to the achievement of personal benefits. I aspired to go to college and to study music, but my mother insisted that I go into the sciences because that is what good students are expected to do. My mother, motivated by her own frustrated ambitions, pushed all of her five children, the girls even more than the boy, to achieve academically. Mother took it hard when my eldest sister left college to get married. And now, years later, my sister has gone back to get an M.A. in creative writing. I know she is doing so because it is a field that interests her, but I also suspect that my mother's words were ringing in her ears all these years.

I went to Birzeit in 1968–69. It was a private junior college then whose student body consisted mainly of upper- or middle-class students. Even as early as 1968, the class structure of the college was starting to change, and there was an influx of students from refugee camps, students who could be there only on scholarships. These students came from the most under-privileged segment of Palestinian society. I met students from Gaza for the first time during an anti-Israeli occupation sit-in held in the village of Birzeit.[2] To me, they were like people from another planet, very different from the well-groomed pampered boys I grew up with, boys who liked Elvis Presley's music, wore jeans, and were politically apathetic. I had never before associated with poor or political Palestinians at such close quarters. Frankly, that day, my sister and I went as spectators, but after the initial discomfort of coming face to face with a different world, I liked what I saw. I admired the intensity and the commitment of those students.

To understand my initial reaction, it is useful to know something about the segment of Bethlehem society I grew up in. It was a conservative segment that was culturally Western, or at least aspired to be. So the more Western you became, the more foreign languages you spoke, the more you traveled, and the more you imitated the West in appearance, mannerisms, and even food, the better. I grew up hearing some people say that the best solution to the Palestinian problem was the internationalization of Jerusalem and Bethlehem; in other words, the rest of the Occupied Territories can go to hell.

My immediate surroundings were vastly different from those of the city of Nablus, for instance. I knew middle-class Nablus women in college, but they were more nationalistic and more socially aware than I was simply because their city was politicized and nationalistic. Not all of Bethlehem society was that conservative, but the segment of society I grew up in as well as a segment of Ramallah society were. Part of the social snobbery involved can be traced to and was reinforced by our colonial education, and it took time and effort to break away from this heritage.

After Birzeit I went to the American University of Beirut (AUB). A strike that started in 1971 over fees became politicized. The Palestinian national movement was at its apex, and there was a lot of discussion, debate, and plenty of materials to read. I felt like a farmer visiting the city for the first time. A new world, culturally Arabic and politically Palestinian, opened up to me. My political education continued when I went to the United States to do graduate work. There, I associated with progressive Palestinian students who helped me think about issues I had not considered before, and the atmosphere of free debate helped me review my past and arrive at a new consciousness. But nothing was as eye-opening as real-life experience in Palestinian villages.

After working in the United States for a year, I returned to the occupied West Bank. The main reason for my return was more because I did not like living in the United States, where competition was stressed over cooperation, than because of my newly heightened national sensitivity. I was hired by the Department of Biology at Birzeit, which had become a university in 1975. There I was, armed with a doctorate in clinical pharmacy from the University of California, San Fransisco Medical Center [1977], ready to work. But the shiny lab I was used to, my security blanket, was gone. I felt helpless and thought that what I had studied was useless and super specialized. In retrospect, my training turned out to be more useful than I had first suspected. We took most of the courses medical students did but with emphasis on pharmacology. So I had enough courses in microbiology, pathology, embryology, and physiology to do research on medical matters without being a doctor. But there was a problem of a different kind, and it centered on my approach to medicine.

I was the product of an education that used the biomedical model, which is the engineering approach to health, a way of conceiving health and body as a machine which can be fixed to operate well again whenever it is broken. Under such an approach, diagnosis is based on lab medicine, and you look for a causative agent of disease. If you cannot concretely document it you deny its existence. Therefore, women whose ailments were not readily apparent were called hysterical, and people were said to have psychosomatic diseases. The main failing of the biomedical model is that it does not take social, economic, gender, and class relations into consideration. That is how we studied medicine in the United States, and I could not practice it that way in the West Bank.

During my first year at Birzeit, I kept threatening to go back to the United States. Finally my friends said that I had to stop being schizophrenic and that I had to leave or to make a commitment to stay. By the end of the first year, I began to adjust to life in the West Bank—and there was a lot to adjust to. In addition to being deprived of working in a hi-tech environment, I had to live in a socially conservative society again. I had been living alone since I was twenty, and single women are expected to live with their families until marriage. Living alone was unheard of, but my excuse was that I needed to live in Ramallah because it was closer to Birzeit where I worked than Bethlehem was. I still had to contend with restrictions society imposes on single women, but the satisfaction I eventually got from my work more than made up for the inconveniences.

One important influence in my professional life is a friend who is both an anthropologist and a public health specialist. I used to talk to her about my research and she would say, have you asked about land tenure? What about people's educational level? At first I thought she was crazy. What does land tenure have to do with medical problems? And slowly, my work in villages showed me that she was right—something *was* wrong with my approach to medicine and with the use of curative and palliative medicine to treat recurrent disease. Often, the roots of the complaint can be traced to malnutrition caused by environmental problems like poverty, bad sanitation practices, lack of education of the mother because of gender discrimination, occupation, or all these factors together.

The most important feature of the health sector at present is the absence of a national coordinated plan for development. There is very little coordination between the Israeli military government, UNRWA, which provides services for the refugees, Palestinian charitable organizations and private institutions, and foreign agencies. Health services are poorly funded.[3] There is also a maldistribution of resources. For example, the West Bank has eighteen hospitals (nine governmental and nine private). Out of that total, six are located in the Bethlehem district where 11 percent of the population lives, and all hospitals are located in urban centers. We were saddled with this distribution of hospitals before the occu-

The entrance to Birzeit Women's Charitable Society is covered with slogans representing all major PLO groups. Photo by Orayb Najjar

pation, but the single most important factor that allows the perpetuation of such a situation is the absence of a national Palestinian governmental authority that is interested in the welfare of people and able to control the direction of development.

The United Nations Relief and Works Agency (UNRWA) continues to run its health services in refugee camps, and as a result, the health situation there became better than in Palestinian villages.[4] UNRWA clinics practiced primary health care, made use of midwives, and were aware of sanitation. UNRWA's problem was not in the programs it established, but in the approach of some of its employees to the people they were serving—looking down on patients, screaming at them, and of course planning for the health of Palestinians in Vienna instead of involving them at every stage. UNRWA's attitude has made some Palestinians reluctant to admit the positive role of UNRWA in health care, but we have to give UNRWA credit for having the right ideas even as early as the fifties; it provided services that matched needs and established clinics where people lived.

Problems of underdevelopment are compounded by Israeli control of every aspect of Palestinian life, including health. One needs to obtain a license for piping water to a village, and a license for installing electricity.

Israeli authorities often withhold these essential basic services as collective punishment or use them as a means of political control. Having laid most of the blame on preexisting and present political conditions, it is important to add that we Palestinians have not been blameless in perpetuating inequalities in the distribution of health services. Individuals and institutions receiving financial backing from outside sources tend to be urban based and politically powerful. Sometimes such backing is given in exchange for political support, rather than because of an established need in the health sector of that area, or in accordance with a national plan of priorities. The rural majority is politically powerless and so its share of wealth has so far remained limited. So any internal changes in health services have to take the question of equitable distribution seriously.

Mustapha Barghuti, the founder of the Union of Palestinian Medical Relief Committees, and I initially got together because we had the same approach to medicine; both of us believed in primary health care and were critical of medical services and medical planning in the West Bank. When we said, for instance, that we should train midwives, the medical establishment accused us of cheapening medicine. By 1981, Mustapha and I began to coordinate our services, and by 1983, it was clear that our approach was becoming—I won't say "correct"—but popular. People responded to the idea of restructuring concepts of health and disease, and introducing the social dimension, and building a health infrastructure compatible with this concept and with people's needs. In each team we have a doctor, a nurse, a social worker, and a village health worker. The team plans for health, taking village conditions and capabilities into account.

Our work in villages started with enlarging on an existing project. One day I poked my nose into a small clinic in the village of Birzeit run by the Birzeit Women's Charitable Society and liked what it was doing. The society began operating the village clinic in 1970. The choice of a clinic was natural because two of the group's members, Georgette Abed and Lama'a Kassis, were nurses. From 1970 until 1978 the two nurses, with the help of a physician, operated a clinic on a volunteer basis after their regular working hours. The project was expanded to include a mother and child health clinic, a vaccination program, and nutrition and health education programs. Because of the limited time and resources of the volunteers, the work remained sporadic and was confined to the village of Birzeit.

In 1978, I saw the possibility of cooperation between Birzeit University and the clinic. Teachers and employees of the university with "health interests" were invited to join the society and a health committee was formed. Our role was to develop and expand the program by securing funding, and by offering technical expertise in the form of research into the needs of the community. This unified primary health care center was to provide curative and preventative services to the university community and the sixteen villages in the area surrounding Birzeit (approximately 25,000 people).

Two women from each village were chosen by villagers themselves and trained for six months in first aid, hygiene, nutrition, and mother and child health. The trainees were then hired by the health center to train other women in their villages, under the supervision of a field nurse. The project started on a modest scale. I had a personal research grant and I hired one assistant. Now the unit consists of twelve people.

Looking back at the events that have shaped my interests and guided my work, I feel lucky that I arrived in the West Bank at a very opportune time in 1978. On the same month of my arrival, a very important event took place—the establishment of the Palestinian Union of Women's Work Committees (PUWWC).

In the health field, 1979 saw the establishment of the Union of Palestinian Medical Relief Committees, whose main mission is twofold: to mobilize rural dwellers and refugees so that they can take part in improving their own health conditions; and to raise the consciousness of health workers by introducing them to the problems of the countryside and the poor. It is as if we all reached a historical point where we decided that something new and radically different was needed. It was as if the West Bank was ready for change and we hoped to provide it. We were lucky because had we come earlier, our ideas would not have worked. On the other hand, we can also say that our ideas did not flesh out without the experience we gained from the earlier failure of the attempts at development in the early 1970s.

In those early years, the Palestinian leadership and the Jordanian-PLO Joint Committee poured large sums of money into the Occupied Territories for development purposes, for "Sumood" (steadfastness) purposes. Yet huge amounts of that money ended up lining some people's pockets and were seen in the form of villas and other luxuries. What had happened was a clear example of misdirected development from above.

I myself slowly learned from trial and error in Palestinian villages what not to do in development. In 1982, we entered a village, armed with our "scientific" knowledge, and, without studying its internal structure, made decisions that sparked old rivalries between clans to the point where one of the leaders of the village simply said, "For God's sake, you have done enough harm already, please leave." The lesson we have learned is that you can't work in a village in the health area, or any area for that matter, before understanding political power relations among families, clans, and even the relations between the village and the nearest town. The failure of earlier development attempts as well as our own mistakes suggested that we needed a new framework for organizing mass movements. We needed, to use some jargon, "mobilization from below," and this is what all those new groups were calling for and practicing. So we started looking for an alternative to the biomedical model and ended up using the social science theory of health, especially the anthropological side of it.

I felt I needed to be reeducated, so I took a year off in 1985 to specialize in development and health at the Sociology Department of the University of Essex, England. What I read there is extremely helpful to me in my work. You cannot separate a social phenomenon into its component parts and study them separately, as in "this is biology," "this is physiology." Nonsense. You need to be grounded both in the medical and social sciences to do an effective job in a developing society.

In countries of the Third World where resources are scarce and where the majority of people live in rural areas, the move towards centralized medicine (hospitals and medical complexes in city centers) usually results in very high costs for health care and little impact on the health of the majority of people—the rural dwellers, which in our case is 70 percent of the population. Now our whole approach centers around locating health care where people are and rethinking about the type of services needed in rural areas.

Our unit strongly advises our health workers to take a minor in sociology. The education of medical personnel is a political issue. We have a situation where we have more doctors than nurses, more surgeons than public health specialists because our system is biased towards curative services. We have reevaluated our medical services, found them wanting, and are trying to put medical development on the right course by linking it to overall national development. We do not conduct studies in the abstract, as we have neither the time nor the resources to enjoy such a luxury. I am particularly fond of conducting "Village Health Profile" research or feasibility studies to set up health projects. We take health indices of the pop-

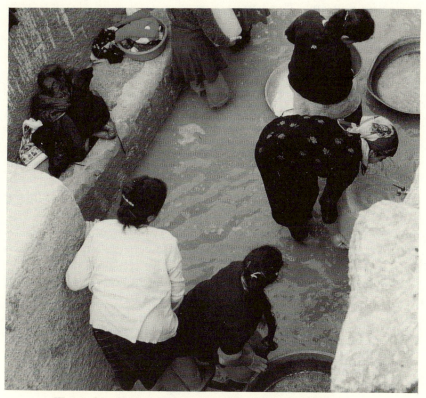

Women from Katanna village wading in water on washday. Photo by
Orayb Najjar

ulation, concentrating mainly on women and children both for biological
and numerical reasons because 70 percent of the population in a Palestinian village consists of women and children. We study that population
from a biological point of view, looking for anemia, malnutrition, parasites, and infant mortality rates. We also look at the social conditions that
create those diseases. A city person with abundant water takes a daily
shower for granted; a village woman who is responsible for carrying the
water supply for her ten-member family, on her head, from a distance of
one kilometer each way views the matter in a different light. Water for her
is a valuable commodity for drinking and essential washing. The lack of
running water and poor sanitation not only lead to disease, but negatively
affect many aspects of women's lives. Over time, the heavy loads of water

cause back problems. The absence of piped-in water indirectly contributes to the undereducation of girls; mothers with large families often pull their eldest girls out of school to help with this time-consuming and necessary daily chore. It is too easy to blame villagers themselves for the unsanitary conditions around them, but the whole society has to take responsibility for the unequal distribution of wealth that puts the rural areas at such a disadvantage.

For a while, Palestinian society was plagued by general studies about health. These studies had a function at a certain stage, but are no longer adequate, at least not as a basis for action. In contrast, our "profiles" yield information about what predisposes a particular community to disease. We found that each area has a different concentration of parasites, and the parasites you see most often in Ramallah villages differ markedly from those in the Hebron district further south. Once we start zeroing in on a certain community, we are surprised at the differences we find between villages. For example, the women of the village of Abu Shkheidem and Kobar are less educated than Biddu women. Biddu is near Jerusalem, and villages close to cities normally educate their women more than villages farther away. Furthermore, UNRWA has a school in Biddu, and that allows even conservative parents to educate their daughters. So from this "profile," we plan a program that meets people's needs and takes into account what they say they want as well as the deficiencies we document.

Our studies are also valuable as a development tool because they offer scientific documentation on how gender relations affect the health profile of a village.

A study of three Ramallah villages showed a 52 percent malnutrition rate among girls, as opposed to 32 percent for boys. In the Ain Dyouk area of the Jordan Valley, 61 percent of all the mothers were found to be anemic, and 51 percent of the girls and 43 percent of the boys were malnourished.[5] In the village of Biddu near Jerusalem, we found that the infant mortality rate for girls was 58 per thousand in contrast to 41 per thousand for boys.[6] Most of the cases of malnourishment were medium to mild, but in another area, we found a woman with a severely malnourished baby girl and begged her to take the child to a treatment center, but her reaction was "I hope she dies." We found that the woman had been married for thirteen years during which she had twelve children at the insistence of her husband who was influenced by his mother. Anyone who has to raise twelve children in two rooms in a house without running water and has to work in the house as well as in the field has a right to be angry, but in a just society, that anger would not be taken out on a baby. Our most startling finding was for the villages that are only three or five kilometers away from Birzeit University. We found that those villages had an infant mortality rate of 91 per thousand! When I tell stories like this to my students at Birzeit, some try to lay the blame for those conditions solely on the Israeli occupation. I answer that, yes, the creation of Israel has disrupted Palestinian society, but that even before the creation of Israel, we had inequalities between classes and sexes. The bottom line is that while now many Palestinians recognize these inequalities and are working to eradicate them, the occupation is preventing those with a desire for change from planning for a new and more just society.

The malnutrition of baby girls is a problem no medical practice can solve. So we did not go to doctors with our findings, but presented them to universities and to the women's groups. Universities need to ask themselves what type of education they are offering their students and to reevaluate their role in the community. Birzeit needs to ask, "Are we using community work projects effectively?"

Safeguarding women's health is the task of the women's movement, or at least should be. Women's organizations need to take up the challenge of changing the consciousness or the relationships that lead to malnourished baby girls. Among our middle classes, malnutrition of girls is not an issue. Where there is poverty, however, the mother gives her son more meat than either she or his sisters get. This arrangement makes sense as social insurance in our culture on the village level. It is the eldest male who is expected to provide for his siblings and for his elderly parents. The girl is simply an extra mouth to feed until she is married. So until there is a true equality of opportunity for women in education and work, this problem will persist in poor areas where resources are now allocated to the "fittest" and most useful. Allowing the persistence of the undernourishment of our future childbearers shortchanges future Palestinian generations.

Inequality between the sexes is not a local problem but a national one, and it would be too much to expect the occupying power to give it the priority it deserves. So take a young sick female, send her to a clinic, cure her, and return her to the same environment and you have done nothing. To effect radical change, we need to establish the idea that health, education, and work are *rights* that should be accorded to all members of society—male and female.

The social, educational, and health problems Palestinians are facing under prolonged occupation has impressed on us the necessity of going beyond factional politics and thinking of Palestinian society as a whole. I can't say that we have been completely successful in totally changing the priorities of the women's movement.

There has always been some tension between national political liberation and women's liberation. In the past few years, however, women's groups have felt some pressure to take a more feminist stand on women's issues. Now there are voices recognizing the importance of women's equality for building an egalitarian nonsexist society. Women's groups are now more willing to address discrimination against women and are willing to cooperate to do something about it. Frankly, people were disgusted with factional politics practiced on every level of Palestinian society–in unions, in institutions, as well as in women's organizations–so leaders had to respond with something different. So when we produced data that confirmed the general feeling in the street of the need for practical solutions to everyday problems, some of these groups felt ready to examine their priorities and plan programs more in step with people's needs under long-term occupation.

So that is how we try to help. I believe our work is a drop in the sea. It will not liberate Palestine, but it is gratifying to see that some of the ideas we are advocating are being absorbed and are becoming part of future institutions. Our work would be useless if it were not for the different women's groups and medical relief committees who use it for planning purposes; after all we are just academicians not practitioners. We live on the fringes of our society and we are isolated from the villages and the refugee camps. We are needed for our technical skills and planning abilities, but our existence is dependent on the groups who live or work regularly in Palestinian villages. I think we are laying the groundwork for a progressive health system for our future Palestinian state.

15 July 1989

When the events leading up to the uprising unfolded in December 1987, I thought they were like other incidents of their kind. Maybe other people more astute than I am recognized the events as being different earlier, but it took me three weeks to pay attention. By January, we knew that the

Intifada was a national revolt against the Israeli occupation. By February, the Intifada was becoming institutionalized. As casualties mounted, we stretched the resources of our clinics to the limit. We had no choice. The first-aid situation was very serious, even critical. We had to care for hundreds of wounded outside hospitals. Even people with medium gunshot wounds preferred to be treated at home for fear of arrest. It was hard to imagine that casualties would become a regular feature of daily life, but they are. Over an eight-month period, medical relief workers treated 36,000 persons from injuries resulting from violence or exacerbation of existing disease. Other groups were active as well, and we drowned in work. We trained village caseworkers for emergencies, combining some first aid with some elements of trauma medicine. In essence, we trained people to know when to stop.

To avoid medical complications, we also delivered 682 lectures in first aid to lay people on how to deal with broken limbs and tear gas inhalation. We published first-aid leaflets, packaged and distributed over 12,000 first-aid kits, and continued with our mobile clinic activities, two, three, or four per day.

To break the uprising, Israelis resorted to heavy collective punishment. During any given week, several towns, villages, and refugee camps would be totally under curfew; in other words, thousands of people were confined to their homes for days on end.

During curfew, it is difficult to convince soldiers to allow patients out of the restricted area, and doctors outside the locale are not allowed in. In many cases, doctors are not even allowed to move freely within their locales. To understand what a curfew means in terms of health, you need to imagine whole areas that suffer from food, water, and electricity shortages, areas where telephones, if found, are deliberately disconnected by the authorities to isolate the village or town from the outside world. Once you think in these terms, you can imagine the type of stress people are under when they have to deal with medical emergencies that range from normal illnesses, chronic illnesses, to gunshot wounds.[7]

First-aid permanent stations were erected in various areas because of the shortage of ambulances and because of our limited ability to keep ambulances running during curfews. The most troubling aspect of collective punishment is that community resources, poor at best, become overextended. Curfews also exacerbate preexisting conditions like hypertension or diabetes. Because of overcrowding, we had an awful lot of respiratory disease in summer. We noticed an increase in pneumonia and in disease that would not have taken the course it did without the long curfews.

Women have done extremely well in coping with those difficulties, and men appreciate their active and indispensable role in the Intifada. The question is, how will we make these changes in the way women are viewed structural in order to make them permanent? When I was making arrangements for getting married, I freaked out at what I had to do. I have been independent, self-supporting, and even family supporting for years. Yet, at age thirty-nine, I needed my father to get a paper from the church (which I had abandoned years ago by choice) to prove I was single. The struggle of women is for legal, social, and educational rights. I have seen too many wives of political men cook and iron while their men *talk* about women's liberation. We have to fight to achieve a more equitable division of labor—inside and outside the home.

Mustapha and I share housework and medical work. We have moved to a new area of research and have recently completed a feasibility study for the care and integration of the disabled into society. We had tried to deal with the disabled before, but realized that disability was not just invisible, but also not fashionable. Because of the UN Decade of Women, development agencies could tie women's needs to developmental issues, making money available for women. Because people considered the disabled charity cases, the responsibility of charitable or religious organizations, it was hard to tie disability with development. There were several impediments: Palestinian society tends to think of disability either as God's will (something that one needs to accept but do little about) or tends to hide the disabled. Then there was the question of priorities. Our society has limited resources, and the going wisdom was that the disabled consume and do not produce, and so they were way down on the list of spending priorities. So to solve the problem of the disabled, you needed to view the issue as one of attitude, but you also needed to think of the practical financial and political considerations.

The uprising changed attitudes towards the disabled overnight. Israeli bullets hit a number of young people in the spine, and suddenly our disabled population grew considerably.[8] One day, these young people were active members of society, the next day they had various levels of disability in a society not equipped to help them. People considered those injured during the uprising heroes and wanted to repay them with good care. People became aware of the problems of the disabled, the lack of facilities

Dr. Rita Giacaman answering journalists' questions about health issues in the West Bank. At left, Wafa al-Baher Abu Ghosh one week after delivering her first daughter (19 July 1986). Photo by Orayb Najjar

for them, and the press began to write about them, and so we jumped on the bandwagon. We want to put the disabled back into society. We have surveyed all the facilities we have and know that we need a system that combines proper physical care for the disabled, with psychological counseling and job training.

I enjoy planning for better health care for all segments of the population. In the United States, there is an established health-care system, and any change you propose has to be incremental. Critics of the American medical establishment cannot change the philosophical orientation of health care whether they think it works for all people or not. In a developing smaller society, planners can make an impact on growing institutions.

The Intifada settled for good an issue that traditionalist elements fought for—the retention of traditional medical practices, and what progressivists pushed for—decentralized health services in rural areas. We now know people have enough sense to accept ideas if they are effective. I do not think that after all these sacrifices, we will settle just for *any* state. We want the state we have declared to be progressive. That is what our work has been all about.

MONA RISHMAWI
Lawyer, human rights and international law

After years of defending Palestinians in Israeli military courts, writing a newspaper column about legal issues, and speaking in international forums about Israeli violations of Palestinian human rights, Mona Rishmawi now heads a Palestinian human rights organization which was given the Carter-Menile Human Rights award in December 1989. Here, she speaks about her work and her views on women and personal status law.

28 August 1989

When I returned to the West Bank in 1981* after studying law in Egypt,[1] I felt that the issues women needed to address were very clear: personal status, equality under the law, and the equitable division of labor inside the home. I felt that women needed to be mobilized on gender issues at the grassroots level. Active women who worked in committees, however, were reluctant to define the women's movement in these terms or to mobilize women on gender issues. In the 1980s, organizers argued that if you mobilize women solely on those terms, you would be telling them that their fight is not with the Israeli occupation, but inside their homes, when their daily lives tell them otherwise. There is not a single family that does not have a relative or neighbor or acquaintance in jail.

When a woman has a son or husband in jail, that is a problem that affects the totality of her life. When a whole refugee camp is placed under curfew, for up to forty days, a woman has to cope not only with food shortages, but with six to ten children out of school, underfoot, for

---

*I interviewed Mona Rishmawi in her home in Ramallah on 4 August 1989, in English, and asked her to speak about her work. The story was written from my notes of the conversation.

Attorney Mona Rishmawi in her home in Ramallah, summer 1989. Photo by Orayb Najjar

extended periods of time, in a two-room house. No one can tell such a woman that occupation does not add to her burden. When a woman's husband, son, or daughter is shot by the Israeli army, nothing else matters but the occupation. When a woman's house is demolished, as collective punishment, after her son/husband/brother is jailed, her main worry becomes getting a roof over the children's heads—then, it is difficult to talk to her about her rights from anything but a nationalist perspective.

Occupation touches every area of life from birth to death, and it certainly determines the educational course of many young people. The organization I work for, al-Haq,[2] has documented many instances where students about to sit for the Tawjihi high school exams are detained and then released when the exams are over without any charges filed against them. The detention delays their applications for college for a whole year. During curfews, *all* high schoolers in the affected areas are not allowed to leave their areas of residence to take the exams.[3] The delay of a whole year before college adversely affects every student, but is especially hard on poor families who plan to send their son or daughter to college. If you are a genuine women's movement, you have to deal with specifics like these. You have to work inside a certain context, and our context is occupation. Women's groups argue that if you ignore the occupation and concentrate only on gender issues, you are encouraging women to fight their main supporters without offering women other means of support.

Women's committees have always insisted that, at least at this stage, taking on a purely gender agenda is too divisive and confrontational because the fight will isolate women from men at a time when women are most needed for the national struggle. I have always resisted this argument, and it took me until the uprising to realize that this approach makes sense, and that the issue for most women is not as simple as I had previously imagined.

The internal dynamics of the Palestinian political scene have to do with power contests between the constituent groups of the PLO. Organized women chose to assert themselves through involvement in the most important struggle for freedom from occupation and thus have positioned themselves as one of the forces that have played a powerful role in the nationalist struggle. Because of their active involvement in resistance, especially during the Intifada, women could not be ignored. And when it was time to declare a Palestinian state on November 15, 1988, women were declared equal by law. The Palestinian declaration of independence affirms that "Governance will be based on principles of social justice, equality and nondiscrimination in public rights, men or women, on grounds of race, religion, color or sex under the aegis of a constitution which ensures the rule of law and an independent judiciary." This document is our own security in the future. Even if I believe that women could have done more to promote a feminist agenda within the platform of each faction, I am pleased that what has emerged in the declaration was a national consensus on sex equality. Of course problems will arise when you start to translate what this equality means into practice.

One positive factor in women's favor is that leaders of women's organizations are aware that they need a more feminist agenda for the future, and that they need to plan for change or else be left behind. I've had conversations with leaders who ask, "How do we change the law? Where do we start? We need to elaborate an agenda, we are ready for suggestions." It is an exciting time. Whereas in the past, gender issues were not a priority, today's women's groups are more conscious of gender inequities and are aware of the danger of letting the gender issue go unchallenged for too long. But events are moving very rapidly and may catch women unprepared.

There are a number of factors working against women in this regard. At a time when women should be most active drawing up plans and demands for inclusion in the new state, the physical needs and hardships of the Intifada are so great that active women are spending most of their energy on caring for the victims of Israeli measures and less time on preparing a women's agenda for the new state.

I have no doubt that in a Palestinian state, we are going to have democracy and elections. The question is, where will women fit into this system? There are various groups that are vying for power, some liberal, some conservative. We need to ask: Will women be included or excluded from these power groupings? Will women be considered a plus or a minus to political groups they belong to? If they are part of leftist factions, they could be considered a plus or a minus to their own group depending on the kind of alliances the leftists need to make to gain power. Will leftist groups underplay the women's issue, for example, for the sake of sharing power with more conservative factions? Another important question is how women define their duty to their own factions. Will women manage to push for inclusion by arguing that it is a political plus for their group to campaign for women's issues, or will they deliberately keep that issue low on the agenda in order to help their own faction win? Will organized women attempt to gain power for their groups or for women? How will the position of Fateh, the largest group, affect women? Will Fateh, which has a conservative and a liberal wing, ally itself to leftists or to conservative Muslims? All those questions have an effect on women, and if women do not pressure politicians and do not get seriously involved in power politics early, their contributions are likely to be forgotten in the scramble for power.

I do not think that questions like polygamy, dowries, etc., will be on the agenda in the near future; these are touchy issues, but because women are starting to be conscious of the importance of effecting change in women's status, my personal conclusion is that this is a very promising period for women. Women have proved they are a political force and that they have a stake in the political process. What they still need to do is to cement those gains and institutionalize them through a slow (but not too slow) process of examination and search for fair legislation for women.

One question that needs to be asked is, is this the time to push for change? Will it distract from other issues? I believe it is time and that this issue is very important to the quality of the state we are planning for. By declaring a state, Palestinians have embarked on a revolutionary course. Revolution does not only mean political revolution, but also a social revolution in gender relations. We have to make sure that sexual equality is not just for public relations consumption abroad. We need a special recognition of women in personal status law.

There are two ways of making law for women in a future Palestinian state. The first is to copy other laws in the Arab world or in Asia, Africa, or Latin America because these countries share our problems. This is not a desirable option because it eliminates the first and most interesting stage of making law which is the evaluation of conditions and creation of an agenda based on those conditions. If we choose the first option, we may end up with nice-sounding principles that are unenforceable because they are very alienated from reality. Laws that descend on people ready made and have not gone through a process of review may have serious flaws. We are now functioning mostly under Jordanian law. When Jordan wrote its laws, it based them on two systems, with different intellectual underpinnings – the British Anglo-Saxon common law and the Egyptian law, which is based on the French Code. There is no original legal thinking in the mixture that resulted. Then the Israelis came; they retained some Jordanian law and made extensive use of the British Military Emergency Law. It is ironic that Israelis themselves have called this Mandate-period law "Nazi" when it was applied to Jews before 1948.[4] So there is a strange "legal" situation in the Occupied Territories, and we sorely need some original legal thinking in preparation for liberation.

Most of the laws that affect women's lives are based on Shari'a religious laws, so we cannot radically change them, but we can choose among the four different approaches and interpretations because some are more liberal than others.[5] We need to take a look at the rights a man and a woman have in contracting a marriage or dissolving it. At present, a man can marry or divorce, then go to court and register the act. But to divorce a man, a woman has to go to court first and publicly explain to the satisfaction of the judge why she needs a divorce. On some issues, we can take advantage of some Islamic rights women do have and publicize them, for example, the right to conduct their own business transactions. In the United States, women had trouble getting credit in their own names before pressure from the women's movement changed that. This issue had been solved centuries ago for Muslim women because Islam allows women to conduct their own business. But there is a great disparity between what Islam allows a woman to do, and what social customs allow her to get away with, and we need to encourage women to insist on their economic rights. Another example: It was not common in Arab tradition for a woman to take on her husband's name, but now it is mandatory.

When it comes to the question of the dowry, guardianship, inheritance, and custody, women's rights need to be safeguarded.

You cannot outlaw polygamy, but you can restrict it by mobilizing the community of women to reject it. Women themselves have to say no to it and find it unacceptable. Women also have to stop thinking of themselves as interchangeable with others just because of their biological function. For example, I met a woman whose fifteen-year-old daughter was killed. The mother is too old to have more children, so she said, "I want my husband to remarry and have ten children." That is her way of making up for her loss and her revenge against Israelis who killed her daughter. Do you tell her her attitude is bad for women's rights?

At present, middle-class priorities for women include personal satisfaction, but this woman's priorities are national. The middle class says, "Have fewer children, educate them, take care of them better." Poorer people have a different agenda, perhaps because they are guided by their past experience with high infant mortality rates. Disadvantaged people believe in quantity as social insurance for their old age. Mrs. Samiha Khalil, president of In'ash al-Usra, encourages women to have a large number of children because she sees childbearing from a nationalist perspective, and she reflects the consciousness of many women here. She represents more women than I do. This is her vision and she is respected for it. To change this type of consciousness Palestinians have to feel that their survival as a people is not under threat. Childbearing practices will change when Palestinian women are confident that they will not lose children to disease or war. This type of change is a long process, and we can help it along if we improve the lives of women through legislation.

I tend to lean towards the second method of lawmaking by tailoring law specifically to the needs of our society. We can elaborate on our agenda as Palestinian women and then translate that into law. We would say for the development of women we need the following system: we need them to stay in school longer and then legislate laws that make education mandatory up to a certain level. Here, a cautionary note: those new laws should be reasonable, realistic, and enforceable. If the laws are too progressive, if there is a large discrepancy between what people practice and what we want them to practice, people will simply ignore the law. In other words, we need to look at lawmaking as a two-part challenge. In the first phase, we elaborate an agenda with the help of women's groups, and then we lead an educational drive in which all organs of the state are involved. We work on the public image of women, on equal opportunity, on reducing women's work through the opening of nurseries at a state level, i.e., we transform some of the private domestic work women do into public work. The state needs to help form good citizens, and raising children is a communal duty.

Having said this, however, I have a few reservations about the purely Marxist analysis used by some women's groups. I find it naive to equate class and gender. I agree that class and gender are related, but some leftist groups tie women's issues too deeply with class issues. It is true that when you create a new and more equitable economic order, you will improve the position of women to a certain extent, especially the poorest among them. But unlike economic systems, which can be imposed on any society from the outside, gender is a cultural issue. Attitudes to gender questions are much more deeply embedded in people's consciousness than matters of class. It is naive to assume that if you eliminate class differences, you will automatically eliminate gender inequality.

Many women are ambivalent about changing anything. We need to work on female consciousness. We have an underlying assumption that all women will be willing to work together for the same goals, but that is not the case. Inequality is so deeply ingrained within the culture that you first have to convince women themselves that they have value. I have seen cases where a qualified woman gives an opinion on an issue, and another woman looks at the nearest male for guidance, as if she needs confirmation of the value of an idea suggested by a female before it becomes even worth considering. I found out that the same kind of conflict exists in the United States. While doing graduate work at Columbia University, I took a course on gender in literature and law, where we read novels that deal with legal and gender issues—a very interesting course, an unusual one for law students. It was hard for the participants, mostly women, not to personalize the issues under discussion. There was a great deal of tension in class, and I talked to the female professor about it. Why is it that people are nervous and jumping on each other? Would it have been as tense if the course had a male professor? Would the gender of the professor make the issues we were discussing more mainstream? I believe that what happens in such a course is that it touches issues you can't distance yourself from. You are talking gender, and it touches your personal and professional life. You are confronted with important questions. You ask yourself: Am I doing what is expected of me as a feminist? If you are dealing with law it is easier. There is this legal language that you share, and in it rules are established. When you talk about feminist theory, people are puzzled because many do not know what you are talking about, you almost have to translate. You have assumed that a group of women are as interested in the issue of sex discrimination as you are, but that is not the case. Often you do not have the language you need to talk to them. When you talk feminism, you are raising a number of issues, and you automatically give *yourself* a number of questions.

People are defined by more than their gender. So I have to ask: Is this the right approach to gender and nationalist issues? Where does my loyalty lie? To my gender as a woman? to my nation as a Palestinian? to my profession as a lawyer? to my family? to myself? How do I keep those different personas from encroaching upon each other? When you start taking this approach, you find that it is tricky to negotiate your path between those different roles. I figure that if a person is happy, she can be productive. But it is not as simple as that.

Update: December 1989

On December 9, al-Haq ("Law in the Service of Man," a civil and human rights organization and the West Bank affiliate of the International Commission of Jurists, Geneva) shared the Carter-Menile Human Rights award with B'Tselem, an Israeli group that also monitors human rights violations in the Occupied Territories. President Jimmy Carter praised the two groups because "In the face of repeated condemnation, harassment, and sometimes even physical abuse, the members of these groups have not wavered in their determination to expose, condemn, and prevent violations of human rights" (*FE* 20 November 1989, 5). Mona Rishmawi and Fateh Azzam, a colleague, accepted the prize on behalf of al-Haq. In a speech delivered in Atlanta, Georgia, where the ceremony was held, Rishmawi said on behalf of her organization:

> For the last twenty-two years, Palestinians in the Gaza Strip and the West Bank—including East Jerusalem—have endured a military occupation which manipulated the administrative and legal structure leading to political oppression and economic exploitation. The fundamental rights taken for granted by other nations have been denied to us, more importantly, the right to self-determination.
>
> The rule of law has been absent. . . . More than 1,290 military orders have been passed in the West Bank, and nearly 1,000 in Gaza amending local law beyond recognition. These orders give sweeping powers to the military and touch every aspect of our lives—economy, transportation, infrastructure, planning, development and organizational activity, education, health, censorship of all media and communication, culture and the arts. . . .
>
> Since its establishment in 1979, al-Haq has documented the full range of human rights abuses resulting from Israeli measures and policies. These include deprivation of life, beatings, expulsions, the demolition and sealing of houses, mass arrests, administrative detention without charge or trial, town arrests, long-term closure of institutions, maltreatment and torture at times leading to death, travel restrictions, denial of family reunification, and collective economic punishments.
>
> On the eve of celebrating the forty-first anniversary of the adoption of the Universal Declaration of Human Rights we can state, with confidence, that the Israeli occupation violates, as a matter of course, every article of the Universal Declaration of Human Rights except one: the article banning slavery!
>
> Given this situation, the Palestinian popular uprising . . . should have come as no surprise. . . .
>
> There is lawlessness at every level: from the soldier . . . up to the military administration and the courts, including the Israeli High Court, which has sanctioned clearly illegal practices like deportations

and house demolitions and routinely defers to the military on all issues related to the occupation. . . .

There is no real accountability. . . . In cases where abuses are so obvious that an investigation actually takes place and the perpetrators are found guilty, the sentences meted out are so lenient as to constitute a green light to the army to continue its policies without deterrent. . . .

On October 18, 1988, Ibrahim al-Mator was seen by other detainees at the Dhariyeh military detention center in the West Bank. Blood was flowing from his head and he was heard screaming, "I am Ibrahim al-Mator. They are beating me to death. Detainees, witness!"

Three days later, Ibrahim was dead. "Suicide," the prison authorities declared. It is our collective duty to answer Ibrahim's call, to witness, to act, so that in the future not only will the Ibrahims of this world be heard and not have to die, but so that they will not have to scream at all (*FE* 18 December 1989, 5).

FIVE

Education, Art, and Journalism

Munir Fasheh writes that "Education has played two principal but opposing roles in the Palestinian experience. On one hand, education has been used by Israel as a tool to control the Palestinians under its domination. But on the other hand, education, both formal and informal, has been used by the Palestinians as a means to survive, to develop, and to express their identity and their rights" (Fasheh 1983: 295).

This chapter looks at how women working or studying in various institutions have used education, the written word, and other forms of self-expression like art to develop themselves and their societies. In every account, there is evidence of the changes that have taken place in the way Palestinian society is assessing its needs and attempting to fulfill them.

When Israel occupied the West Bank in 1967, it clashed with the population when it changed the curriculum, censored textbooks, or deleted parts of books. Palestinians resisted Israeli changes in the curriculum and clung to its contents fearing that any change in the status quo would lead to the Judaization of education. But in time, some educators began to realize that, even with the nationalist content that the Israelis had deleted, the books and, in fact, the whole educational system as it existed before the occupation had serious shortcomings that made it unresponsive to the problems Palestinians were facing.

A reevaluation of the educational system came as a result of the establishment of various volunteer groups and the spread of informal education that included community-oriented volunteer work, theatrical and folkloric groups, children's programs, publications of books and magazines, women's organizations, health-care projects, and adult education. Volunteer groups proved more flexible and better suited to community needs than the formal educational system (Fasheh 1983: 306–7).

People were aware that reform was needed, but between 1975 and 1982 education researchers assumed that any reform would take place within the system Palestinians had inherited from Britain and Jordan. Between 1982 and 1985, researchers began to reevaluate not only their earlier published surveys, but also their previous assumptions regarding "appropriate education" and reforms (Ricks 1985: 9, 11). Two areas benefited from this reevaluation, neither of which are directly under Israeli supervision: literacy training and preschool education.

Literacy Training:

Literacy training went through several stages. In the 1950s, charitable societies like In'ash al-Usra were especially concerned about the high rate of female illiteracy and so became pioneers in offering literacy classes. The societies, however, used children's books in their classes and lacked a coordinated plan of attack against illiteracy.

Jordanian government statistics for 1961 revealed that the rate of illiteracy for women over fifteen (on both sides of the Jordan River) was 84.2 percent. This figure dropped to between 73.3 and 80.5 percent in 1967 and to between 36.3 and 59.3 percent in 1985. The decline is the result of an overall Arab drive that targeted the years from 1977 to 1991 for eradicating illiteracy (Khader, *Al-Kateb*, September 1988: 53, 56).

In 1976, Birzeit University established experimental classes in the villages around the university with the purpose of developing a literacy curriculum, and by 1982, the center was handling sixteen classes in seven centers teaching 127 women and 3 men. In 1978, adult literacy programs were established as a cooperative project between Birzeit and the Higher Committee for Literacy, which coordinated the work of all charitable societies involved in literacy education, and later any other groups that offered literacy classes. Birzeit then moved into teacher training and curriculum development and supervision, while the societies did the practical teaching (*1982 Yearbook*, Birzeit University). Women's committees also started becoming active in the field.

The first segment of this chapter describes how Palestinian institutions have arrived at a new understanding of the problems of illiterate women, an understanding that is changing their way of dealing with the learners. Writing samples by newly literate women explain their reasons for joining the classes and record what they have to say about the Palestinian experience.

Preschool Education

Various groups have become involved in preschool education over the years. The efforts started with charitable societies and gained momentum with the interest of women's groups in the provision of services at the kindergarten level. Since most of the schooling is under the control of the Israeli government, preschool education offered different groups an opportunity to have an impact on the education of their children through restructuring Palestinian education.

The most successful effort to date has been the creation of the Early Childhood Educational Center. What distinguishes the center from other institutions is that it has not indulged in factional politics and serves all groups equally—leftists, rightists, fundamentalists, and Christian church groups. The account of Assia Habash introduces the obstacles facing a principal when she attempts to improve teacher training under occupation, while taking the need of her students to express their national sentiments into account. Habash also chronicles her efforts to restructure and improve kindergarten education through teacher training.

Artist Vera Tamari, who taught art at the same school Habash ran, describes both how she encouraged students' self-expression and how she herself dealt with the expectations society has of an artist living under occupation. Vera discusses the role of the artist under occupation and stresses the liberating effects of creativity.

University Education

In the Palestinian experience, the education of women and their entry into the work force were extremely important for the changes that took place in their lives. Statistics between 1948 and 1967 show an increase in the male/female ratios in all stages of education. Writes Dearden, "The fathers of better-off families who went into exile after the creation of Israel no longer put all their savings into land and property but paid out much more than before on educating their daughters—as they had always educated their sons. . . . So everywhere in the Middle East, Palestinian women are serving as doctors, head mistresses, school and university teachers, administrators, nurses, secretaries and in the less advanced countries are providing a living example of how, in a Muslim society, women may lead useful outgoing lives without loss of dignity or principle" (Dearden 1976: 15).

Yet the opportunity to get an education was not and still is not available to all women equally. According to Islamic law, women automatically inherit a fixed proportion of their fathers' property. This creates pressure on them to marry within their own family to prevent loss and fragmentation of their family's land. The customary pattern within Palestinian society has been marriage among cousins. Fadwa Hussein, who relates her story below, had to cope with family pressure to marry a cousin she did not want. Education and the expanding horizons of village life have given Fadwa an inarticulate but strong sense of her individual right to freedom. She hasn't analyzed her situation or identified her struggle with the national goal as many other women do. She has simply persevered doggedly with her education, seeing it as a means of escape from the cage of social oppression. A few years ago, her dreams would have come true. Educated Palestinians were welcomed, indeed relied on, in the expanding oil-rich Gulf countries. Now, like her uncles, Fadwa is finding out that circumstances have changed and her expectations are unrealizable. The oil boom is over, jobs are scarce, and Palestine's many graduates are finding the Arab world has no room for them. A little over a year after Fawda was interviewed, *Al-Nahar* newspaper wrote on 3 June 1986, that 30,000 workers and their families returned to Jordan from Kuwait after having lost their jobs there.

In contrast to Fadwa, Tahani Ali, who comes from the same village has different expectations for herself. She takes it for granted that education is her right and that her parents will support her. She also takes it for granted that she is going to have a career in the area of her specialization. The differences between the experiences of these two women illustrate the great disparity in the position of different Palestinian women in the same society—sometimes in the same neighborhood. The stories also show that

The literacy program in the village of Kobar has twenty-six students, 1985. Najiyyeh Abu Hajj on right. Photo by Orayb Najjar

these two women face different problems, Fadwa with Palestinian society itself and Tahani with the Israeli occupation.

The chapter ends with stories of two journalists, Wafa al-Baher Abu Ghosh, born in 1961, and Mary Shehadeh, born in 1901. The women differ on the utility of higher education for women, but both are concerned

Fihmiyyeh el Barghouti, left, and Basimah Kasim rehearse the play they have written for the women of Kobar center. Photo by Orayb Najjar

with what child care means to women and how relations with Israel have affected Palestinians in general.

Literacy

Initially, illiteracy was viewed as merely the inability to read or write and was depicted as "a disease" that has to be wiped out from the otherwise "healthy body" of society. Illiterates themselves were regarded with a mixture of pity and disdain and were viewed as ignorant, marginal, negative, and uncreative beings. Thinking about the subject has changed, and now many planners realize that the presence of illiteracy goes hand in hand with the prevalence of social injustice and class and gender oppression (Khader 1988). The reasons women give for their illiteracy bear out that conclusion, says Aisha Nasir, fifty-six: "When I was a young girl, only rich people educated their daughters and poor people who had the opportunity educated their sons. So not a single woman my age was educated in my village." Nadira Salah explains, "Bad luck played an important part in my illiteracy. I was the eldest girl, and my mother had one child a year and I was expected to take care of it."

But why do women choose to register in literacy classes? Interviews suggest that they see literacy as a form of empowerment. Reading helps them take the right bus, sign their names on vouchers, read the Quran, and write letters to their relatives. Some have more mundane reasons for wanting to learn, says Najiyyeh Abu Hajj, forty: "I decided to join Kobar's literacy classes because I like to watch foreign movies on television and it is frustrating not to be able to read the Arabic subtitles. I can, of course, ask my younger sister to read them aloud, but she gets tired of it, and I don't like to impose on her." One twelve-year-old girl joined her mother's literacy class because she could not function in the school system. Another woman joined because she is a poet and wants to see the poems she has been composing since 1936 in print.

In most developing countries, literacy programs are run and financed by the government and so have the weight and resources of a state behind them. Literacy programs are able to use radio and television broadcasts to reach illiterates and to teach and retain them. In the West Bank and Gaza, however, Palestinian institutions with limited budgets have taken on government functions without having control over radio or television stations in the Occupied Territories.

Literacy teachers depend on word of mouth or work through existing organizations to advertise their services. Teachers sometimes use plays to draw the attention of villagers to the advantages of literacy and to encourage women who have doubts about themselves as older learners to join classes, as this play by literacy teachers shows.

EDUCATION IS LIGHT

A play written by the teachers of the Atara Village Literacy Center.

UMM ISSA: Hey, women, you've been going to the literacy center for two years now. Tell me, have you gained anything? What nonsense: "After his hair turned white, they sent him to the Kuttab."

UMM MOHAMMAD: You mustn't think that we have wasted all this time.

UMM ISSA: Show me what good it has done you.

UMM MOHAMMAD: I'll tell you. Yesterday I received a letter from my son and I read it myself. I didn't need to go to the girl next door and reveal my family secrets to her.

UMM ISSA: I don't believe you can read by yourself.

UMM MOHAMMAD: You don't believe me? Let me read part of it. (Reads)

UMM ISSA: So you only know how to read letters?

UMM MOHAMMAD: Oh no, we've learned a lot of different things. For example, do you know how night and day happen, and how the seasons change?

UMM ISSA: Is this a trick? When we go to sleep, it becomes night, and when we wake up, it becomes day.

UMM MOHAMMAD: (Laughs) No, that's not the way it happens. Night and day happen because the earth is round and revolves around itself.

UMM ISSA: Yeee. You are hallucinating! Hush, don't let anybody hear you.

UMM MOHAMMAD: Why, Umm Issa?

UMM ISSA: Because it's the sun that revolves around the earth.

UMM MOHAMMAD: No, that's wrong. You be careful not to let anyone hear you.

UMM ISSA: So what's the truth then?

UMM MOHAMMAD: The earth is like a ball. If you put a light in front of it and turn the ball, you notice that the side facing the light is lit and the other side is in the dark. That's how night and day happen. You must have heard that in the United States it is dark when we have light. That's the way it is. The earth moves and not the sun.

· · · · · · · ·

UMM ALI: You educated people are atheists. You say that rain does not come from God.

UMM MOHAMMAD: Didn't you hear about education in the time of the Prophet? He used to teach women, and especially his wife Aisha. He even said, "Take half your religion from this Hameera," and he meant, "Learn from her."

UMM ALI: Yes, I heard about the Prophet, and I even heard that the Quran encourages learning and education.

UMM MOHAMMAD: Right, you must have heard that the Prophet, peace be with him, was illiterate until he was forty, and then had a revelation, and was told "Read" three times, and he answered, "But I am not a reader," until he read what the revelation told him to and he recited the Quran.

UMM ALI: Yes, I've been hearing that since I was a little girl. I even heard that the Prophet decreed that each captive from Bader who teaches ten Moslems to read will be set free.

UMM MOHAMMAD: Well, since you are aware of these things, why do you not believe that adults are able to learn?

UMM ALI: You know, I think you are right.

. . . .

UMM ISSA: Hmmm. What you are saying makes sense. You seem to have benefited from the school while Umm Ali and I missed this opportunity. I wish we had registered and learned.

Women who join classes are eager to give their opinions on all kinds of subjects, including the Intifada:

In the name of God the Compassionate

In the absence of Arabs and in stealth, the state of Israel was established on the coastal plain of Palestine. The case was forgotten by the international community. After Israel occupied the rest of Palestine in 1967 the owners of Palestinian land started asking for their land after the international community turned its back to them and the Arab world had forgotten them.

On that basis and after forty-two years of occupation the Intifada erupted in Palestine and it included every city and village of the Palestinian land. This Intifada which rose with a stone taught oppressed people how to revolt against injustice to win their rights.

The glorious Intifada will continue to present victims and martyrs until the Palestinian people regain all their legitimate rights and establish their independent state on the hallowed soil and it is a revolution until victory.

Badia'a Omar
November 21, 1989

The joy of those who learn to read and write is unmistakable and can be seen in the letters to relatives that are written in class:

In the name of God the Compassionate
June 23, 1983.

Dear sister, Greetings,

I miss you a great deal. I never imagined that, one day, I will hold the pen and write you a letter but I have fulfilled my wish and joined a literacy center. I am now in the fifth grade. I read the Quran and I read the paper and I help my daughter Huda with her lessons.

My greeting to you and a greeting is the end.

Your sister,
Umm Mohammad

Despite coordinated efforts to eradicate illiteracy, researchers agree that progress has been slow. Literacy programs lack resources for reaching those in need of classes. Programs are understaffed and underfunded and those who operate them find it difficult to graduate the number of people who register. Retaining learners until graduation remains the most difficult problem. In the Occupied Territories, the number of people who registered for classes in 1986 was 2,451, 95 percent of whom were women between the ages of fourteen and fifty. Of that number, only 258 women "graduated" fully literate. While this number constitutes an improvement over 1980 where only 150 learners graduated out of a total of 5,475 learners, the number of women who drop out is still too high (Khader, *Al-Kateb*, September 1988: 71).

An encouraging development on the literacy front has been the entry of women's committees into the field. Although different women's groups have had mixed success with keeping their classes running, PFWAC has declared that "Eradicating illiteracy is a nationalist mission, and an important step to raise the social reality of women." The committee's policy is to offer literacy classes in every one of its centers, and it is actively working on methods to retain women in classes by the provision of child care and by making the curriculum more meaningful to the women by adding general knowledge and nationalist information to literacy (PFWAC *Kifah al-Mara'a* [Women's Struggle], June 1984: 65).

ASSIA HABASH
Former principal, kindergarten education specialist

After teaching psychology at a men's teacher training center for twelve years, Habash directed the UNRWA Ramallah Women's Training Center at Tireh between 1975 and 1983. Habash describes the problems she had with UNRWA officials while trying to modernize the vocational training offered to women refugees, and the problems she had with the Israeli military governor whenever her students demonstrated against the occupation. After cofounding the Arab Studies Society, and while working on her Ph.D. while her daughter was completing hers, Habash founded the Early Childhood Training Center. Here she describes how she and her staff overcame the initial resistance to the changes they were making in kindergarten education.

24 June 1985

My father was unusual.* He was always proud of my achievements at school and encouraged me in my education. During my last year in high school the Jordanian government was offering scholarships for studying nursing in England. I thought of applying for one—not that I'd ever wanted to be a nurse, but because it seemed a good opportunity to visit another country. My father asked me, "First, do you want to be a nurse? Second, do you want to accept a scholarship that commits you to working afterwards in whatever part of Jordan they want to send you to?" The truth is he was discouraging me from applying because he wanted the satisfaction of paying for my higher education himself.

I applied instead to the American University of Beirut (AUB) and was accepted. I didn't try for the Beirut College for Women because I knew the academic standard was lower. At that time, 1954, it was unusual for a girl from a conservative middle-class family to travel abroad alone and go to a coeducational college. There were only three or four girls from the whole of Jordan in my class at AUB. My father supported my going there, but all the rest of the family, my uncles and aunts, were against it. Even my mother would have preferred that I go to the Beirut College for Women. Luckily my father was the head of the family, so his decision was final.

When I told my father that I wanted to marry a man I'd met at the university, he had no objections, although it was unusual then for a girl to

*The first part of the story was done by Kitty Warnock, who interviewed Assia on tape in English in the spring of 1985, and then transcribed and edited the interview. Kitty knew her slightly at the time. I interviewed Assia in July 1986 and August 1989, and she used Arabic and English during the interview. I worked from the notes of my conversations with her. I also visited the Zababdeh center in July 1986 and her office in Jerusalem several times to see work in progress in 1989. I asked her about her life and then added specific questions about her work in children's education. Assia sent me several letters, reports, and workbooks to update my information.

Assia Habash and her daughter Deema in their home in East Jerusalem, 1986.
Photo by Orayb Najjar

choose her own husband—most girls didn't have the opportunity. I was
very lucky to have both a father and husband who supported me in my
education and my career. You sometimes find one, but rarely both, even
now. During my professional life my husband has shared responsibilities
in the home, and when I decided recently to pursue my education, he
backed me up. He is proud of supporting both me and our daughter in
working for our Ph.D.s. in England, she in biology, I in early childhood
education. When I travel to attend seminars or conferences, people still
ask, "What kind of woman is this?" Even my Ph.D. advisor in England
thinks it is out of the ordinary for a woman of my age and marital status
to leave home to study.

Being a woman has not caused me insuperable problems in my professional life. There is, however, one great disadvantage all women work
under here that is not generally recognized, and that I was not able to
overcome. Women are so much more vulnerable than men to real or
imagined scandal and gossip: people are always frightened for their
daughters' honor and ready to assume the worst.

My first experience of the fear for women's "honor" was in my first job
as an educational psychology instructor in the UNRWA Men's Training

Center in Ramallah. I started in 1961 and was the only woman in the whole of Jordan to be employed in a men's institution. There had always been men teaching in women's institutions because of a shortage of qualified women teachers, but not the other way around. When the then minister of education, a religious man, came to visit the center, I used to disappear, because we didn't want him to know that there was a woman on the staff. In the twelve years I taught there I was not promoted, and this was because of my sex. If I had been made chief instructor, my duties would have included inspection of the trainees' dormitories. The UNRWA directors could not risk putting me in a position that would have been so shocking to the community. A woman going into the men's rooms would have been quite unacceptable.

The problems I've had because of being a woman have been less difficult to deal with than those inherent in being a local staff member in the hierarchy of UNRWA. The agency provides Palestinian refugees with some essential services in health, education, and welfare, but UNRWA is an international body, and its policy making is done abroad. The aim of these planners has been to help Palestinians, but only to maintain basic services. Palestinian staff with ideas in development more compatible with the needs of society are actively discouraged. UNRWA officials are always frightened of upsetting the host countries in which they work.

My efforts to improve and modernize the courses in the Tireh center were always frustrated. For example, a few years ago UNRWA was given $500,000 for its vocational training program. I put forward a plan for the development of important courses that don't exist in the Occupied Territories for training physiotherapists and X-ray and dental technicians. My plans got no response from UNRWA, who gave almost all the West Bank's share of the money to the Men's Training Center.

When the Tireh center was opened in 1961, the courses were designed by UNESCO experts from all over the world. The programs were very good at the time, and our graduates were highly valued wherever they went to work. But a long time has elapsed since then, and only superficial changes have been made.

In 1980, during a visit to further education colleges and polytechnics in Britain, I came across many fascinating new developments and realized that our program, which UNRWA was so proud of, was twenty years out of date. I made some initial contacts with one of the colleges I visited, with a view to improving the training of our teachers. My superiors in

UNRWA reprimanded me severely for taking this initiative without authority from them: "We know what is needed. It is not for you to decide what improvements to make."

On another occasion I expressed a wish to update the equipment used in the center. I knew that modern educational technology could improve the speed and efficiency of our training. For example, girls were coming to the center from impoverished refugee-camp backgrounds where they had hardly had any opportunity to see machines. A typewriter keyboard was something new for them, and it could take them three months to learn to use one. With new techniques we could cut their learning time down to a few days. More important, we had to develop our courses to keep up with modern office technology. I said to the UNRWA field director, "Unless we modernize the center, no one will want to employ our graduates. We've got to teach the trainees how to use computers, word processors, telexes. . . . " His reply was, "Why do refugee girls need to know about such sophisticated equipment? There is no need for such things; the West Bank and Gaza are not ready for them."

You see how colonial his mentality was? He thought our refugees are poor and backward and so is our society, so we need only the most basic training. I explained to him, "We are not preparing students only for today. They will still be working in thirty years' time, and already most offices in East Jerusalem have telexes and computers."

It wasn't only the attitude of UNRWA officials that obstructed my aspirations for the center. The whole political situation in the Occupied Territories holds back development. Education is bound to suffer when it is regularly interrupted by the military authorities closing down schools, colleges, and universities for various reasons. Directors of educational institutions face a tremendous, insoluble conflict. Their desire to improve the standard of education is at odds with the students' need to express their national feeling. If the students demonstrate, the military authorities close the college; if the college is to stay open, the students have to be prevented from demonstrating in support of their people. What should the director do? He or she is caught between the pressure from the students demanding their right to express themselves and the pressure from the institution's governing body and the military authorities to suppress the students' activities. The occupation authorities try to make all heads of institutions in the Occupied Territories cooperate with them. I refused. Far from supporting me, my superiors in UNRWA felt that I was making

unnecessary problems. It was my refusal to cooperate with the military
government that caused most of the friction between me and UNRWA.

I think the military picked on me particularly because of my firm
beliefs and stands. During the time I was there, Tireh was harassed more
than any other higher education institution in the West Bank. Every time
the girls demonstrated, I was called in to the military governor's office and
lectured on how to run the center. The girls only did the usual things
students do in demonstrations—they would come out onto the road in
front of the center and burn a few tires and chant for two or three hours.

Often they were provoked by soldiers or local collaborators—the Village
Leagues—coming by and driving around outside the center. I used to say
to the military governor, "Tireh is so far from the town of Ramallah,
nobody sees when the girls come out onto the road to demonstrate. Why
don't you just let them alone and let the trouble fade away?" But he was
afraid of trouble escalating and would never accept my suggestion. He
always sent soldiers out and arrested a few people.

Once the soldiers took some photos of girls throwing stones. The military governor showed me the pictures and asked me to identify the girls.
Although they had scarves over their faces, I knew exactly who they were,
but I said to him, "How do you expect me to know every one of my six
hundred and fifty trainees? I don't know them." The deputy director of
UNRWA, an American, was with me at the time. He obviously wanted me
to comply with the military governor's order to avoid trouble. "Look
here," I said to him, "if you ask me to do this I will resign, right here in
front of the military governor. It's not my job to identify girls for the
Israeli army!" He reported my noncooperation to the director. It was
because of incidents like this that UNRWA decided to dismiss me.

We had one very funny incident. One day the military heard a rumor
that there were some explosives hidden in the center. Out they came in
force to search us. Trucks, jeeps, half-tanks, the military governor of the
West Bank himself. It was like a military parade. The soldiers rampaged
around all day and found nothing, then just as they were leaving, they
noticed a flower bed that we had planted with the center's initials. In
English, our initials are RWTC—Ramallah Women's Training Center. In
Arabic, they were MTF—Markaz Tadriib il-Fatayat—which also stands for
Munazzamat al-Tahriir al-Falastiniyyah—the PLO! You should have seen
the governor's face when the soldiers brought him to look at it. I laughed
so much. "What do you think this is?" I said. "We've had these initials

since before the PLO began." But the UNRWA director, instead of defending our right to use our own initials, felt that he had to apologize to the Israelis for what he called our "mistake."

Another time the director lectured me for two and a half hours about how I should not be biased against Israel. "You are a United Nations employee. You must be impartial." "First and foremost," I replied, "I am a Palestinian. You can't deny me my national feelings." "No, I can't, but I can ask you to keep quieter about them."

It was after this exchange that the campaign to dismiss me began. I suspect that UNRWA made a deal with the Israeli authorities. The military government was bringing a case against me, charging me with responsibility for some forbidden books and posters that had been found in the center. I think that in exchange for the case being dropped, UNRWA promised to get rid of me.

My dismissal was the second and clearest example in my experience of the handicap I mentioned earlier, that women are so much more vulnerable than men to scandal. Disagreements between me and UNRWA, stemming from my refusal to compromise with the occupation, built up over a period of years, and eventually UNRWA decided that I was an obstacle in the way of its smooth relations with Israel. Being a United Nations body, however, UNRWA could not announce publicly the actual reason for my dismissal. UNRWA officials had to find or create some other excuse that the community would accept, and this was where they exploited the fact that I was a woman and working in a women's institution.

Rumors of improper behavior in the center were spread all over the West Bank and Gaza (where many of the trainees are from). Because Tireh is a girls' college the public was ready to believe these rumors and be shocked by them. The ruse would not have succeeded if it were a men's college because nobody would have cared about such insinuations.

I challenged my dismissal, and my case was taken before UNRWA's Special Panel of Adjudicators. The panel found that the charges UNRWA had made against me were baseless and ordered my reinstatement. This put UNRWA in a tricky situation: How could they back out of their commitment to the military government?

I must admit that UNRWA has made some contributions to the progress of women here by providing education—vocational training in particular. The courses in the West Bank have been in traditionally accepted "women's subjects," it's true, but that's unavoidable when you have single-sex institutions. In UNRWA centers in Syria, female trainees can enroll to be radio and television technicians or study engineering drawing, and in Jordan there are coeducational paramedical courses.

We tried an experiment in breaking the sex barriers here. When we opened a new paramedical course in Tireh, half the students who joined were men. There were twenty men among six hundred and fifty girls. Each man had sixty or seventy admirers! Men were not used to coeducation, and the attention of so many women had a very bad effect on their personalities. When they went back to their dormitories in the men's centers on the other side of Ramallah, they were teased by their envious roommates. But the last straw was the political situation. Whenever the military authorities imposed a curfew for days on end, we had a problem on our hands–getting men back to their dormitories. We couldn't let them stay overnight in the center. I used to take three of them at a time in my car, breaking the curfew seven times to drive them secretly across Ramallah. In the end I had to say, "This is impossible. Either we have a completely integrated coeducational system, or nothing."

For women's status to improve, the aims and objectives of education have to change. The number of educated women is growing, it's true, but it is not yet changing people's fundamental attitudes. We follow the Jordanian system in the West Bank, though I don't see why UNRWA shouldn't opt out and establish its own system. We need to have a more progressive curriculum that will establish equality between the sexes in all aspects of life.

24 June 1985

The year 1985 was one of the most exciting and productive years of my life because I finally discovered what I wanted to be when I grew up: Someone who improves kindergarten education in the West Bank. Actually, as early as 1960, I realized that something had to be done about our kindergarten education. True, I had ulterior motives; I was not satisfied with the type of education my children were getting, but I retained my interest in doing something about it long after my children had grown. In 1963, I submitted a proposal to charitable societies for an alternative experimental kindergarten program, but it was rejected. I turned to other matters, but political events in the area and our reaction to them redirected my attention to the crucial early years of our lives. I was convinced (as many people are) that the early years have a bearing on the critical thinking of people and that it helps shape their national character. Our own past has certainly not been stable enough for the development of a good educational system. We have had a succession of four different political administrations since the beginning of this century—Ottoman, British, Jordanian, and Israeli. Our educational system is a strange mixture of the contributions of those periods. At the end of British and French colonial rule, Arab regimes retained the educational systems that colonial rulers left behind and made only minor modifications on them. Such systems were designed to serve the rulers—to create bureaucrats—not to produce problem solvers. As Palestinians, we never had control of our own educational system.

In 1967 education suffered a setback when Israel occupied the West Bank and Gaza. Israeli authorities retained the books that were used under Jordanian rule after making changes in history and geography books. At present, the level of general knowledge of our children is pitiful. About a week ago, some children, ages nine to fifteen were interviewed for computer camp by a Palestinian company offering scholarships. Some did not know where the Golan was, most knew very little about Palestinian history, and some were not aware of what happened in 1948 when the state of Israel was established at the expense of Palestinians. While Israelis are to blame for the changes in curriculum, for the long closure of schools after demonstrations, and for the unwarranted transfer or dismissal of teachers as a form of punishment, the sorry state of education is also caused by our teaching methods—the "chalk and talk," the rote learning, the idea that knowledge is something one uses to pass exams with, instead of information one needs for real life. No wonder our professors complain that students get to the university with poor critical and analytical thinking skills. Such skills do not come from studying "great men" history about the exploits of rulers and caliphs or "great battle" history with its share of dates and names, but from studying history in a more realistic way—by drawing lessons from history and by tying the past to the present.

The fragmentary nature of the educational system can be seen most clearly in kindergarten education. We have UNRWA preschools, religious (Christian or Muslim) kindergartens, private institutions, as well as those run by women's groups and charitable societies. The location of these schools was not determined by detailed study of the needs of each area.

A 1987 survey revealed that in the 353 preschool sites covered, we have about 200,000 children four years old and under, and assuming that 10 percent of them are eligible to enroll in kindergartens, we can tentatively conclude that existing kindergartens only serve one-fourth of the children in need of such education. There is also a problem that is even more serious than the shortage of kindergartens—the problem of quality.

An al-Najah National University study of twenty-six kindergartens in the Nablus area conducted by university students under the direction of Dr. Ahmad Jaber concluded that most of the kindergartens surveyed concentrated mainly on the affective domain and only secondarily on the cognitive domain. Most teachers involved in kindergarten education have only high school diplomas and lack professional training. Few teachers have experience with using materials that enhance the development of the child, and most perform the duties of first grade teachers by concentrating on the three R's. At the same time, children's language, self-esteem, and physical development are neglected. Kindergarten teaching is a low-prestige job. Working conditions are poor and teacher salaries range between 40 and 60 dinars a month ($100 and $150). The physical setting of the kindergartens is poor. Many buildings have not been designed for that purpose and are overcrowded. Faced with this situation, we realized that because of a lack of funds, we cannot deal with inadequate buildings, but we can make an impact on teacher training. We can remove those oppressive desks preschoolers have to sit on. We can allow children to act their age, and we can remove the teacher-as-dictator from the classroom. If children have a creative preschool program where learning is a pleasure, then they may carry the love of learning with them into the first grade. So we may not be able to change the curriculum in primary schools under Israeli occupation, but we can change teaching strategies making class time activity oriented. We could also stress the development of individual children by enriching their environment. Such a change would place children at the center of the educational process and would take care of their cognitive, psychomotor, and affective development. And to do that, we have to reach teachers.

So under the name of the Arab Studies Society, we designed a project that we called the Early Childhood Research Center (ECRC). The aim of the center is to develop and upgrade preschool education in the West Bank. In addition to teacher training, we have created a library and resource center, a toy- and educational game-making center. We conduct

A child and a teacher demonstrate to other children the steps of the Dabkeh, the Palestinian national dance, at Zabandeh school. Photo by Orayb Najjar

workshops in model kindergartens that use curricula and methods developed by our early childhood education experts.

The first time we advertised for teacher trainees with degrees in psychology or education we received 135 applications, some from people with Ph.D.s. We did not take overqualified people because we knew that they would not be able to adapt themselves to the requirements of the job. We chose five women and three men to encourage men to enter preschool education. We have established six model kindergartens in six different areas of the country. We expected the Hebron conservative area to be the most difficult to work in because it is the least developed, but administrators interested in kindergarten education there were most cooperative, shattering all our stereotypes about that part of the country. By far the most original project is one that we have established in the village of Zababdeh in the north of the country.

While looking for a place in the north, we were told about a Palestinian priest, the principal of an elementary school who was receptive to new ideas. We were attracted to that village also because it had something not many other locations possess—space. Zababdeh had a large old unused church, abandoned for a new one. We sought the help of Kathy Bergen, a Canadian, then the associate country representative for the Mennonite Central Committee, Jerusalem. The Mennonites provided the funds necessary for renovating the church and, thanks to the Latin Patriarchate.of Jerusalem who gave permission for the renovation, the building became a kindergarten for 120 children. Dr. Jacqueline Sfeir, a Palestinian specialist in early education who was teaching at Bethlehem University, was hired to design the training program for teachers of the Zababdeh kindergarten. Initially, it was hard to convince anybody that "active learning" and activity centers were worth trying. After the first week of training, one of the teachers announced: "This is not a class, it is a zoo. My conscience does not allow me to take a salary for this." Teachers saw child-directed education as threatening. They saw their role as transmitters of the alphabet and numbers, and the kindergarten Dr. Sfeir had designed had activity centers that children moved between. Parents were just as unhappy as teachers. If their children were not learning their letters and numbers in notebooks parents could see, what were they doing all day? So both teachers and parents wanted to stop the project. Dr. Sfeir called both parents and teachers for a meeting, explained what was going on (one more time), and asked for their indulgence until Christmas, promising that if they did not like what was happening by then, they had the option to go back to the old system.

With promises of a way out, teachers gave up active resistance to the program, but Dr. Sfeir noticed that they did exactly what was prescribed and were very literal about it. Because of their insecurity, they needed to hang onto her instructions and her exact words. When teachers noticed that students were calming down and asking excellent questions, they told Dr. Sfeir, "This must be a clever bunch," in other words, resistance was still there. Christmas vacation came. Evaluation time came and the results were so good that even the teachers were impressed. That was a turning point. Teachers and parents voted unanimously to stick to the program. Dr. Sfeir now works with the Zababdeh school as a consultant and sometimes uses it for training other teachers. The experiences of Dr. Sfeir were repeated in other areas as well. We now know that change can take place.

We are trying to spread this type of education, but very cautiously. Some of the teachers' groups who visit to observe do not realize that it looks as if the educational process is self-propelled, but that a great deal of preparation goes into keeping the children interested in the play centers and in keeping things running smoothly. The interaction that takes place between the teacher and the students, and between the children them-selves, is very subtle and indirect. We want the idea to spread, but not without guidance. Child-oriented learning looks deceptively simple to carry out to the outside observer. It is easy to copy, but hard to make work. As Dr. Sfeir said, "Someone may have all the right ingredients but not the cake." One could end up with a fiasco. We see the role of our center as protecting the integrity of this method so that it can be applied correctly.

The West Bank is going through a difficult political period. There are competing political groups, each offering different solutions to Palestinian problems. Perhaps the most unusual aspect of our program is that we are not working for a Palestinian faction or group but for the whole country. Our independence from different factions is reflected in our choice of bene-ficiaries for our courses. We have approached or have been approached by people from al-Aqsa nursery system, Muslim brothers, the Latin Patri-archate of Jerusalem, the kindergartens of the Jordanian Red Crescent Society, as well as women's leftist groups.

My husband Ziad has caught my excitement for the project. "You seem to be so fulfilled," he says. "What a waste of years. I wish you had a chance to work on such a project when you first proposed it in the sixties." My husband has always been extremely supportive of my work outside the home. He is a real feminist and he believes in equal rights all the way. If he disagrees with something I intend to do, he says, "Here is what I think, but you do as you like." We have two children. Our daughter Deema says that her father is more liberated than I am.

Deema, twenty-seven, has recently received a postdoctorate research award after she received her doctorate in plant physiology. She has decided to marry a British lawyer. My son Samer, twenty-four, has decided to marry an American woman he met while studying in the United States. I would have preferred them to marry Palestinians and objected at first, but once I was convinced that that is what they really wanted, I had to accept their decisions; as they both pointed out to me, I had raised them to be independent. Deema knew ahead of time I could not argue with her because she is mature. I did try to reason with Samer. I said, "You are still young, think about it longer," and he said, "Oh, you are so traditional!" Both Deema and Samer's bride will be married in traditional Palestinian dresses, and I feel good about that.

27 June 1989

My life was going along fine when I had the shock of my life. My husband died of a heart attack. Losing him was totally devastating. But what added to my pain was my experience with trying to renew my passport. I discovered that from that moment on, I had to be called "Assia, the widow of Ziad Habash." I can understand being classified as "widow" in an official form, but to have that as part of my name on my passport was awful. Here was a man I loved, someone I shared twenty-eight years with, years full of life, and yet, I had to be reminded of my loss for the rest of my life. I turned the world upside down trying to change my newly acquired title to no avail. I got nowhere at the passport office, so I went to the Jordanian Ministry of Social Affairs—they phoned the Ministry of Interior—nothing worked. I was told that I could revert back to my father's name. I said "Look, I had a wonderful life with that man, I used his name, I do not want to negate my time with him, I just do not want to be tied to him in sorrow." No use. So according to the Jordanian personal status laws, I have no standing of my own. My age, my work in public life, my education, my experience—all those things count for nothing. What is important to the passport control people is my status as a *female* in relation to a given male.

After I repeated my story to people, I heard horror stories from other women on the subject. An unmarried female professor wanting to renew her passport was asked if she is "a spinster"—that is a classification that can go on a woman's passport! A woman who had the wedding ceremony performed (Kateb al-Kitab) but whose marriage was not consummated or was annulled for any reason will be called "Nashizah" (recalcitrant woman, shrew, termagant). If she wants that word removed, she had to be classified as "divorced," even though she had never lived with a man. Although it takes two to marry and divorce, and although some women die before their husbands, men are never classified according to their sexual status or their tie to a woman. No man is a widower, no man is divorced, and no man is a bachelor.

A group of us is now talking about personal status laws. Not just griping, but trying to examine them and see what we can do about them. A female lawyer, a Muslim, is now looking at the Shari'a laws. We have got to fight for issues like inheritance, divorce, and custody rights, and it is not going to be easy. What is happening in the West Bank is a true revolution, and if we do not make use of this upheaval to work on the legal position of women we will lose an important chance. We have to build on the gains women have made *now*. Otherwise, when we have a Palestinian government we will need to fight to gain our rights. That is why what girls study in kindergarten and school matters.

I have high hopes for the kindergarten project and hope that, eventually, we can increase the number of trainees we take in every session. Last year we had thirty-two trainees in Hebron and fourteen in Jerusalem. This year, we had eighteen, thirty-two, and fourteen trainee teachers in Nablus, Jerusalem, and er-Ram. We do different types of training. We diagnose a kindergarten and start from where people are. That is why we are hesitant about sending people to train abroad even when we get scholarships. Most kindergartens in richer countries are well stocked and full of toys and games, and we do not want our teachers to get the impression that without the colorful plastic and the ready-made stuff, they cannot have a successful kindergarten. We demonstrate through our model kindergarten what can be done with local material that costs little. We have a toy workshop, we do pictorial training, we work on empowering teachers by concentrating on their human relations with children. We discuss

استيقظ الطفل وقد بال في فراشه

The child woke up and found that he has urinated in his bed.

• تبوّل لا إرادي من شدّة الخوف بعد سماع القصيج خارج البيت •   ٢٥

Uncontrollable urination caused by fear brought on by loud noises outside the house.

Drawings taken from a booklet on handling children's fears of the occupation.

mother-child relationships, communication with children, respecting children, involving them in activities, and involving members of the community in children's education. We discovered that it is hard for teachers to retain all that training and that we need to have follow-up sessions. We arrange whole-day visits with teachers and provide them with other types of support. We are proud of a tape of children's songs we produced, and during the uprising, we felt the need to help parents tackle children's fears, so we produced a booklet with a lot of drawings on how to handle children who are unusually traumatized by events. What do you tell a preschool child when she wakes up and finds soldiers in her house and senses that her parents are powerless to protect her? How do you deal with children who start bed-wetting because of fear? The booklet is distributed to teachers and is supposed to be shared with parents.

Preschool education will not change overnight, but we have to start somewhere. I know we are on the right track.

Update

Since the interview, the center Assia heads published a five-volume children's workbook suitable both for mothers who want to work with their children at home and for kindergarten teachers. The exercises and ideas were, in part, compiled from kindergarten teachers in the last few years.

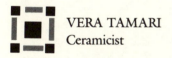

VERA TAMARI
Ceramicist

Vera, one of Palestine's few female professional artists, has studied in Lebanon, Italy, and England. Her work includes paintings, drawings, pottery, and glazed ceramic tiles. Here, she talks about her upbringing and work, and about the expectations people have of artists in a society under occupation.

It was easy for me to become an artist because both my parents were interested in art.* My mother did something very unusual at the time—

*Kitty Warnock interviewed Vera in English in her studio in Ramallah in April 1985. She taped the interview and worked from the transcript. She asked Vera about her career as an artist. She knew Vera only slightly at the time.

Vera Tamari in her studio in Ramallah, 1986. Photo by Orayb Najjar

she stayed in her convent school in Jerusalem for an extra year after she finished high school to study some arts and crafts; then when she went back home to Jaffa she made a little workshop in the corner of the house and took drawing lessons by correspondence from an art school in Paris.

After she married, she couldn't develop her talent, but even now I rely a lot on her artistic judgment. My father was a connoisseur and collector, and both of them went to exhibitions, read, and knew about world art. Most important, they taught me to love nature and appreciate beauty.

What made it even easier for me was that my brother, who is several years older than I, decided to quit his studies and become an artist. He's really an artist, in his personality, much more than I. He'd always shown talent and my parents had encouraged him, but it was difficult for them to accept his becoming a professional artist. He was their only son, and they expected him to have a distinguished career in physics. They were embarrassed when people asked them, "What does your son do?" and they had to answer, "He's an artist." In the eyes of people here that was the same as saying, "He does nothing." It was much easier for them to accept that my sister and I should be artists.

The only thing a woman could do then, in the mid-1960s, was to be a teacher or a housewife, and you could combine being an artist with either of these—you could be an art teacher, or you could stay at home and paint and have a little corner to display your little works. It wouldn't offend society or undermine your parents' status. A girl was not thought of then as a professional.

There were no four-year universities in the West Bank at that time, and not many women went into higher education. But my sister went to Beirut College for Women, and it was natural that I should follow her. Two years after I graduated, a vacancy came up in the Art Department of the UNRWA Women's Training Center in Tireh, Ramallah. I didn't want to teach, but the director persuaded me, and I accepted the job.

It was the best thing I ever did, really. I had to take girls who had no background whatsoever in art and train them to be art teachers. They had done no art since they were eight or nine years old and they were completely inhibited. They were forced into the art section because they were academically too weak for any other subject. They hated it! I tried to be kind and encouraging, and took them on trips until we got over their fears. By the end of the two-year course they were transformed.

I'm not boasting; the experience we had was something very special. My aim was to make them not artists, but people who could use whatever materials they had around them creatively, not necessarily producing beautifully finished end results. They couldn't understand at first why we didn't have drawing lessons or paint landscapes full of Swiss chalets. But gradually, through experimenting with materials, they became aware. Then they began naturally to understand composition, and at the end they could recognize good quality work. We studied teaching skills as well, and they became very good teachers.

All they had learned went to waste when they started working, because art is almost totally neglected in our schools. They got jobs in UNRWA schools in the refugee camps, but not as specialist art teachers. They somehow fell into the old pattern of wanting to please the headmistress by doing whatever extra Arabic or history she asked them to do. If they did have an art class, they'd do the conventional things, copying something, or sticking macaroni onto paper and painting it silver. Horrible!

Because of their background they were shy, not aggressive enough to impose their ideas on anyone, and they got no support from anywhere. It wasn't my job to follow them up, and the UNRWA inspectors who came around did not usually agree with my methods.

I was too modern for them. Besides, the girls had no materials to work with. In college, in addition to the usual paints and colors, we'd done a lot of work with scrap materials that I had collected for them—old magazines, fabric, all kinds of things. But in the refugee camps they didn't even have scrap materials. They don't have any magazines or scraps or cloth. Nothing. It was really sad.

I think there is less art taught now than there was then. There is a new syllabus which is even more theoretical, less practical. This affects the whole of our lives. How can you repress creativity in a child? If you have a creative mind you can excel in anything. It's through experimenting, through feeling, touching, arranging, and organizing, that you develop your talents. If a child does not have the chance to do this, he or she becomes rigid. When our students come to a university, they are desperately rigid. It affects everything they study later on.

Another essential result of art education is becoming sensitive to things. It's important to one's whole being, being aware of the environment, of nature, or colors. Without this awareness, people take things for granted. They don't notice the different kinds of trees, colors, and they don't stop to analyze or think. They don't even feel things emotionally.

Pupils here are rather encouraged to suppress their feeling and reactions to things. Art training would develop people's self-confidence and individuality, too. Once you start doing things by yourself, cutting and pasting paper or whatever, thinking about it and experimenting and making your own decisions, of course you become more confident in everything. I don't think art is being given much importance yet, even in kindergartens. It's considered a luxury.

I left teaching after a few years because I wasn't growing anymore. I wasn't doing any work of my own and growing artistically. I felt suffocated. I'd been to a couple of summer workshops abroad, and that's where I discovered clay. I'd never handled it in my life before, but I loved it. I decided to travel to Italy and take a practical course in ceramics.

When I came back I set up my own workshop to pursue making pottery. It was wonderful to be able to concentrate on my own work at last, and I produced quite a lot. It wasn't easy for me though. I got so lonely! All my life I'd been surrounded by students, colleagues, and friends, and now I had to work all alone and learn to program myself. It was hard to define the kind of work I was doing. I didn't have the discipline of doing industrial production, and there wasn't much outlet for what I made. The few people who did like my work had already bought as many pieces as they wanted. I was sitting day in and day out in my workshop, without any interaction with other potters—there aren't any other studio potters in the West Bank—or with anyone who understood what I was doing. I had two exhibitions anyway. They were a mixed experience. People enjoyed my work, but they were saying, "Oh, it's fantastic, it's beautiful," while I knew that I still had a long way to go.

Nobody realized this. They accepted what I was doing and would have been happy if I did the same for twenty years. No one was going to encourage me to develop. There's no public that understands ceramics here. Perhaps people are developing a feeling for painting, but ceramics has become remote from their lives. In the past, pottery cooking pots and water and storage jars were everyday objects, especially in the villages, and so now people associate pottery with backwardness. Their sense of values has changed, and they'd prefer to look at a crystal vase rather than at a crude pottery thing.

I began to make tiles using themes from village life. People liked these. They didn't understand the material still, but they did relate to the subjects. I never had to repeat myself. I visited villages and was always picking up new impressions of people, objects, scenes. I have lists of commissions that I haven't yet done, but now I think I've outgrown this period. In the future I may use more Islamic themes.

All the time I try to keep a balance between making tiles and making pots. I really love working on the wheel. It fulfills some internal need. I love the motion and the life in it.

I never overcame the problem of loneliness. I was always either at home or down in the workshop, out of touch with people, without any stimulus. I decided I needed some kind of training to give me a new push, and that's why I went to England two years ago. I looked for a course on Islamic or Palestinian pottery from a technical as well as historical angle, but I couldn't find anything that was both practical and academic. I joined the Islamic art and architecture M.A. program at Oxford, which was the nearest to what I wanted, but I didn't put my fingers in clay once while I was there. It was a great strain being thrown into such an academic approach, when I hadn't studied for nearly twenty years and was used to working with my hands every day. But it was a wonderful experience. The teachers were very good, and I've come back with a completely new kind of knowledge that I never expected to have.

Is my art political? Political enough. I consciously try to do something that is connected with this area. I express myself through the colors of Palestine, village and landscape scenes, traditional motifs. I think I was the first to use designs adapted from traditional embroidery. The rounded shapes of pots are like the rounded shapes of women and the embroidery patterns fit naturally onto pots.

My art probably doesn't stir violent emotions in people. It won't start a revolution, but it makes them happy inside because they are related to it. At an earlier stage, when everyone was trying to express political feelings using obvious symbols in art, I thought maybe I should be more explicitly political. I tried using doves and chains and things. I couldn't express myself in this way at all. I made drawings with political ideas in mind, but I was never impelled to finish them. I felt that they weren't profound enough, or that the clay wasn't meeting my goals.

A nation must have art. Just as you want to raise a child to be sensitive, you want a people to be sensitive and aware. Most of our art is political though, and there are dangers in that. Political art expresses and maybe purges people's feelings about their situation, and it is useful if it shows people abroad what we are experiencing, but such an approach used exclusively doesn't teach people to enjoy art for itself and doesn't develop their sensitivity. Some of our artists have fallen into the trap of using the same political themes and symbols over and over again. We've lost a lot as far as self-expression goes.

Whenever artists have produced very personal painting, without any political motifs, they have been criticized. Palestinian leaders know the importance of art—of creative art as well as of preserving our heritage. There was a museum in Beirut, a very good exhibition of the best works of Palestinian artists all over the world. It was destroyed in the 1982 Israeli invasion.

Artists have been working here for only ten or fifteen years, and the oldest of them is not yet forty. They are still finding their way. They studied abroad after the 1967 war, came back here, and got enclosed. They have no contact with art movements in the rest of the world. At the same time they have not developed a really local style, because they are still influenced by their teachers and their books. The symbols our artists use— doves, chains, clenched fists—are international socialist symbols. If the quality of work here improves, a Palestinian style will develop in time.

We have an active organization now, the Association of Artists in the West Bank and Gaza Strip. The idea began about fifteen years ago when a group of artists realized that art needs some sort of organized support. It took some time to work out, and has had its ups and downs, but there was an exceptional period a few years ago when we had several exhibitions traveling around the West Bank and Gaza and abroad. Art was absolutely not known at all to the general public at that time, but masses and masses of people came to these exhibitions. It was wonderful! They were glued to the pictures, they'd come up close and touch them and examine every detail. They hadn't been exposed to paintings much before, and they didn't know how to just look at a painting and absorb it personally. They wanted the artist to explain everything. It was a good experience for the audiences and for the artists themselves, a great encouragement to the artists to develop what they were doing. There were some very strong painters here then, but many of them have since left the country.

The association has revived recently, and we are trying to be better organized. Our projects include: exhibitions abroad, publishing books about Palestinian art, training programs, and workshops. Funds are always a problem, but we will do whatever we can. Recently, we had a joint exhibition with some progressive Israeli artists. It was an important event politically rather than artistically. It raised some conflict in the community: many Palestinians prefer not to have any contact with the Israelis at this stage, but we artists believe that this is the right time. The quality of the work in the exhibition was rather weak from both sides. In the future I hope we'll be able to have a joint show of better quality, where we can really learn from each other and show good art, not simply demonstrate that art exists.

I don't find any particular problem with being a woman artist, although there are few of us. The public does find it strange that I use clay, use a machine, and get myself all dirty. They expect a woman to be sitting in a neat room behind an easel doing little paintings. I remember once a doctor came to my workshop to commission something. He must have come straight out of the operating theatre; he still smelled of antiseptic and looked very pale and clean. He felt so out of place in my mucky workshop that he couldn't bring himself to buy anything!

With the other artists, my relationship is fine. If it's not very close, that's not because of my sex but because they are all painters. My work takes much longer to complete than theirs so I am cut off from participating wholeheartedly in all their exhibitions.

My life is entering a new phase now. I've recently joined the faculty of Birzeit University, where I'll be teaching an academic course in Islamic art history. I'll enjoy being involved with people again, but at the same time I'm worried that I won't have time to work creatively. Soon the university will be opening a Faculty of Fine Arts, and then I will be able to teach practical courses. I'm very much looking forward to helping students experience pottery.

Update

Vera took part in a 15–21 November 1988 ten-woman exhibition in East Jerusalem. She published with architect Suad A'amiri *The Palestinian Village Home* (London: British Museum, 1989). In November 1989, Vera took part in an exhibition with three of the most well-known painters in the Occupied Territories—Nabil Anani, Suleiman Mansur, and Tayseer Barakat. Interviewed by *Al-Fajr*, English weekly, 6 November 1989, Vera said,

"What inspired me in my recent work are countless ancient pottery shards which can be found scattered all over the countryside. They are a testimony to the historical continuity on the land. With no seeming interruption, the past and present embrace one another. Pottery making is an organic process intimately tied to the earth. I find this link more pertinent in my work these days."

In her studio in Ramallah in August 1989, one could also see two three-dimensional scenes of demolished houses, still wet. Vera said that those scenes were inspired by the increasing number of demolished houses in the Occupied Territories.

When Birzeit University was closed, Vera started inviting the neighborhood children to her studio. A number of clay pieces made by the children could be seen on her table.

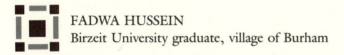

FADWA HUSSEIN
Birzeit University graduate, village of Burham

Twenty-four-year-old Fadwa Hussein lives in the village of Burham. Many of the problems Palestinians are experiencing are caused directly by military and political oppression. Fadwa's story illustrates another kind of problem particularly affecting some rural women: the conflict that occurs when rapid economic change creates new expectations that clash with old assumptions.

May 1985

My father died in 1971, when I was ten and my sisters were one and two.* Our mother left us with our father's family and went back to live with her mother, and she was persuaded to remarry almost at once. She was still young. Her brothers thought she should not be alone, and her mother told her, "You have not had any sons. For the sake of the family, you must marry again and try to have some." Everybody, including my mother, agreed that grandmother was right. It's the custom here

*Fadwa was a student of Kitty Warnock's at Birzeit University, and a cousin and friend of Kitty's friend and collaborator, Hala Salem. Kitty taped the interview in English at Fadwa's uncle's house where she was living in May 1984 and then transcribed and edited it.

that a woman who loses her husband before she's had any sons must marry again.

She couldn't keep us with her when she remarried because we belonged to our father's family, and anyway her new husband would have refused the responsibility of bringing us up. I don't know if she was unhappy about losing us. I wasn't allowed to see her much, and wasn't even told that she was marrying and going to live in another village. I came home from school one day and saw my grandmother carrying my two-year-old sister who was screaming, "I want my mummy! Bring back my mummy!" That's how I learned what had happened.

I don't blame my mother for abandoning us. It wasn't her fault. It was the fault of the customs, and her mother, and all her brothers and brothers-in-law. She wasn't clever or strong enough to resist them. Her ideas have changed since then, and now she feels that what she did was wrong. I feel sorry for her. She hasn't been happy with her second husband, although she did have the son who is supposed to justify all our sufferings.

When my mother remarried, we girls stayed with the eldest of our father's brothers in our village, Burham. His wife didn't want anything to do with us so I had to leave school to look after my baby sisters. After I'd been absent for two months, the headmistress got worried about me, because I had been a good student, and she came to our house to see why I wasn't coming to school. When she saw our situation, she was shocked, and she arranged for my sisters to be taken to an orphanage in Bethlehem. People in the village still talk about what a disgrace it was to the family, that none of my uncles could manage to look after the two little girls. Luckily my sisters have been very happy, and they have had a better life and a better education than they would have had they stayed here.

I went to live with the second of my father's brothers. His oldest son Ibrahim was good to me, and I enjoyed school, so for a while I was happy. Then in 1978 Ibrahim got a ten-year prison sentence, for political reasons, and I was left at the mercy of the rest of the family, who hated me for some reason. Perhaps they were jealous because I was better at school than any of them. They tried to make me leave school and go out to work. When that failed, they forced me to do a lot of jobs in the house so that I couldn't study properly. I had to wash the dishes and tend the goats. Even on the day of my final exams I had to fetch water from the spring a kilometer away. I always had to get up at 5:00 A.M. and could only study late at night. I don't know how I managed without getting ill or giving up hope. Nobody encouraged me, not even my mother. She wasn't allowed to visit me often, and when she did she was trying to persuade me to get married, like most mothers do.

I was accepted as a student at Birzeit University, but that didn't bring me any independence. An unmarried girl can't live her own life here even if she is a university student. Her relatives think she should do whatever they tell her. I was still living in my uncle's house, dependent on him, and his family was still fighting against my education.

One of their tactics was to take away any money I had so I couldn't do anything without asking them. I managed to save a little secretly, and I gave it to a cousin in another house to keep for me. When the time came for me to pay the fee to register for the second semester at the university, I went to fetch the money from her. My uncle saw me on the way, and when I got home he asked me suspiciously what I had been doing. I had to make up a story, to protect my kind cousin, but by the evening he'd heard from some village gossip where I'd been. He flew into a rage because I'd lied to him.

It was the last week of the semester, and I had two exams the following day. I'd spent most of the day studying. Besides, it was Ramadan (the month of fasting), so I hadn't eaten or drunk anything since before sunrise. You can imagine how weak and tired I was feeling. My uncle beat me, then locked me in a room without any food. He meant to keep me there all the next day so I couldn't go to take my exams. By chance, one of our neighbors heard the row, and he went and described what was happening to a university teacher who lives in the village. The teacher reported it to the university's student council. At 8:30 A.M. the next morning, I heard a knock at the door—it was the teacher and members of the student council come to fetch me. My uncle was afraid of them and let me out without saying a word.

I arrived to take my exams one hour late and in such a state of shock that my hands were shaking and I forgot everything I had studied the day before. I passed anyway! I realized that I couldn't go on living like this, and nobody was going to help me except myself. When the exam was over, I went to the village clinic to show the doctor my bruises. I was going to report my uncle to the police for beating me. But on my way to the police station I met another one of my uncles, and when he heard what I was doing, he stopped me. He couldn't allow me to bring such dishonor on the family.

I moved into the student hostel for a while, but although the university let me stay there without paying when I explained my circumstances, and I worked in the kitchens and in the library in all my free time, I couldn't make ends meet. I was relieved when another of my uncles came and fetched me to his home. He came partly because he was sorry for me, but mainly because he felt it was a dishonor for the whole family to have driven me out of the village.

It wasn't only my education I had to fight for. I was also determined that I would marry when and whom I chose, and this brought me into conflict with everybody. When my father died, he left me some good land, with olive and fruit trees, and my uncle wanted to keep it in the family, so he decided I should marry his second son, Maher. I hardly knew Maher, as he'd been exiled for suspected involvement in resistance activity, and what I knew of him I didn't like. Besides, I was sure that it would be the end of my education if I married him, so I refused. All of my relatives were against me, even my mother. They all agreed it would be wrong to let the land go out of the family. I had to use a mean way of getting them to leave me alone. I'd been given a scholarship for the university from In'ash al-Usra. If I left without graduating, I'd have to pay back to In'ash al-Usra the $400 that they had already paid for my university fees. I said to my uncle, "O.K., I'll marry Maher, but you'll have to pay back In'ash al-Usra's money, won't you?" I knew he'd prefer to let me finish studying rather than pay, so I was safe.

The next problem was, what was I going to do after I graduated? There is almost no work here, and I couldn't possibly leave home and live by myself. It's unheard of for a girl to leave home before she is married, especially a village girl. But how could I stay here in the village, dependent on my uncles, unwanted, and with nothing to do? The best solution would be to get married. Through my mother's sister, who lives in Amman and visits the West Bank regularly, I heard that the son of their other sister in Kuwait was interested in me. In 1982, when he heard that Birzeit University was closed by the military government for seven months, he came to Jordan and sent our aunt over here to fetch me. I got a permit from the military authorities to go to Amman, but at the bridge crossing I was turned back by the Israeli security men. No explanation—they never tell you why. I've never been involved in political activity in my life, so I

Fadwa Hussein with one of her twins in a one-room house in the village of Burham, 1985. Photo by Orayb Najjar

suppose it was because of my other cousins. My cousin was ready to wait for me – I think he loved me already, although we had never met – and after a lawyer had worked on the case for six months, I finally got permission to leave. We met in Amman for three weeks in the summer of 1983, and we got engaged at the end of that time.

My fiancé had to go back to his job in Kuwait and I had to finish at the university, so we didn't meet again until we got married a year later. I wasn't afraid. He's a good man and he respects me. I'm sure we'll be happy together. He has been working and saving his money for five years so that he can marry and then go on studying. We'd like to go to the United States to study for masters' degrees.

I'll miss my village with its hills and trees and pure air, but I've heard that life in Kuwait is good. Palestinians are rarely granted citizenship, but salaries are high, so as long as you have a job, you can be comfortable. We have to accept the restrictions. Where else can we go and find work? The worst problem my husband and I might face is with his parents. They will want us to have at least ten children! They had only three, so according to our society's customs they have the right to demand that their son give them plenty of grandchildren. If it were up to us, we would only have four or five, but it is not a matter for us to decide alone. My husband has to think of his parent's wishes as well as ours.

Update

A few months before Fadwa's marriage a group of Shiites threw a bomb at the United States embassy in Kuwait. As a result, the Kuwaiti government has placed restrictions on the entry of any non-Kuwaitis into the country and has stopped granting visas to any Palestinian except those who have jobs and work permits. Being married to a long-term resident is not enough to gain Fadwa entry into the country. She knows of a dozen other young women in villages around Burham, and a "whole club of us" in Jordan, who are trapped like her, unable to join their husbands except for short visits. Fadwa's husband is using all the influence he can muster after twenty years of living in Kuwait to try to find her a job, but it will not be easy. Meanwhile she is living on whatever money he can send her in a single rented room in her village.

Fadwa's inability to find work is not making her feel that all her efforts have been worthless. In common with many Palestinian women of the present generation, her ambition was not to be an independent single career woman, but to become what she is now: the educated wife of a professional man. From her still fairly traditional point of view, her plans have been crowned with the greatest possible success: she has given birth to twin boys (at the end of May 1985). Insofar as she shares her society's valuation of women primarily as mothers, she is proud and fulfilled. She has taken her sons to Kuwait to show them to their father. Fadwa is allowed to stay in Kuwait as a visitor for four months, and she is content for the present to ignore her university economics textbooks, which are sitting on a shelf beside her wedding shoes, a testimony to her un-completed struggle for personal self-determination.

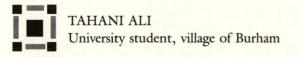

TAHANI ALI
University student, village of Burham

When Tahani registered as a freshman in 1983, her biggest problem was in decid-ing whether to study engineering or physics. Yet when the Israelis closed all insti-tutions of higher learning indefinitely in January 1988, Tahani found that her problem was in graduating with any kind of degree. She describes how the closure has affected her future plans, and how she and her village of 250 have reacted to the Intifada.

When I sat for the Tawjihi high school exam (science track),* my average was 88 percent.[1] This meant that I could get into engineering school at Birzeit University, with its entrance requirement of 86 percent. Even though I got higher grades in my engineering courses than in physics, I decided to transfer to the Physics Department. I changed my major because after examining my reasons for wanting to be an engineer, I had to admit to myself that I was into it for the prestige attached to the pro-fession, rather than because of any special interest in the field, whereas I was very interested in physics as a subject.

I came to like physics in high school, and it took special circumstances to get me properly introduced to the subject. Even though our high

---

*Tahani was interviewed in Arabic in August 1989. The account was updated by letter. I asked Tahani to tell me about her life and university education.

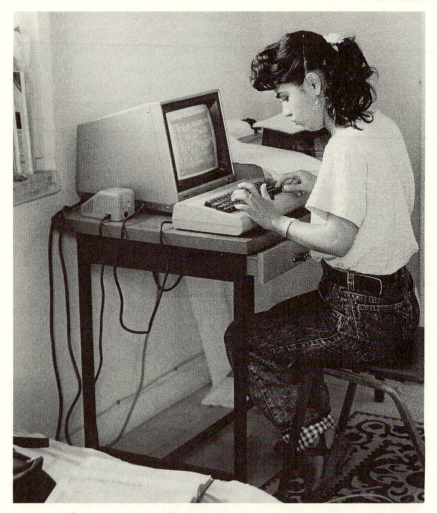

Tahani Ali in a makeshift classroom, a house Birzeit University rented to continue some classes after the closure of the university, now in its fourth year. Photo by Orayb Najjar

school had a reputation for being the best in the district, our physics teacher was not teaching in her area of expertise and was not doing a good job. Then the Israelis closed our high school down, and a university student majoring in physics gave us remedial lessons and showed us how exciting physics can be if explained well.

I think I chose to study science because we live in an age where we need to shun romanticism and use our logical faculties. My university career, however, was anything but logical, and was as turbulent as the political situation. Because of repeated university closures, my first semester was extended from four months to eight, and the university was closed several times before the Intifada. With repeated closures, it was difficult to start studying again whenever the university reopened. I was afraid of expecting a normal semester, afraid of putting all my energy into studying for fear of getting disappointed again with yet another closure.

I entered Birzeit University in October 1983, and I still have not graduated in 1991. As science students, we were at a disadvantage even when our department tried to make up for classes. For example, when the Israeli authorities closed down the new campus for a total of three months in 1984 and 1985, we had no access to our physics labs there. So while the arts students took regular classes at the old campus and in other buildings, we took only the theoretical part of physics, and all of the science students were given incompletes with the understanding that those grades will be removed after the completion of lab work.

We thought the closures that ran one, two, or three months were long, but when the Israeli authorities closed the university this last time during the uprising, we felt that the open-ended closure was a disaster. Indefinite closure is psychologically debilitating because it put our future on hold. It is bad enough that, for many university students in other fields, jobs are scarce and the future does not look bright. But with no graduation in sight, the future looks even more bleak.

After the last closure, I went through a period of depression. Despite all my resolutions about trying to be self-motivated, I found it difficult to study on my own. It is hard to sit with a book when the Occupied Territories are going through an upheaval of this magnitude, when people are getting killed, injured, or imprisoned every day. Study needs a certain peace of mind, a feeling of normalcy, and occupation and repression are not normal states of affairs. We needed help to concentrate, we needed to feel there was some kind of structure in our lives. The decision of Birzeit University to continue teaching despite the military order forbidding it to do so helped raise student morale.

There is no regular university where students gather. The campus, closed by military order, is deserted, and the town of Birzeit looks like a ghost town. The walls of the town are covered with slogans, and shops are closed most of the day because of the strike. But Birzeit University has rented a number of houses in the nearby town of Ramallah and is using them as classrooms. Classes are kept small; only seven students are supposed to be taught at one time to avoid drawing attention to the buildings. But our makeshift university has given me a push and has made me work quite hard, even harder than I worked when I was at the university. I think crisis brings out the best in people. Because only a few of us are supposed to be here at any one time for fear of Israeli crackdowns, I can spend more time on the computer and work more closely with our professors, whether they are Arab or foreign. Today, for instance, I am working with Dr. Mike Sealey, an American who is working extremely hard with us, putting in extra time to make sure we go over what we have missed. Dr. Sealey's efforts, and the efforts of other teachers, have made me regain confidence in other human beings and in my own abilities. At the university, some professors seemed remote and inapproachable, but because we have fewer students now, and because we are working in a small area rather than in lecture halls, our professors are spending more time with each of us, and so we have the chance to get to know them, as well as other students, better. We all feel that we are in this together and that we have to make it work. It appears that the more determined Israelis are to stop us from educating ourselves, the more we feel the need to study.

Without a campus, the university cannot of course offer all the classes students need, but as time passes, more subjects are being offered. For example, last summer I was taking two courses; in January 1990, I took three courses and a seminar. I now feel that I am making progress towards my degree.

Comparing notes with other students, I can say that we are now serious about our study because professors are willing to risk arrest for our sakes. My days are busy. I leave my village of Burham at 7:00 A.M. to be at our makeshift university by 7:40 A.M.

Although I was born in Jerusalem, I lived in the villages of Burham and Birzeit when I was a child. We lived in Birzeit to enable my mother to teach in town without having to hassle with irregular public transport between Burham and Birzeit. But after we bought a car, and after water and electricity came to Burham, we felt we could move back to our village by the end of 1980; after all, we owned a house and some land there.

Like other villages, our small village of 250 has experienced the uprising firsthand. When Israeli authorities closed all schools in the West Bank, we set up education committees to help the thirty to thirty-five students in our village, the way university students helped us when our high schools were closed. I taught science to fifth graders, math and science to ninth graders, and Arabic to high school students. Some children really enjoyed our type of school. One fifth grade girl kept following me around after classes. She said she wished I were her regular teacher and added, "Why don't you become a doctor, so that if I become sick, you can cure me." She wanted me to be everything to her.

Because my mother teaches at the Birzeit Preparatory Girls School and my father is the principal at the Burham Elementary School, volunteers turned to them for help. My parents gave us tips on teaching and advice on visual aids. While teaching science, I decided to venture into practical first aid. I asked the children if anyone had recently been stung by a scorpion, a common occurrence in villages. It turned out that one of the children's brother had been stung the day before. So I asked, "What did your mother do?" and we went from there to talk about fact and fiction in treating bites. I tried to make my teaching interesting, but I emerged from the experience with added respect for teachers and felt that specialization is really needed to transmit knowledge. So even though we did what we could for the children, we realized how much they were missing by staying out of school for so long. I would like to teach physics when I graduate. I think I am lucky I chose this field. Unemployment is rife, but scarcity in the field will enable me to work—besides, I enjoy the subject.

The closure of the schools hurt people educationally and financially. My father was placed on half salary when his original salary was barely sufficient for us to start with.[2] My mother works for UNRWA, and because of the drop in the rate of the Jordanian dinar, her salary dropped to 60 percent of its value. And here I am, eager to help support the family, not knowing when I will graduate. Even with two wage earners, our finances are tight, and I have no idea how refugees with occasional employment cope.

In addition to the disruption of school during the Intifada, we had to deal with regular Israeli attacks on our village. The Israeli Captain Maher calls us "Mushaghibeen" (troublemakers); we prefer to think of ourselves as merely active. The Israeli authorities have tried to turn some of our villagers into collaborators, but were unsuccessful. We discovered a collaborator from the nearby village of Kobar. The man was taken to the mosque where he gave up his weapons, admitted that he was a collaborator, and repented. After the confrontation with the former collaborator, Israeli soldiers raided our village, and when they did not find the young men they were looking for, soldiers entered some homes and poured rice sacks into sugar sacks, ruining both. During the search, soldiers also used foul language and cursed women.

The authorities have resorted to collective punishment against us. Two young women, Kifah Yusef and Khulud Abdul Rahman, wanted to study nursing in socialist countries, but they were refused permission to leave the Occupied Territories. Some young men were not given "good conduct" papers that would allow them to go to Jordan. Israelis also forbade anyone from the village from going to Jordan starting from the beginning of the Intifada until nine months ago. Then there was the war of slogans.

Wherever you go, the walls are covered with slogans listing the dates of strikes and encouraging people to resist occupation. On one of the walls someone had written "Long Live the Intifada." Israeli settlers came and wrote instead, "The Intifada is dead and buried. Long live Israel," and they also wrote something in Hebrew and drew a star of David on our wall. As you can imagine, the writing was immediately painted over, but the star of David was left intact, and next to it someone wrote "= Hitler."

We do not have many means of resistance at our disposal, but we are boycotting Israeli products. We have one small grocery in our village, and if you go there, you will see only local products.[3] Before the Intifada, I used to care about nice clothes. Now we all think of money differently; we donate money because we realize there are people who are much worse off than we are. When women's committees set a target of five thousand sweaters for prisoners, every house in the village started knitting; we contributed two sweaters.

Our village also got involved in agricultural work. The neighborhood committees distributed chicken, seeds, and saplings. We used chickens for fresh eggs, and we tilled our land. We planted okra, cucumbers, tomatoes, beans, and mulukhia. Because we are a large family, the garden could not satisfy all our needs; besides, water is expensive, and you need careful planning to make a garden cost effective. Some plants did not do well; yet, that garden meant a lot to us psychologically. All villagers planted, and having a garden became a symbol of resistance, a sign of our belonging to the Palestinian nation, a way of returning to our roots as farmers, a way of getting in touch with the land. It is strange how one thing leads to another. The Intifada changed my whole belief system.

Things that were distant before became almost necessities. I find myself searching for my roots. I've been wearing Western dress all my life, but for the first time I started thinking of making an embroidered Palestinian national dress. I have also reexamined my own taste and reevaluated my real needs. I used to collect earrings, and I own about eighty or ninety of them. I no longer buy them; I also no longer buy perfume. My priorities have changed and so has my outlook. I used to try to live normally because I wanted to forget about long-term occupation, as if it is something that will go away if you ignore it. Now we all realize that we have a role in ending that occupation, and not buying Israeli goods is the least we can do. At first I looked at Israeli goods on Jaffa street in Jerusalem but did not buy them, but now I have stopped going there to shop. I feel terribly out of place in the Israeli section of Jerusalem. I see soldiers and remember what they do to people, so I shop only on the Arab side of Jerusalem. We need to support our own factories; even though our merchants have distribution problems, we should help by seeking out Palestinian products.

The Intifada created a sense of solidarity among people. There is a sense of excitement at the unfolding events. There is no illusion that it is going to be easy to get rid of the occupation, but now we have hope and feel there has been some movement. The walls tell the whole story. On every special occasion, we are greeted with photos of Yaser Arafat or George Habash on electricity poles, and believe it or not, people have managed to hoist flags on tall cypress trees. Once soldiers came at night and looked for slogans, books, and clothes and forced us to show them all our papers, including private papers. With the occupation, you feel that there is no sanctity to any home. One night Israeli soldiers came while we were all asleep, and when we did not open our door immediately, they pulled off our outside gate and rushed in. I was dreaming and woke up feeling disoriented, and I was terrified when I opened my eyes and found soldiers in my bedroom. I was in my nightgown. After they left, I put my robe on, and that night slept with it on. From then on, my robe was like my security blanket. I had to have it close to my bed in case of another intrusion.

People have different reactions to the same event. When my eighteen-year-old sister Jumana, who shares the room with me, woke up to the soldiers, she looked at them with all the contempt she could muster and then turned her back to them and faced the wall.

Israeli soldiers use devious means to enter villages undetected by the youths who guard every locale. Soldiers simply expropriate Palestinian cars and tell their owners to come pick them up at the police station a few hours later; then they disguise themselves with the Kufiyas (the Arab headdress) and use Arab cars with the blue license plates to enter villages. No matter how they get in, the way soldiers treat people is atrocious. Once I was in the house of a woman whose son was wanted. Soldiers came and turned the house upside down and hit Umm Shakib, the mother of the young man they were looking for. The five-year-old child in the family wet herself out of fear. Soldiers finally picked the son up and took him away in a helicopter. The family was incredulous when it received a bill for the helicopter ride! What kind of mind will send you a bill for imprisoning your son? One does not know whether to laugh or cry on such occasions.

During one of their searches, soldiers found rubber bullets collected by children as souvenirs. I was amazed at how upset the soldiers were to find them. I do not understand how Israeli occupation authorities think. They want to hit you and break you, but do not want you to tell anyone, as if the rubber bullets found by the villagers on the ground and collected as evidence of the thick firepower is evidence against us and not them.

My eight-year-old brother Maher used to be scared every time soldiers came, but with time, he started to react differently. "Take me with you to the Naqab prison," he would say, because there were young men there he knew. When soldiers asked, "Are there young men in your house?" Maher would say, "No, come right in and search," instead of cowering behind one of us, as he did earlier. One soldier was so annoyed by Maher's chatter and seeming nonchalance that he shouted "Shut up!" He is not the same young boy he was at the start of the Intifada. We have all changed— irrevocably.

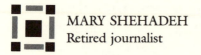

MARY SHEHADEH
Retired journalist

Born in 1901 to an educated family that encouraged her to write, Mary Shehadeh met her husband, editor Boulos Shehadeh, through the articles she sent to his paper. Boulos encouraged her to write for his newspaper and for radio. Mrs.

Mary Shehadeh in her home in Ramallah, 1985. Photo by Orayb Najjar

Shehadeh also lectured all over Palestine. She was the first woman to speak to an all-male audience in Gaza, and she was the first Arab woman to lecture in Jaffa in 1931. Here, she discusses her career that spanned twenty of the most turbulent years of Palestinian history. She also talks about her public-speaking activities and her involvement in the women's movement.

I have had two schools in my life—my father and my husband.* I was born in Jaffa on December 28, 1901, the eldest of seven children. My father taught Arabic, French, and Greek at the Greek Orthodox school in town. I loved reading, and my father encouraged me by pulling out books from his extensive collection and saying, "Now that you are ten years old you are old enough to read these." So I always grew up knowing that there was a difference between formal education and real learning.

Father, Sarrouf Spiridon Wahbeh, worked for *Al-Akhbar* newspaper in Jaffa. Even as a child, I had access to magazines and newspapers published in different Arab countries whose journalism was more developed than ours. I think I was about fourteen years old when Mary Ajami, the owner of *The Bride,* a women's magazine in Syria, saw something I had written and asked me, through my father, to contribute to her magazine. I sent her an article about my impressions of my first visit to Syria. She published my contribution and wrote me a letter in which she said, "You have talent, and you will have a bright future." Her encouragement meant a great deal to me; people cannot build themselves alone and need support, and I was lucky to get it.

My mother, one of the few women in her age group with a high school diploma, also encouraged me to read and study, but she wanted me to learn to embroider, too, and taught me herself.

Father was planning to send me to medical school in Greece after I graduated from high school, but when World War I broke out, he was drafted into the Turkish army. In 1915, the Ottomans ordered the evacuation of the Jaffa area, so our family moved to Damascus. Conditions were harsh. We sold our jewelry and then our clothes to buy food. Our situation did not improve until my father deserted from the Turkish army and

*The excerpts from Mrs. Shehadeh's writings as well as some of the details of her life were taken from a paper titled: "Mrs. Mary Shehadeh: A Biography," written by Laila Faik Mir'ea in 1984. I interviewed Mrs. Shehadeh at her house in Ramallah in 1985. Mrs. Shehadeh used Arabic and English. I asked her to tell me about her life and work in journalism. I wrote her story from my notes. I also corresponded with her son, attorney Fuad Shehadeh, 26 March 1990, who provided me with some news clippings about his mother's lectures.

took us back to Palestine. We still could not return to Jaffa, however, because of the British blockade of the port. The family remained in Nablus for six months in a one-room house and slept on borrowed mattresses. Mother and I earned some money by selling our embroidery. And although our income was low, we were better off than we were in Syria. When we returned to Jaffa, we found our house totally stripped of furniture. Our trees and vines also suffered from three years of neglect in our absen.

By the time I was nineteen, the schools that were closed for the duration of World War I reopened. That gave me the opportunity to teach Arabic and English in the mornings and sewing and embroidery in the afternoon at St. Joseph's School in Jaffa.

In 1919 a newspaper appeared in Jerusalem, "Meraat Al Sherk" [*sic*] (*Mirror of the Orient*).¹ In 1921, the paper introduced a column called "The Pens of Ladies" which ran articles by pioneers in the women's movement such as Asma Toubi and Kudsiyyeh Khursheed, and it also solicited contributions from readers. My father drew my attention to the articles. Father would say, "Look! Look! You can do better than that. You should send in an article."

I started writing, and the owner of the newspaper, Boulos Shehadeh, liked my articles so much that whenever I was slow to write, he would write urging me to continue. About three years after I sent my first article, Boulos decided he wanted to meet me. At first, he was under the impression that I was my father's sister and so thought that I was much older than I was. My father asked me to write and tell Boulos who I was. Boulos then asked the principal of my alma mater, the Friends' Girls' School in Ramallah, about me. He also wanted to know whether my father would mind a visit from him. The principal told him that I used to be one of her best students and that I graduated from high school at age fifteen. She also said she did not think that my father would object to the visit. Boulos came to our house and asked me to write for every issue. Soon after we met, we realized that we had a great deal in common. Boulos said, "This is the woman I want." He asked an Arabic teacher, Hanna Salah, to intercede with my family. When Boulos asked for my hand, Father at first did not approve. Boulos was a widower with two children and was born in 1883. Father wanted me to consider the age difference, and the fact that Boulos was nineteen years older than I meant that he was bound to die before I did. I said, "Look, ages are in the hands of God. A young man may die in an accident any day." Father was not swayed by my argument, but finally said that since I was so sure of my choice, he would not stand in my way.

We were married in 1923. My marriage opened up new horizons for me, mainly because we moved to Jerusalem, which was the center of intellectual, social, and political activity in Palestine. Our social life was busy, and our house was like a literary school. Writers and journalists from all over the Arab world visited us, and just listening to their dinner conversations was in itself educational.

Once we invited Mahmoud Azmi and Khalil Mutran, two Egyptian journalists to dinner. That same evening, my husband's older and more conservative brother came to visit. When he saw that I was ready to join the guests, he took me aside and said, "I see that you are all dressed up and prepared to sit with the guests. It is not customary for a woman to sit with the men at the table." I told him that I would just serve the food and leave. When Boulos heard of his brother's advice he was quite upset and said, "This is none of his business. Whose wife are you anyway?" and made me sit at the head of the table despite my protest that there was no need for us to upset his brother.

Boulos and I had two children, Fuad and Najla, in addition to Mary and Aziz from his first wife. When the children were young, I raised them myself although I hired help for the house. I worked at the paper whenever I could. But when the children got older, I placed Fuad, Najla, and Mary in boarding school in Bethlehem and went to the paper almost daily. I was responsible for selecting materials from foreign newspapers and magazines; I also chose articles for publication from the contributions of our readers from all over Palestine, especially from Jenin and Nablus. From time to time, I wrote articles myself.[2]

I was extremely interested in the question of women mainly because of my belief that the status of women determines the status of a whole society. On November 14, 1925, I published a call in *Meraat Al Sherk* that was titled, "A suggestion that I hope will be taken." In it I called for the formation of women's societies to help the needy. I said that it was shameful that Egyptian and Syrian women had formed societies ahead of us, and I suggested holding a bazaar to help famine-stricken people in Syria. The response to my call was good, and so I wrote again and suggested that a few influential women I named could get together and discuss the formation of a society. Although we always announced these activities in the newspapers as charitable in nature, we were determined to discuss politics but could not advertise that because we needed a license from the Mandate government to operate any society.

We deliberately called the committee the Committee of Arab Women because up to that point, the societies in operation were divided along religious lines. We wanted to get Christian and Moslem women to work together, and we succeeded.

We held our meetings in Jerusalem. We later changed our name to the Society of Arab Women. I toured the country and gave speeches to women's gatherings, and we formed societies in Nazareth, Jaffa, and Acre. I was also elected to the executive committee of the Women's Congress in Palestine in 1929.[3] Our newspaper took great interest in the proceedings and reported our demands in great detail.

Although as a teenager I was always called upon to give speeches welcoming visitors to our school, I was very nervous about speaking to the general public. I was once invited to give a speech to the Gaza Youth Club. At first I refused because it was an all-male audience and I would be the only woman in the room, but my husband urged me to accept. In those days, few men wanted women to do any public speaking both because it was not "proper" and because some men did not want women to upstage them, but my husband was always there, telling me I could do it. It was not easy though. I was sweating and so nervous I could hardly see the page. Because of the nationalist content of the speech, the audience clapped very hard. By the time I spoke to the Haifa Literary Club, I was more relaxed.

I got into trouble over the speech immediately (see Excerpt I). The British governor of Jerusalem, Ronald Storrs, phoned me and warned me not to give any political speeches. He said, "If you do not close your mouth we will send you to the Seychelles Islands. . . . I am not joking, I mean what I say." The British government also sent a memo to its employees (including my brother-in-law) warning them not to attend any of my speeches. Oh, what a pity. The country of Palestine was lost; its people were lost!

My husband tried to salvage what he could by being active in the "Defense Party" whose motto was "take, and then demand more," but we were attacked for our position, and look where our refusal to salvage what we could has gotten us.

The British warning against political speeches was effective. When members of the Haifa Literary Club invited me to speak to them, they asked me not to talk about politics. I started my speech by saying how amused I was because some people thought I was a politician. So I said that I was going to speak about politics—the politics of the family (see Excerpt II).

In my view, the mother is the primary care giver in the family. She is a school to her children. I used to write criticizing women who allowed their maids to raise their children.

My ideas about higher education for women have changed over the years. When I was fresh out of high school, I believed that a woman did not need higher education because if she gets too attached to a career, she will neglect her children. If she studies and stays in the kitchen, that is also a waste. Why have a career you cannot pursue? However, from my own experience and from observing others, I noticed that housewives do not necessarily spend their time with their children, but waste it visiting or gossiping. I thought that perhaps it is better for them to get a university education and work outside the home. But, in all circumstances, a woman should not neglect her home. If she is a good manager, she can take care of career and home. I hate the idea of men helping with the housework except in extreme circumstances. If a man has free time he should concentrate on his career. Instead of helping with the dishes he should read books or articles pertaining to his career. If he is a doctor, he should spend time reading medical books. Housework would consume valuable time. If a woman is a lawyer, it would help if she married one; if she is a nurse, it would help if she married a doctor because she would understand his work and help him.

A woman can have free time if she is organized. She does not have to clean the whole house every day. She should set aside one day for heavy cleaning. If she wants to work outside the home part time, she can manage. If it is full time, she should hire help, although now it is difficult to find help who can clean the house as well as they used to in the old days.

In my time, there was a great intellectual chasm between men and women. Because women were not allowed to obtain an education, men felt superior to them. Today, the chasm between the sexes has narrowed. He's educated, she's educated. He understands, she understands. I know a young female lawyer, Mona Rishmawi, who worked for my son who is a lawyer. He believes she is very clever. Mona's case set me to thinking about equality. When she gets married, it would be a pity if she worked only in the home. She and her husband would have to hire help. In contrast, take the situation of my own mother. She was intelligent, well read, and had a high school diploma, yet Father did not even want her to leave the house to buy groceries. He liked to spare her the hustle and bustle of the marketplace and bought everything for her, including her embroidery thread. Today, women's movement is not restricted the way it used to be thirty or forty years ago.

I myself depended a great deal on the encouragement of my husband. It was he and Ajjaj Nuwaihed, the director of the Palestine Broadcasting Service, who urged me to write for radio in 1941. At first, Ajjaj said, "Since your husband has no time to write, why don't you write a foolscap page of five minutes of radio air time, and if I like it, I will give you a regular slot." I did, and the five minutes were increased to ten, then to fifteen by the third year of radio work because we received a lot of letters. The item that drew most comment and discussion was called, "In the West, marriage is a beginning; in the East, it is an end." That program dealt with the exorbitant amounts of money required for marriage and for furnishing houses. I got the idea for that item from observing a Jewish friend of mine. She was a dentist from Britain and had rented a room that she used as a clinic during the day. At night, her couch doubled up as a bed. I compared her attitude to that of women who feel they had to have big houses and show them off. One listener wrote, "This is a new kind of literature we have never heard before. We want more programs of this nature." Others asked for the program to be repeated, and a few objected to what I had said. I also wrote a number of programs on child care.

Today, I listen to the radio and I am not impressed with the kind of programs that masquerade as talk shows. The material is not well researched, and the ideas are shallow. I used to read two to three hours in preparation for each segment.

Today's journalism is no better either. We get complimentary copies of daily newspapers and I read them all. Newspapers lack the depth that used to characterize papers in the twenties or thirties. Perhaps the paucity of materials can be attributed in part to the strict Israeli censorship that Palestinian papers are subjected to; when journalists tell me about their experiences today, I realize that even though we had heavy British censorship in our time, Israeli censorship is more severe.

My dear husband died in 1943. I could not bring myself to write, lecture, or work in radio. I was drawn out of my seclusion only once by a very dear friend who begged me to give a speech at the women's society in Bethlehem in 1945 on Mothers' Day. In that speech, I said:

> I have often read material by famous contemporary writers about women, and it invariably starts with this expression: "Women have an important role in society." As if those writers, God forgive their sins, believe that society consists only of men. . . . I would like to remind these writers that without women, the world walks on legs of dough.

When the Arab-Israeli war of 1948 broke out my son Fuad and I were traveling on the Jerusalem-Ramallah Road when we were shot. Fuad was wounded in the shoulder, and I was wounded in the thigh and in my lower arm. Because the bullet entered one way and came out the other, I lost part of the bone, and I lost most of the mobility in my lower arm. So after that, writing was physically difficult. But even psychologically it was hard to write because we led unsettled lives after the war. We moved to Amman in the fifties and then returned to Ramallah where we are living now.

When you look at the period we were living in, and the historical events we have witnessed, you will realize that we have not had an easy life. We have lived under Turkish, then British, then Jordanian, and now under Israeli rule. But we always tried to do the best we could.

I think people must be guided by one motto: "Enjoy whatever you do." If you eat, do so with pleasure; if you sleep, relax and enjoy it; if you do a job—any job—try to immerse yourself in it. But I think the secret of a happy life is finding a career that suits you, one that you commit yourself to. I was lucky I found a career and found people to encourage me to pursue it. A woman needs a man to depend on, and I have lost that man, and that is why when Boulos died I could not write or lecture.

I lived with Boulos for twenty years. They were happy years. My time with him passed as if it were a single year.

Excerpt I: *Speech believed delivered in 1931 at the Gaza Youth Club*

In this town which is ravaged by war that turned it upside down, in this eternal city that armies from many nations and tongues could not vanquish, . . . stands an Arab woman, for the first time in the history of the city, standing on the podium, raising her voice high in a gathering full of men, . . . to salute those gentlemen who invited me to speak because they are the sons of people whose name was recorded in history as an example of intellectual development that has accompanied human beings from the time of creation until today–that development which no nation can last without in the field of struggle. . . . If I come up short, gentlemen, please forgive me; we women are still at the beginning of our modern revival, and the reason is that men wanted us to be weak, and that weakness, which men have caused unintentionally, was the cause of weakness in the whole nation.

The nation, gentlemen, is composed of two pillars, a man and a woman; if a woman is weakened, so is man; if she is strengthened, so is he, and they cooperate to reach the greater goal every nation that is struggling aims for, glory for eternity, honor, independence, and freedom.

Gentlemen, the Arab countries have never needed in any single day of their history the efforts of their men and women as they do in these days when we see all nations competing in the field of nationalism to ensure their existence in the journey of nations. . . . In this age where brother is against brother, . . . a cannon needs to be met with a cannon, a sword with a sword, an army needs an army, money needs money, and learning needs learning . . . [mentions looming danger of enemies "who want to devour these holy lands of our forefathers"]. . . . Who of you is content with the condition Palestine has come to, politically, economically, or socially? If anyone is content with this situation he is no son of Palestine, because Palestine does not carry slaves on its soil . . . and a free man is one who sacrifices for his country, and always repeats what the poet said,

Biladi wa in Jarat alayya Azizatun,
Waahli wa in Dannu alayya Kiramu.
(My country, even if it mistreats me is dear
And my family, even if it withholds things from me is generous.)

. . . If you want to serve your country, place before your eyes that your country is a sacred trust from your fathers and forefathers, so you should hand it over to your children and grandchildren, and if you come up short, know that the soul of those heroes that opened up this country with their blood will be displeased with you from the world of eternity, and it will say: "Great ancestors, but lousy progeny." You cannot reach your goal as long as the seeds of disunity and corruption are everywhere. . . . He who seeks glory stays up nights, and when I say "stays up," I do not mean in coffee houses, casinos, or bars with billiard tables or with gambling, but between books and papers, studying languages that allow you to stand among other nations, . . . and teaches you perseverance and hard work.

One of the many duties of a young man to his country is to be independent and full of initiative because a country cannot be revived by dependent citizens. . . . A young man . . . with a free Arab spirit refuses to be enslaved or humiliated by other nations . . . and the young man who depends on others to free his country for him will not see independence with his own eyes, because independence is always taken and never given. . . . I call upon our youth to rebel against old worn-out customs if they stand in their way. . . . Renewal will not be possible without calling white white, and black black. . . .

We women like only the man with a strong will and a great spirit and unending ambition. We do not like to see our young men bewail their luck, complain about the times. . . . A man with a strong determination creates his own luck. . . . The people of the United States said they wanted to be independent, and they fought the greatest nation on earth until they gained their independence. The will of Washington gave America its independence. The will of Mustapha Kamal kicked out the Greek armies and the allies from his country and created new Turkey. If you want a new Palestine for us, all you have to have is determination. . . . The country needs you. . . . Long live will and long live strength. . . . [You] must not be content with slavery, colonialism, poverty, and ignorance. . . . Poor countries have no place under the sun. The struggle between nations today is nothing but economic struggle so that each nation can gather as much as it can [suggests hard work to make the country richer]. . . .

Let's go forward. Forward . . . for the sake of Arab nationalism . . . forward for the independence of our country, yes forward, so that we can see the day when our Arab flag, which has flown over most known lands, is flown over these parts. I hope this thriving club which includes most of the youth of Gaza will stamp out bigotry and every obstacle that stands in the way of the development of this country. I hope that the club will always call for unity between Arab Moslems and Christians, and that youth will rise to the highest level and walk towards freedom, towards glory to the ranks of eternal heroes.

Excerpt II: *Speech read before the Haifa Literary Club,*
13 November 1932

Ladies and gentlemen, when a delegation . . . came to me to ask me to
speak before this club, the first thing they warned me about was not to
talk about politics. . . . It appears that members of the club . . . were
misled by what newspapers wrote about me. But I would be the first to
tell you, even though my husband is a journalist, that newspapers do not
tell the truth most of the time. My husband is going to criticize me bit-
terly tonight for saying this. . . . To tell the truth I do not understand
politics. Men who are highly educated . . . are still children in politics, so
what about women who have not yet started their intellectual lives.
Believe me, the disasters that are now upon us have come by way of politics. I am ashamed to say that the rich among us is a politician, the poor
among us is a politician, the worker is a politician, and so is the student.
Wherever you go, you hear people speak as if our ambassadors are all over
Europe and the U.S., . . . as if our planes were so numerous that they
have no place to land. . . . But my speech tonight is political. . . . This
afternoon, my words will not be about politics as people understand it,
but it will still not depart from politics. Which politics? Not the politics
of the Mandate or the Balfour Declaration, not the politics of total independence or valiant death, . . . or not the policy of "take, and then
demand more" that my dear husband invented. . . . I will discuss the politics of the family, the politics of family structure, the politics of married
life. Such politics, I believe, is the basis for building civilizations and
nations, the foundations for real independence, the basis for nationalism,
the basis for freedom, equality and immortality. If the masses call, "Long
live the country," I call, "Long live the family." If they call, "Long live
political independence," I call "Long live economic independence."

In Palestine these days, we find a nation of orators. Every week, a gathering is held in one of the towns where orators compete . . . and vie with
one another in the field. . . . As if this were not enough, I have also been
thrust among the male speakers (I beg God's forgiveness [in jest]) and
female speakers. Every time I visit a town, its club asks me to speak. And
why? So that it be said that women too are partners in this political awak-
ening. . . . But ladies and gentlemen, our cause is not a matter of lectures
in clubs, or protests in newspaper columns. The future of our families
does not depend on these protests, or on speeches or speech makers, but
on marriage in which the soul of a man and woman meet in understanding. . . . The happiness we seek is in our homes . . . we clap in admira-
tion . . . for a male or female speaker but it does . . . no good to the

domestic bliss that we seek. . . . Happiness will not enter houses if the family connection is disjointed. . . . A philosopher said that if we can solve the problem of the family, we can solve the problems of the world. . . . A number of philosophers from Plato, to St. Augustine, to Erasmus, to Karl Marx, to Bernard Shaw tried to tackle that problem, but despite their noble ideas, they could not do so satisfactorily. . . . Today's family is different from yesterday's, and the family of the twentieth century is different from the family of the nineteenth.

And the most important source for friction within the family is what we call mental incompatibility between a man and a woman. . . . Let me give you an example of what I mean. A man might see a woman and is taken by her beauty, he thinks of nothing else, he asks for her hand without knowing anything about her habits, manners, and nature. After the month they call the honeymoon, her real nature begins to emerge, and he finds that she is in one valley and he is in another. He might like to save, she might like to waste. She might be tidy, he might prefer confusion. He might like to read and she might prefer playing cards . . . he might like her to wear simple clothes, and she might like fashion from the modern city. A woman might like her husband to spend his time at home, and he might like to spend his time outside the house. . . . What kind of family and what kind of affection can survive all those contradictions? How can we get communication? . . . Can a young man and woman test for it before marriage? [Suggests that it can be to a certain extent, but that it is hard to find out because each partner appears at his/her best during courtship, so she stresses compromise.] How can it be achieved given the fact that neither man nor woman is an angel? If a man wants a woman to be perfect he won't find one, and if a woman wants a perfect man, she will not find one except in Plato's Republic, and we are not there yet. . . . [Suggests compromise so that partners can help each other in this troubled world.] Man, do not think that a woman was born a slave at home. Woman, do not think that a man was born to slave for you, to work so that you can splurge on whatever you like. . . . [Suggests tailoring income to need and not imitating others when you cannot afford it.] . . . If a certain employee, for example, can have whisky in his house and can travel to Europe every year, and his suit costs ten pounds, and he smokes the best cigar, why should you, a simple employee whose salary does not enable you to act like him, imitate him, with the result that you will lose your future. Yes, the needs of life are many, gentlemen, but the wise person can do without many of them . . . intellectual civilization is not the same as material civilization, which by itself cannot make a happy family. [Quotes an Arabic poem about imitation.] . . . The reason for this misfortune [that results from blind imitation] is the great intellectual difference between men and women. Men were educated before women, and the number of educated men far exceeded the educated women by ten to one. This is not women's fault because male schools were more numerous and better equipped than female schools. Take a man who had higher education, and a woman who is almost illiterate. The joy of this man is reading, and she is involved with her clothes and makeup, so how can there be understanding between such a man and a woman? We are not asking that women be philosophers, but on the other hand we do not want a woman to be illiterate or semi-illiterate so that if a man talks to her, he would find some pleasure and happiness. . . . If educated males constitute 50 percent, the same proportion of women should be educated so that we will not have this great deep gap between men and women in the East. It is useless to call for political or economic independence . . . if the woman is weak, has no opinion of her own, and is unable to progress as times change. A nation is as strong as its women.

Woman, don't be ashamed of working in your home and taking care of your kitchen. The cause for the breakup of a number of homes is the neglect of the kitchen. I have read about many famous women who won millions who still spend time taking care of the kitchen every day. [Mentions an empress and a queen who were not ashamed to tend to the kitchen and warns against blind imitation of the West.]

And you, young man, you ask woman to fulfill her duty to you, but you also have duties you have to undertake for her sake. First of all, a woman has a soul, just like you, she can feel pain, so do not be hard on her, and just as you want to see her smiling, she wants to see you smiling too, she also does not want to see you spend your money on matters that do not benefit the family . . . and do not spend your nights away in taverns and bars. . . . If we want to imitate the West, why don't we imitate it in real civilization, persistence and perseverance, self-sufficiency, independence, and in valuing nationalism. . . . Woman, I direct this word to you, you are the only one who accompanies a man in all stages of his life . . . be the mother that inspires independence and the love of country in your child, the spirit of honor and sacrifice . . . teach him as a youth to shun worldly pleasures and to be a sincere nationalist, teach him to be the man of the future, and that he has a great responsibility towards his nation and his country.

WAFA AL-BAHER ABU GHOSH
Journalist

Wafa, unmarried and ambitious, dreamt of making something of herself—of becoming the minister of information of a Palestinian state. Wafa's marriage and her attempt to hold a full-time job and raise two children under the age of four have modified her ambition. She now longs for a job where she can control her time and discusses the frustration of writing features that do not pass Israeli nightly censorship.

23 April 1985

I had never planned to be a journalist.* I grew up wanting to be a lawyer, to be close to people and to defend their rights. I am not sure when I changed my mind. Maybe it was when my teacher praised my compositions, but I reasoned that advocacy journalism is the closest thing to practicing law.

When I announced my intention to study journalism at Yarmouk University in Jordan, my immediate family did not object to my career choice, but my sister's husband tried to talk me out of it and to convince my mother to advise me against it. He said, "Study Arabic language and you will have your life all planned out for you. You will be a teacher, and will know what you are expected to do, and your hours will be regular." I told him I couldn't imagine myself standing in front of a blackboard and that I've always wanted to have an exciting rather than an easy life.

My sister, his wife, is thirty-one years old and he is forty-two. I believe she has domesticated herself. She never leaves the house without him. As

---

*I interviewed Wafa on 23 April 1985 in Ramallah in Arabic, and the interview was taped. I asked Wafa to tell me about her life and then asked her specific questions about her work as a journalist. Very little editing was done to the first part of the interview. I updated the story when I visited Wafa's office in Jerusalem on 30 June 1989. In that interview, I asked Wafa about censorship of her work. I later visited her home, met her children, and asked her about her domestic life.

Wafa al-Baher Abu Ghosh researching an article in the house she shared with her mother in the Old City of Jerusalem, 1985. Photo by Orayb Najjar

time passed, she began to find her life normal. "Sometimes," he tells her, "I think I admire your sister more than you because she argues with me." But in truth, we don't just argue, we quarrel. We have more heated battles than the battles of Beirut on matters of principle, and we once stopped talking to each other for two years.

My father died three years ago, so I live with my mother, my brother, and his wife in a two-room house in the Old City of Jerusalem, just inside Jaffa Gate. My two brothers are quite progressive. One, an electrician who works in Saudi Arabia, urges me to go to graduate school, which I may yet do. The other is a tailor. He lives with us, does the same job as his wife, and shares housework with her. He reacts to my writing and suggests topics I could write on, and is proud of me. My mother is not educated, but she is quite reasonable and listens to good arguments. She believes that I should let my conscience act as a remote control unit. I leave the house to do investigative reporting and do not have to tell her where I am going—she trusts me.

After I graduated from the University of Jordan in Amman, I applied to most magazines and newspapers in East Jerusalem. Perhaps my expectations were too high, but I was shocked at the way I was treated. "Yes, fill out a form, we will call you." But they did not even have the courtesy to write to tell me I was rejected. They did not seem to understand that when lower middle-class families like mine invest in a college education for their kids, they sacrifice a great deal to make ends meet and are anxious to see their children established. Some of the men I met were all puffed up in their offices. They looked at me as if to say, "Who are you? Here we are with M.A.s and Ph.D.s and here you are, a mere recent graduate." I keep hearing, "Journalism needs fresh blood," but when fresh blood like me applies, older and more established journalists and administrators treat us like nobodies, instead of individuals with potential.

In most newspapers, there is something like a pyramid in administration, and when one applies for a job, people who have already found their niche in the paper are anxious to assign the newcomer a place in the scheme of things. While I was being interviewed, for instance, the owner of the newspaper asked if I would make a cup of coffee for my boss if asked. I said, "Definitely not." I explained that I had no objections to making coffee for my boss or for a colleague as a friend, but not as part of my job, and even then, if I were busy, I would expect them to do the same for me. The owner muttered something about the pyramid of administration, but the matter was dropped.

I was hired at *Al-Sha'ab* Arabic daily. There are few Palestinian women journalists working today, and most are not involved in investigative reporting. In some newspapers, women are not respected for their intellectual abilities. I once asked what a female journalist at another newspaper did. To my surprise, her colleague blurted out: "First and foremost she receives guests at the paper, then. . . . " He was talking about a woman with an M.A. degree in journalism, one who wrote articles even as a teenager! In my paper, I was relieved to discover that my colleagues are not sexist and deal with me as an equal.

The first salary I was offered was 40 Jordanian dinars (about $100) a month, although the Association of Arab Journalists has recommended 120 dinars as the absolute minimum pay. But even 120 dinars is not a living wage. Most of us in journalism are not in the business to make money. But we need a salary that begins to cover the expenses of our food and clothes. I have since bargained for 20 more dinars and I almost quit to get it. I felt I was in a good bargaining position because I was offered another job and could afford to stand firm.

When I write, I find myself drawn to social issues. For example, I reported on the Israeli attempts to shut down the Hospice, the only Arab hospital in the Old City of Jerusalem, because the subject concerns low-income families. My editor wants our paper to have a regular women's page, but I do not feel ready to tackle it. I feel that I am still training to be a good reporter. I am in the same position as a professor of mythology I have interviewed. He said he'd been working only on a small area of mythology, "Mythology in religion in the Bethlehem area," for ten years, and he's still "floating on the surface of mythology." If that is how this specialist feels, then I can say that I am still at the shores of investigative reporting. I see myself as slowly moving in the direction of writing about women, but not before I've broadened my knowledge of Palestinian society.

I hesitated about tackling the women's page for other reasons. To be credible, such a page needs to appear regularly and has to be fair to all women's groups. To do a good job, I need to meet women's committees in different locations. I do not own a car, and neither does my paper. Public transportation, especially to villages, is unreliable. I cannot afford to waste the whole day just to get a small item. It takes stamina to be a journalist here, and maybe eventually I'll start a women's page.

The Israeli occupation touches all facets of our lives. It affects the amount of effort journalists put into news items they report. Every journalist knows that it is useless to turn a news item about the release of a political prisoner into a human interest story, to see how his or her family fared in his or her absence. We censor ourselves because we know that every night, every single item, including advertisements, has to be shown to the Israeli censor. Reporters now have a formula for prisoner stories: "So and so was released from such and such a place after completing a sentence of X number of years"—end of item because that is all that will get by the censor.

The difficulty of getting decent political commentary published has resulted in the emigration of political analysts. This brain drain has provided Kuwait with a respectable number of editorial writers who emigrated there and left us with few analysts. Palestinian journalists flourish in the freedom allowed in Kuwait. They benefit from the ability to spend as much money as they need on a story, to travel wherever the story takes them, while Palestinian journalists in the Occupied Territories, in their own country, live from hand to mouth and see their editorials canceled regularly.

Because of the need to stand up to Israeli designs on us, a curious situation has developed where we don't have journalists in the full sense of the word; we have political cadres working in journalism. This is understandable: papers are the only means we have of reaching the masses. We do not have control over a radio or television station in the West Bank or Gaza, nor are we allowed to organize or hold public political meetings. Lack of unity between different groups has not been good for journalism. Until recently, what we had was a political map, and journalists were living on different parts of it. Each paper served a different political faction, and there was competition, but little communication, between them. Also, communication between journalists and readers was vertical. It was more like "information giving" and less like communication. The fact that few papers have regular letters to the editors exacerbated this problem. Our journalism needs a central planning authority. I do not want to sound as if I am a fan of centralization per se, but in developing countries, it is essential to draw up a communication policy, to institute guidelines for journalists, and to uphold journalistic standards; otherwise, underdeveloped countries will graduate underdeveloped professionals.

The establishment of the Association of Arab Journalists in the Occupied Territories in 1981 was a positive step. Through it, we are tackling our relations with the owners of the papers, our relationship to our readers, and our standards as professionals. The association is by no means perfect. There is still friction between political factions, but I believe that, in its own limited way, the association is playing the role of a Palestinian government. When I criticize friction between people with different political orientations I do not mean that I want everyone to have the same ideology. I just mean that our differences should be pushed into the background for the sake of the cause that unites us: working for an independent Palestinian state.

Women, of course, have a role in the creation of the state. When I see a Palestinian woman who has managed to obtain a Ph.D. or excel at a career, despite the obstacles placed before her by our patriarchal society, I consider her an exceptional person. I feel that the talent of a great num-

ber of Palestinian women has been underutilized. People's expectations of women, that their primary function in life is to be wives and mothers, leaves a deep impression on women and nips their ambition in the bud. Women spend their teenage years, and even their university years, dreaming about marriage. Those dreams impede women aspiring for fulfillment in careers.[1]

I hope that my own marriage will not affect my ambition. I got engaged in the summer of 1985. I am delighted that the engagement has not drastically changed my life; it has simply given me more freedom because my future is now more secure (in the traditional manner) and I can be left alone to pursue my career. One of my colleagues asked me whether my fiancé, Awni Abu Ghosh, was leftist or rightist. When I said "leftist," he said, "Then you are compatible." I found it refreshing that he did not ask whether Awni was rich or poor, but asked about the way he thinks—which is just as well, as Awni is totally broke and jobless!

Awni and I decided to marry when we were in high school. Then I went to college and he went to prison for five years for nationalist reasons. Frankly, I worried about how we would fit together after his release, but I was delighted to discover that he read voraciously and educated himself in prison, and that we still have a great deal in common. My mother seems like a quiet woman, but she can be stubborn if she wants to be. At first she did not approve of my relationship with Awni. She worried that Awni would find it difficult to support me. I made her understand that he is the only person I intend to marry and that I see our poverty as a passing phase that we will enjoy telling our children about. Awni is seriously talking to the editor of one paper about a job in journalism and I hope he gets it.

We are both relieved that the engagement ceremony is over. While Awni's family were officially asking mine for my hand, he was sweating so much you could wring out the handkerchief he was using to wipe his forehead. I was sitting there clenching my fists. When my family finally approved, he exclaimed that he never thought he'd live to see this day!

Awni tells me I can do anything I want to do. He says, "You are special, I am not important, and I will try to provide you with the atmosphere that will allow you to excel in your work." I hope that he continues to feel that way. I believe that you can evaluate a man by the way he reacts to women. I am just lucky that he was the boy next door and that he is the person who will share my life. I tell him that constantly.

One thing we are sure of: we are going to be poor for a number of years and we have to postpone our wedding until we can find a place to live. There is a problem of not having access to land in Jerusalem. The Israeli authorities make it hard for Palestinians to build there so it is hard to find an affordable place to live. We are both from Jerusalem and feel sentimental about the city, and would like to live here.

I like the city, and I like exploring places I have not been in before. Once I was doing a story and asked a woman of seventy for directions to get to a certain house. When she heard I was a journalist, she showed off her knowledge by reciting poetry. She then said, "I wish my family had not married me off at the age of eleven. I am intelligent, I would have been the minister of information. I made up for it by educating my children: one of my sons is a doctor, the other an engineer."

I have thought a lot about what she said. I too would like to have children when we can afford them, and I have rosy dreams for them. I read that a pregnant woman can even have an effect on her unborn child because it can hear music. But as I see it, my most important role as a mother will be to teach my child how to think, how to analyze. I live in a different time from that old lady. I do not have to live my life through my children. I have to make something of myself. I would like to be somebody important in the future. I too would like to be minister of information in a Palestinian state, and in time, I would like to write a book about the Palestinian experience.

You ask why I chose to be a journalist. I think it is because I love to talk!

Update: 1986

When Wafa's editor, Akram Haniyyeh, asked her to start a women's page, she was afraid of not being able to deliver it once a week by herself. Haniyyeh understood her concern for quality and hired another young reporter, Abla Ya'eesh, to work with her. The page was different from any other women's page in the Occupied Territories at that time. The two reporters and their editor decided that the Palestinian woman they were writing for and about was not the well-made-up or fashionably dressed self-involved woman other publications often portrayed; *Al-Sha'ab*'s woman was a hard worker and provider who did her share of work outside the home as a farmer, laborer, teacher, or professional. Each week, the paper examined a different locale, concentrating on the rural areas. "Women in Balata Refugee Camp" (3 June 1986) examined development in women's centers (literacy, child care, and basic services). Another regular item, "A Face from My Country," focused on women in nontraditional careers. The 18 February issue, for example, featured "Women as Engineers," the 13 May issue ran "Women as Dentists: Between the Sparkle of the Title, and the Problems of the Profession," the 3 June issue featured pharmacist Hania Shafi. A regular medical column discussed medical problems, often with women doctors, or introduced the readers to institutions run by women: "Fayzeh Zalatimo: A Success Story in Administering a Medical Lab" (20 May 1986). Although the women's page stressed the achievements of Palestinian women, it also exposed discrimination against them. A recurrent topic was the unequal treatment of male and female babies: "The Traditional Question Still Goes: Boy or Girl?" The article was subtitled: "But these days they are also asking 'how is the mother doing?' " Another hot topic is the high rate of female high school dropouts, good students who are forced to leave school to get married or to help around the house. On 13 May 1986, *Al-Sha'ab* ran "When the Mother Is Absent, the Oldest Girl Performs More Than One Role," an article critical of pulling the eldest daughter out of school to care for her siblings. *Al-Sha'ab* also covered topics of interest to college women, for example, "Finding a Room: An-Najah University Women Face a Chronic Problem" (25 February 1986).

Feminist women writing abroad were also given space on the women's page: e.g., a piece written by Ghada Samman, a Syrian writer, "The Tribe Interrogates Ghada Samman" appeared on 12 November 1985. On a less regular basis, the paper also published articles as well as statistics about women's struggles abroad, e.g., "Angolan Women's March" (5 November 1985).

Wafa left *Al-Sha'ab* and took a job with *Al-Bayader al-Siyasi*, a bimonthly magazine, in part because she found it hard to live on her salary. She no longer writes exclusively about women's affairs, and although other papers have women's pages, no paper has allowed its women's page editors to spend as much time on investigative reporting as Haniyyeh did.[2] As a result, many of the items on women's pages are assembled from other publications or from what reporters derisively call "Reporter Scissor."

30 June 1989

Practicing journalism during the Intifada has not been easy. Since November 1, 1988, twenty-five of my articles have been canceled by the Israeli censor. Censorship hurts. In a daily newspaper, if your work is not published one day, you see it on the next day. In a bimonthly magazine, when fourteen days go by and there is nothing, you feel as if you are unemployed. Even people who know you do not realize the extent of censorship and ask you, "Why have you not *written* anything lately?" I wrote an article about how women in the Dheisheh refugee camp were faring with the imposition of long curfews and with attacks from Israeli settlers—the article was completely censored. I wrote an article about the house General Ariel Sharon acquired in the Muslim Quarter of the Old City of Jerusalem. I felt qualified to explore the subject because I've lived in the Old City all my life, I know its every corner, I understand the dynamics of the place, and I know people there and can gauge how they feel. That article was censored. I wrote about Israeli attempts to take over the Arab Electricity Company in Jerusalem, but the whole article was censored with the exception of an interview with Mohammad Watad, a member of the Israeli Knesset. Running only that interview would have distorted content, so we did not run the article.

To avoid excessive censorship, we have to write in symbols. Sometimes those symbols work, and at other times they appear convoluted even to me when I reread the articles at a later date. For a while, we were not allowed to say "martyred"; we did not want to say "died" because a young person who is shot while resisting the occupation, say, while throwing stones, or writing slogans, is not simply dead—she or he died so that we can be independent, so we wrote things like "was lost" or "was united with the soil," or "his mother waited for him, but he did not return." We were and still are forced to resort to sentimental words that we are not quite happy with because we want to communicate that the death of that youngster is not to be considered normal.

The censor sometimes crosses out materials in a haphazard fashion. Sometimes he deletes words because he does not know what they mean. The censor once deleted the word "Duma" (dolls) which without accents resembles the word for "Dammi" (my blood); the censor also crosses out the most important segments of many stories. On Mother's Day, for instance, I wrote an article that was anchored on the theme of the mother of a prisoner who has visited and waited for her son for eighteen years. I also interviewed a number of other mothers. All the interviews were passed except the one about the prisoner's mother. I was left without a theme and without a structure. So censorship complicates the normal creative process, and you have to produce material for three issues to have enough for one.

During the Intifada, the national leadership has asked us in pamphlets to observe a general strike to show our rejection of the occupation. Newspapers and magazines have remained open, as they should, but that constitutes a heavy burden on employees because on many days, public transport is on strike, and many, like me, do not own private cars but are still required to be at work by nine. Sometimes, I stand in front of my house with my two children for fifteen to twenty minutes to catch a ride. We wait, and it is either too hot or too cold. The children fidget. I shudder when I think of their getting sick. As if the inconvenience is not enough, we pay exactly one-third of my salary for transport. My husband is progressive and educated, yet the minute we have difficulty with transportation he says, "Quit work, stay home." If this is how he feels, you can imagine what it is like for women married to conservative men.

My husband and I start the day by taking our two children to my mother or to his. So here we are, so-called "modern parents," yet we are forced to depend on the older generation to raise our children because the child care facility close to our house is full. Then I have shopping problems. Because of the strike, shops open from nine to noon only, and we get a half-hour break during that time. My life is stressful enough without being restricted to doing all my shopping in half an hour. On three or four days a month, everything is totally closed.

I used to have an idealized image of marriage and raising children, but both are more difficult than I had imagined. I think it is easier to chisel a rock with a needle, or use a shell to empty the ocean, than deal with children. I am now in awe of women who have six to twelve children. I find myself defending housewives when I hear someone calling traditional women ignorant. What do you expect? Just consider what it takes to prepare Arabic food for six to twelve children every day. Just think of what it takes to keep those children clean—just imagine the washing and ironing. Rural women have even harder lives than the rest of us because they also work in the field and may not have electricity or running water. Peasant women have two jobs but get no money for doing either, certainly not for farming. Working women in cities can at least have stimulating lives at work, but housewives with large families have few options.

Then, of course, there is the guilt. I cannot escape the feeling that, as a working mother away from my young girls most of the day, I do not do enough for them or spend enough time with them. Awni used to do a great deal of the housework before he went to work himself; now we often have disagreements over housework. I write three articles a week. I do most of the shopping and almost all of the housework and cooking. I realize that my husband is starting a new business, a news agency, and so needs to take time to develop it, but it does not solve my problem.

I also feel pressure of a different kind. I have two girls, and it is time to have "the boy." I have read about a kit that helps determine the sex of the baby. My sister had seven girls and three boys. Her husband, a pharmacist, would have been happy with fewer children, but she insisted on having that many even though all those pregnancies were hard on her emotionally and physically. I do not want to be in the same position she is in. I want to try for a boy but do not want more than four children. Older family members and one religious woman said to me that I should be content with God's will, and that I will have a boy if God wills it. But I said, what if it takes seven pregnancies? I tell skeptics that if one can, with logic and science, decrease the number of children, why not?

I am overworked. After putting in a whole day chasing interviews, I long to go home and relax, but I have to attend to the needs of two children under four. Sometimes I feel so exhausted I am tempted to quit work, so I stay at home for a day, and I go crazy. So I now feel that I am at a crossroads: if my husband's new press office starts making money I intend to do free-lance work; that way, I will be able to control my time. On the other hand, I know I will miss my work. Although there is some drudgery involved in some of the work I do, I find it challenging to convince sixty people to give me their political opinion on the phone in these tense times when people all around them are getting arrested. I have to talk to many more than sixty people to get sixty interviews, but getting this many is a test of my persuasive ability. I am also very proud of a couple of interviews I have conducted recently. I asked Faisal Husseini nineteen good questions and did not return home until eight. In all modesty, I believe that in my interview with Sufian al-Khatib, I asked very courageous and frank questions.[3]

I long for professional independence that allows me to do what I like best—writing. But at the same time, I want a larger measure of control of my working hours. I long for national independence, both because of the oppressive nature of our lives, and because I would like to write freely about Palestinian subjects. A journalist has a special place under an occupied press as well as in an independent state. I have no doubt that we will get our state. People cannot be oppressed for long. Look at other revolutions—Cuba, Vietnam, Namibia. We are now playing a waiting game with the Israelis.

A journalist said that our state is only a stone's throw away. I like that, even though I do not expect it to be easy to get a state. How soon we will get one will depend on how much we manage to "root" the uprising, and on how patient we are in accepting the many sacrifices that are yet to come.

SIX

Conclusion

Forty years after the dissolution of Palestine, the Palestine National Council (PNC) issued a declaration of independence on 15 November 1988, in which it asserted the principle of equality between the sexes. But on the ground, women still have a long way to go toward equality because of several contradictions between the expectations people have of them and the types of lives they lead. Areas of concern are the balance between the nationalist issue versus gender relations; women's education, health, and work; women's image in literature; and the difference between women's role in society and their status in it.

The Nationalist Issue vs. Gender Relations

The question of gender inequality was not on the agenda of early Palestinian women's organizations for the same reason interest in inequality is still weak today: Palestinian women, like men, were consumed by a desire for independence, to the exclusion of other issues. Activists were aware of the need to improve the status of women, but they argued that such reform will have to wait, both because it will detract from the main issue of the struggle for Palestine, and because

254

Such measures of reform can only be introduced by National Governments, or by persons deriving their authority from the people. A mandatory power finds itself unable to embark on any scheme of reform which in its opinion may arouse the least religious susceptibility of any community. . . . If Palestine had a legislative council elected by the people, it could introduce any such reformatory measure [raising the age of marriage] without making itself liable to or risking any criticism or attack (Mogannam 1937: 53, 54).

But the dismantling of Palestine meant that the dream of a Palestinian national government was not realized, and that no scheme of reform was instituted to improve the status of women in Palestinian society in the diaspora. Since 1948, several constraints have marked the Palestinian experience: Israeli occupation, exile, emigration, physical hardship, and refugee status.

After a period of dependence on the United Nations and Arab regimes to solve the Palestinian-Israeli dispute, Palestinians concluded that they have to take a much more active role in charting the course for their own future. The PLO, which was initially created with the help of Arab governments, became a vehicle for Palestinian nationalism. The organization created institutions that represented the various sectors of Palestinian society, including women. But the General Union of Palestinian Women (GUPW) in various Arab countries was much more involved in recruiting cadres for the struggle for Palestine than in researching the condition of women or in instituting legal reforms to improve their status. Fateh, the largest constituent group of the PLO, for instance, insisted on keeping identity cards for its commandos with space for more than one wife who could claim benefits.

The creation of the first of the four women's committees in 1978 introduced changes into the structure of women's organizations in the Occupied Territories. Those new forms of organizing took account of the mostly rural nature of the Palestinian population, and shunned top-down decision making in favor of empowering village- and refugee camp-based committees. On the positive side, individuals and organizations have moved away from welfare towards encouraging self-help and "mobilization from below," as Rita Giacaman put it. But the raison d'être of the women's movement—recruiting women for the national struggle—persisted well into the 1980s. The committees continued to stress the nationalist role of Palestinian women, sometimes at the expense of gender issues. To date, not a single group has managed to present its vision of women's role in Palestinian society other than in broad generalities of wanting women to work "side by side" with men. No group has yet come up with a blueprint for what Palestinian society needs to do to improve the education of women, their health, their work opportunities, and their legal status, but there are a few changes worth noting.

Amal Nashashibi, an independent woman active in developmental and educational affairs, has noticed that women's groups have in the last few years realized that they had to start paying attention to the gender discrimination issue despite their early reluctance to do so. The committees' personal experiences with the weight of traditions pulling women down, as well as their interaction with independent Palestinian women and international feminist groups, challenged the leaders of women's committees to produce something concrete on the effect of gender discrimination on development. Until recently, public calls for a more progressive consciousness for both sexes have been the missing link in the attempts to empower women. And while Palestinian educators are calling for a radical change in education to stress issues relating to class, and to encourage abstract thinking, the women's movement has not yet adopted a call for dealing with the stereotyping of women in the curriculum. The impetus for such change is coming from female academics and independent women who have always been interested in gender and legal issues. Increasingly, one hears that there is no contradiction between being a nationalist and a feminist. Sociologist Eileen Kuttab, also the coordinator of Beisan's Women's Research Committee, said that women suffer cumulatively from national, class, and social oppression, but that "national liberation does not contradict liberation of women from traditional conventions" (Tawfiq, *FE*, 24 December 1990: 8). So, on the positive side, there is evidence that a number of women on the West Bank are no longer restricting themselves to general statements about women, but are also gearing up towards a clearer definition of women's issues. This new interest in cementing the gains women have achieved so far is further fueled by the threat women are now facing from the growing influence of the fundamentalist movement. The ability of Hamas to intimidate even activist women in Gaza to wear a headcover has alerted West Bank women to the danger awaiting them if they leave the women's issue to the conservatives. But a number of areas still compete for the attention of women's groups. Below is a review of the issues where contradictory demands on women are made and a summary of what women's organizations are doing about them.

Women and Education

In the Palestinian experience, the education of women and their entry into the work force were extremely important for the changes that took place in the role of women. In 1930 Palestinian women represented only 20 percent of the total number of students in (British) government schools (Miller 1985: 103). Statistics between 1948 and 1967 show an increase in the ratios of male to female in all stages of education. In the 1985–86 school year, UNRWA had 13,079 boys and 15,489 girls in elementary schools, and 5,558 boys and 6,185 girls at the preparatory level (ninth grade) (UNRWA Staff 1986: 8). And while the total number of students sitting for the high school exam increased by 280 percent between 1968 and 1984, the number of girls who took it went up by 386 percent. In 1968, there were 2.5 males for every female taking the exam; by 1990 the ratio will be 1.5 for arts and science. For the arts stream of Tawjihi alone, the ratio will be almost one to one (Rouhana, *FE* 1985: 7, 10).

Education has helped many women enter the labor force. When the foundations of Palestinian society were shaken and the Palestinian community was dispersed after the 1948 Arab-Israeli war, the need to confront the crisis subsumed many pre-1948 values that may have rejected the whole concept of a woman's becoming the center of a family's extended and effective network. Suddenly, the national crisis left no choice but to extend the role of women for the survival of the community. Palestinian women's support of their elderly parents and their help sending brothers and sisters to college when there was virtually no other means of survival helped change the role of women (Khalili 1977: 164–65). Three facts need to be remembered, however: education is not equally available to all sectors of Palestinian society; males are still given preference over females in high school and university education; and females are encouraged to marry young. Women's groups attempt to empower women by providing literacy education and training classes for a number of traditionally female professions, but the women's committees have no programs that specifically concentrate on the education of women or the retention of women at school. And, although members of the women's committees sometimes intercede with parents and convince them to allow teenage girls to remain in school, there is no organized committeewide, nation-wide effort to encourage committee members to stress the importance of education.

Women's Health

Women's reproductive role is adulated in Palestinian society. Women are told that having a large number of children is a national duty. Samiha Khalil, head of a women's society, talks about reproduction in political terms. Even PLO Chairman Arafat exhorted women to have no less than twelve children each when he talked to gatherings in places like Abu Dhabi. Without women buying into the need for seven to twelve pregnancies each, there will be a shortage of fighters for the "revolution." Without their bearing their sorrow over the loss of their children with dignity, there can be no martyrs either. But this rhetoric over the joy of reproduction as the heroic reproduction of community has not been matched by a commitment by the Palestinian leadership to devote resources to the care of women who give birth in difficult conditions. Rural and refugee women have not received their share of health care, and not enough money has been spent on mothers in the past.

The establishment of the Union of Palestinian Medical Relief Committees (UPMRC) in 1979 and the consciousness of its members of the need for preventive medicine have provided the Palestinian community in the Occupied Territories with a blueprint for progressive care for women and their children. This type of health care is based on solid research on rural conditions for women in studies like those conducted by Dr. Rita Giacaman. The mobile clinics UPMRC use, run by volunteer doctors and health professionals, serve remote and rural areas. Under this new health care system that has spawned imitations by different groups, women are served well. Women's groups with ties to these health care projects are on the right track in making health care a women's issue. The services women's committees bring to villages in cooperation with medical groups increase the credibility of the committees with the rural population. Although plans for a nationwide health care system are still in the making, the fact that part of the delivery of that care comes through women's groups and reaches the most needy is very encouraging.

Women and Work

Despite the increase in the number of educated women, illiteracy persists in rural areas, especially among older women. Undereducated women who are raised with the assumption that they will work only at home face contradictory demands. They are expected to give birth to and raise a large number of children, but many, such as Umm Ibrahim and Samar Suleiman's mother, also support those families because of absent male wage earners. When women from underprivileged backgrounds work for survival, their educational level enables them to do only repetitive factory jobs, which keep wages low and unions out, or labor-intensive low-paid sewing jobs. Often, women are not given higher education because of the assumption that they will marry and that a male will support them, whereas many become the main supporters of their families and, like Zahira Kamal, send siblings to college.

The number of Palestinian women working outside the home has been increasing steadily over the years, as women have gained additional skills through access to education. But there is a reluctance to take their role as professionals seriously. The main reason for that reluctance is that child care and housework are still seen as primary duties. Asked for his opinion on women's work outside the home, Faisal Husseini, a leading nationalist in the Occupied Territories, gave an answer that is typical of the general feeling about women and work: "I am not against women going out to work, but in my opinion, the natural place for a woman is inside the home. In her home she faces the most difficult of tasks: building the family and raising children. If there is a financial need, however, and if a woman can . . . combine outside work and tasks of the home, I have no objection to her going out to work" (Najjar and al-Khatib 1986: 15).

The tactics of the women's organizations and the programs they sponsor stem from an understanding of this sentiment. Women's committees stress the provision of child care *and* provide it. PFWC, the largest women's committee, at one time had 1,504 children in its kindergartens. In that respect, the committees differ from the women's movement in the West in that, like Husseini, most female organizers assume that child care is women's work, and so by providing child care, they see themselves as helping free women from *their* responsibilities. Despite rhetoric about changing women's role in society, the programs that the committees undertake do not seek to change the role of women, but attempt to make it easier. Women's committees also seek to empower women through offering them literacy programs and job training. These programs are successful in that they help recruit women who would not otherwise be able to participate in any activities outside the home. The issue of men doing more housework and parenting is raised only by a minority of educated women, and is not on the agenda of the women's movement at this time.

Women's Image in Literature

There is a contradiction between women's actions and the portrayal of women in literature. Although attitudes toward women have evolved since 1923, some complain that the image of women in Palestinian literature has not changed from the "all-providing mother, obedient wife, romantic lover of old." Women find their way into literature, says Dr. Hanan Mikha'il-Ashrawi, "not as portraits of themselves, but as the embodiment of the unattained, the perfect goal: fertility, lush land, the womb of society, Palestine itself." Furthermore, adds Ashrawi, who a few years after making that statement held the position of dean of arts at Birzeit University, women's realistic role in tradition—that of peasant—is also used, but such women are depicted as completely lacking in self-consciousness. "Very few writers deal with women as conscious beings who handle their own problems" (Pesa, *FE*, 8 March 1985: 11).

While women's organizations have not yet taken an official position on writing about women, female academics are increasingly raising the issue. Dr. Ilham abu-Ghazaleh, who teaches linguistics at Birzeit University, has conducted a content analysis of poems written between December 1987 and May 1989. Abu-Ghazaleh found that even in those national poems inspired by the Intifada, poets stress the physical appearance of women (long hair, tiny waist, her image as bride) rather than their action. Poets also dwell on women's biological function or her role as childbearer or housewife ("guard the fetus, you its mother," "kneaded by women," "she hung her steadfastness" like clothes). When a woman reacts in poetry, she reacts passively (gazed, cried, felt, waited, missed, was awakened, cries, slept for years, alone, sad, patient, silent, thinks, has secrets, is surrounded by wolves). Women are depicted as emotional, tormented beings (women's cries for help, cries like a child, shy, complains). All the verbs used to describe women's action suggest that women talk rather than act.

While women in real life rush to the streets daily, rescue young men, and sometimes, like Haniyyeh Ghazawneh, die while doing so, women in the poetry of the uprising do not seem to participate in the street, but are told what is happening out there when men return. Women are not even given the chance to interpret events but are told what those events mean. Commenting on the depiction of the relationship between women and men in those poems, abu-Ghazaleh observes that women are either totally negated by their absence, or are depicted as incomplete beings. And what is worse, she adds, is that all of this passivity in depiction took place at a time when women in every neighborhood were more active than they have ever been. So abu-Ghazaleh called on writers to use literature as a revolutionary weapon to change consciousness (abu-Ghazaleh 1989: 65–76).

Despite these persistent images in poetry, there are some improvements in references to women in nationalist leaflets. Islah Jad, who teaches cultural studies at Birzeit University, analyzed the content of the secret leaflets of the Intifada to count the number of times women are mentioned and the type of mention they receive. Jad notes that the first pamphlet signed by "The nationalist forces in Gaza," and distributed by the Islamic movement urged "women and children and old people" to take part in a funeral held on 16 December 1987. As pamphlets started to appear on a regular basis, women were also addressed "People of martyrs, giants of the revolution, youth, students, workers, farmers and women, let us burn the ground under the feet of the occupiers" (Call No. 1, 10 January 1988). This type of address, says Jad, is different from the 1936–39 formulation addressed to "[male] Youth of Palestine, men, old people [masculine], young boys."

To honor women in the 1930s, one called them "society ladies"; this changed to "the sister of men" in the revolutionary period. Finally, women and girls seem to have earned the right to names that describe their individual actions, says Islah Jad. *Nisa'a al-Intifada* of March 8, 1989, called Manal Sammura "al-Shinnara" (the sparrow). The fifteen-year-old girl was shot on 25 October 1988 while rescuing a young man.¹ Academic institutions are also becoming sensitive to the inclusion of women. The 1990 calendar issued by the Palestinian Academic Society for the Study of International Affairs (PASSIA) in East Jerusalem listed the dates on which important Arab and world leaders died. Martin Luther King's death in 1968 was listed and so was the date on which Swedish Prime Minister Olof

Palme was killed in 1986. PASSIA, however, did not list the date on which Fatmeh Ghazzal, the first Palestinian woman to die in combat, was killed in battle in Wadi Azzam on 26 June 1936. In 1991, the research center included that date as well as other dates that show the contributions of women to Palestinian society. Incidentally, the calendar listed the Jewish New Year for the first time also in 1991.

Women's publications are slowly becoming important vehicles for discussion, instruction, and participation. All women's groups have issued special Intifada publications that recount the heroism of individual women with titles such as, "A Flower Pot Against the Army: Umm Abdullah" (PUWWC *Newsletter*, 8 March 1988) and "Women of Shu'fat Refugee Camp: "Neither Shamir nor Rabin Scare Us after Today," "Even the Mother of the Bride Is Not Left Alone," "Mrs. Tamam Awad: Our Foreheads Will Remain High Until We Regain our Palestinian Identity," "Hajjah Zuhur Anati, 80, and Another Heroic Tale," "How Umm Abdullah Threw the Soldier on the Ground," and "She Received the Body of her Son with Ululations" (UPWWC, March 1988). One publication advised women to advertise their involvement by writing slogans on walls, and women have done so.

In a December 1990 conference held by Beisan Research Center, a workshop was devoted to women in the press and in literature. The workshop recommended the creation of a women's press center and women's magazines and the awarding of prizes for research on women's issues (Tawfiq, *FE*, 24 December 1990: 8). This interest in women and language is a relatively new phenomenon.

Women's Role and Women's Status

There is no doubt that women take an active part in the Intifada. But have their contributions affected the way society perceives them? In trying to answer the question of whether their contributions have enhanced their status, Najah Manasrah writes that even though we can see that change has touched the role of women, and even though we can feel optimistic about the increase in women's participation, we ought to differentiate between change in the role of women and change in their status within the general population. Although role changes will eventually lead to improved status, that improvement will take place slowly because of a number of other factors such as the environment, culture, and education

(Manasrah, *Al-Kateb*, August 1989: 54–58). The distinction Manasrah makes between role and status is an important one, rarely made by people who write about women. That distinction is especially ignored by analysts who use the increase in women's activism interchangeably with the change in women's status. Many pamphlets by the resistance movement equate women's willingness to be imprisoned or to die for the cause and society's acceptance of her sacrifices with improvement in their status.

Taking part in the national struggle, however, has not automatically been translated into gains in rights and status, but the experience women are gaining in the national struggle is serving them well in raising their consciousness for the need to fight for equality during and after liberation. Says one newsletter,

Let's Work from Today on establishing women's rights to full equality with men in all rights and duties in our independent Palestinian state (The Higher Council of Women in the Independent State of Palestine, 8 March 1989, Woman's Packet).

But change is hard because of fundamentalist opposition to women's involvement in social life; of the belated interest of women's committees in gender-related issues as opposed to nationalist issues; and the inaction of liberal men. Explains novelist Sahar Khalifah, in the name of one character talking to another,

They [liberal men] would like the continuation of the status quo because it is in their interest. They benefit from the economic participation of their women, they benefit from the participation of their women in politics, but they do not require themselves to exert any effort in developing a more advanced consciousness towards women . . . they require a woman to be [politically] conscious to a certain degree, but balk when she understands . . . because it means questioning their privileges because the day will come when she will ask, "Does development mean that I should be exploited more. A union says that a worker has to be aware of her responsibilities as much as her rights, so where are my rights with you, with the union, with the revolution and with the country?" Then he will say, "When we are free, we will free you."

The woman hearing this conversation says:

—But they do not hear us.

—How could they, when we do not open our mouths?

—But if we open them, they say it is silliness.

—The important thing is that we open them while we are on stage. They will not hear us if we are below the stage. Over the stage, over it. On the stage.

Sahar Khalifah responding to critics of her feminist novel *The Sunflower* (Khalifah, *Al-Kateb*, September–October 1981: 83).

It appears that women have finally found a forum, a stage, and are slowly exploring new areas of involvement. In a conference sponsored by Beisan Research Center, speeches delivered by the participants in a one-day conference on 14 December 1990, exhibited signs that a process of reevaluation of women's role is under way. A man in the audience admitted that there is "a stream in Palestinian society opposed to women's freedom" but that the topic is not mentioned in any of the many nationalist political functions. The significance of admitting that the gender issue has been slipped under the rug should not be underestimated. Others in the audience called for the conference to take a firm stand on the question of the "hijab" because such a stand represents the democratic freedom of people to wear what they will.[2]

Sociologist Lisa Taraki, an authority on Islamic movements, noted that while the movements in different countries are not homogeneous, they all command the wearing of a head cover, have prohibitions against women working outside the home, and expect women to go to segregated schools and workplaces. Taraki posed the question in terms of the dilemma of reconciling the requirements of an Islamic life and the requirements of contemporary life. Faisal Husseini said that the conflict between old and new ideas should not be fought at the expense of women and by the imposition of the headdress (Tawfiq, *FE*, 24 December 1990: 8, 9).

The fact that different political groups were represented at the conference means that a new alliance is emerging between those groups and the women who have struggled with them for all these years. It appears that the success of Hamas (zeal), a religious organization, in challenging the leadership of the PLO in the Occupied Territories, as well as in forcing Gaza women to wear conservative dress, has impressed women with the necessity for immediate joint action to combat the conservative trend.

The stated aim of the conference was "to shed light on social problems faced by Palestinian women and to reaffirm the importance of female progress and participation in the struggle for national liberation and democracy." Reports of the conference show that the participants did that

NOTES

INTRODUCTION

1. Wellesley Editorial Committee, *Women and National Development: The Complexities of Change* (Chicago: University of Chicago Press, 1977); A. Smock, ed., *Women: Role and Status in Eight Countries* (New York: Wiley 1977). Sheila Rowbotham's *Women, Resistance and Revolution* (London: Penguin, 1972) has long sections on women in the Algerian, Cuban, and Vietnamese independence struggles but only a brief mention of Palestinian women.

2. L. Beck and N. Keddie, eds., *Women in the Muslim World* (Cambridge: Cambridge University Press, 1978); and UNESCO, *Social Science Research and Women in the Arab World* (London: Pinter, 1984). Most social science writing about the Middle East pays little attention to women of minority groups; two recent symposia published by *Peuples Méditerranéens* (1983 and 1988) are unusual in this respect.

3. E. Sanbar, "Le vécu et l'écrit: historiens-réfugiés de Palestine," *Revue d'études palestiniennes* 1.1 (1980).

4. The interest in Palestinian cultural institutions in the national cultural legacy developed after the resistance movement had revived peasant customs as part of a "culture of resistance."

5. For an introduction to the Palestinian resistance movement, see Abu Iyad with Eric Rouleau, *My Home, My Land* (New York: Times Book, 1981), and Helena Cobban, *The Palestinian Liberation Organization: People, Power, and Politics* (New York: Cambridge University Press, 1984).

by openly standing up to fundamentalist coercion of women and b
ducting four workshops to discuss various aspects of women's educ
work and legal rights, and political organization. These developi
show that the Palestinian women's movement is finally coming of age
there is no doubt that the success of the women's movement will de
on whether those workshops will move from making calls for actio
those different fronts in need of attention to actually drawing up con
programs stemming from their vision of the role and status of wome
Palestinian society. The trick is to move women from being "sister
men" to sisters of women as well, whether the occupation persists f
while or whether it is lifted in the near future.

6. When first formed, it was PAWA (Association) and became PAWU (Union) in the 1940s. I use PAWU here and PAWA when speaking about the early period.

7. A list of these associations is given by Y. Haddad, "Palestinian Women: Patterns of Domination and Legitimation" in K. Nakhleh and E. Zureik, eds., *The Sociology of the Palestinians* (London: Croom/Helm, 1980), 167. Comparison with Mogannam suggests that it is incomplete.

8. Ted Swedenberg notes the stereotypical nature of accounts of women's role in the Great Rebellion: "Problems in Oral History: The Palestine Revolt of 1936," *Birzeit Research Review* 2 (Winter 1985–86).

9. See R. Sayigh, "Palestinian Women: Triple Burden, Single Struggle," special issue on "Les Femmes et la modernité," *Péuples Mediterranéens* 44/45 (July–December 1988).

10. See Laila Jammal, *Contributions by Palestinian Women to the National Struggle for Liberation* (Washington, D.C.: Middle East Public Relations, 1985), 18, for the names of Nablus women who fought with the Arab Salvation Army.

11. About 780,000 of the 1.3 million inhabitants of Palestine (60 percent) became refugees (Lesch 1983: 48).

12. Jammal, *Contributions*, 23, lists: Dar al-Tifl al-'Arabi, the Red Crescent Society, The Society of the Wounded Militant, The Orphans' Home, The Family Welfare Society, The Home of the Girls' Orphanage, al-Makased Society, and In'ash al-Usra. Five of these were in Jerusalem, two in Nablus, and one in al-Bireh.

13. In 1965, the Israeli Communist party split into two factions, the New Communists, Rakah, most of whom were Arabs, and Israeli Communists, most of whom were Jews. Al-'Ard (the Land) is a group established by Arab nationalists in 1964 to further the interests of Palestinians who became Israeli citizens in 1948. Israeli authorities refused to register the group as a political party, despite its acceptance of the right of Jews to an independent state. The Israeli Supreme Court upheld that decision, and the minister of defense banned the group (Gilmour 1980: 113).

14. Samira Khoury gives her life history in Didar Fawzy, "Palestiniennes de l'interieur," *Peuples Méditerranéens* (22/23, January–June 1983).

15. Karameh is a battle that took place between Israel, the Jordanian army, and the Palestinian commandos Israel was trying to dislodge from that border town on 21 March 1968. Commandos insisted on participating even though they had only light weapons against the heavily armed Israeli army. As a result of their "martyrdom decision," the battle became a turning point for the fortunes of the guerrillas. Thousands of recruits flocked to volunteer to fight with the Palestinian resistance movement after Karameh (Hirst 1977: 284–86).

16. R. Sayigh, "Palestinian Women and Politics in Lebanon," paper for symposium on Women and Arab Society, Center for Contemporary Arab Studies, Georgetown University, Washington, D.C., April 1986 (in publication).

17. Joost Hiltermann writes "the women's movement has suffered less from Israeli repression than the labor movement, most probably because of the occupying power's estimation that the women's movement had little influence among the

population. The popular uprising in 1987–88 has proven the authorities wrong: in fact, the women's committees showed themselves to be far more effective in mobilizing the population than the trade unions" (Hiltermann 1988: 401).

18. Rita Giacaman, "Palestinian Women and Development in the Occupied West Bank" (Birzeit University, mimeo, n.d.).

19. The GUPW in Lebanon (1969–82) was allocated a small yearly budget by the PLO/resistance movement. In Palestine, one of the activities of the PAWA was to collect donations for the national movement.

20. See R. Sayigh, "Palestinian Women."

21. Lajnat al-'amal al-nissa'i, *Hawla awda' al-mar'a al-filastiniyya fi al manatiq al-muhtalla: dirasa maydaniyya* (Ramallah: al-Bireh, 1980).

22. The PUWWC is affiliated with the Democratic Front for the Liberation of Palestine, the Union of Palestinian Working Women's Committee (UPWWC) is affiliated with the Communist party, the Palestinian Women's Committee (PWC) is affiliated with the Popular Front for the Liberation of Palestine, and the WCSW with Fateh (see Chapter 4).

23. Peasant uprisings against land sales for Zionist settlements took place in 1886, 1901–2, and 1910–11 and would certainly have involved women. J. Tucker discusses comparable spontaneous actions by Egyptian women against British soldiers in *Egyptian Women in the Nineteenth Century* (Cambridge: Cambridge University Press, 1985).

24. Figures based on a report by Shahin Makarius, 1883, cited in S. Graham-Brown, *Education, Repression, Liberation: Palestinians* (London: World University Service, 1984), 15.

25. Cited by A. Zahlan and E. Hagopian, "Palestine's Arab Population: The Demography of the Palestinians," *JPS* III.4 (Summer 1984), from Ottoman sources.

26. Quoted by Mogannam (1976), 253. The quotation is taken from a letter sent to her by the government chief secretary.

27. Birzeit College did not begin to offer a four-year program until 1972, after several years as a junior college. Bethlehem University opened in 1973, followed by al-Najah, Gaza, and Hebron. Graham-Brown, *Education*, 82–86.

28. M. Hallaj, "The Mission of Palestinian Higher Education," *JPS* 9.4 (Summer 1980), gives the ratio as 20 per thousand, compared with a ratio of 4 per thousand for the Arab world as a whole.

29. Graham-Brown, *Education*, 84.

30. Educational figures for five Palestinian camps in Lebanon (1979) show that 35 percent of females above ten years were illiterate, 30 percent could read and write, and 3.1 percent had gone beyond the last (intermediate) level provided by UNRWA (PLO Central Bureau of Statistics, Damascus, 1980), 226.

31. An exception is Lila Abu Lughod, *Veiled Sentiments* (Berkeley: University of California, 1986). But see *Peuples Méditerranéens* 22/23 (January–June 1983) for the poem of a Kabyle woman, Thassadit, first written down after her death. Also, in

the same issue, N. Hammouda, "Les femmes rurales de l'Aures et la production poetique."

32. Shelagh Weir, *Palestinian Costume* (Austin: University of Texas Press, 1989), gives an excellent account of the "language" of Palestinian embroidery.

33. See H. Granqvist, *Marriage Conditions in a Palestinian Village*, 2 pts. (Helsinki: Societies Scientiarum Fennica, 1931, 1935). The British government made marriage of girls under sixteen illegal, but the custom continued.

34. Equality, or *kafaah*, is cited by J. Esposito, *Women in Muslim Family Law* (New York: Syracuse University Press, 1982), 128, as a principle of Hanafi law. Palestinian practice suggests that it is widespread.

I: *COPING WITH THE LOSS OF PALESTINE*

Umm Ibrahim Shawabkeh

1. In 1948 the United Nations established an emergency body to give aid to Palestinians refugees. In 1950, the agency became the United Nations Relief and Works Agency (UNRWA). It is still providing housing, some food rations, medical services, and education for those up to the age of fourteen, and some vocational training to nearly two million registered refugees in the West and East Banks of Jordan, Gaza, Syria, and Lebanon.

2. A census was conducted three months after the occupation of the West Bank. A number of Palestinians who happened to be out of the country studying abroad or working in the Arabian Gulf or elsewhere were left without an identity card, and without the right to live in their country. The family reunion scheme was established whereby a family can apply to have its relatives return and obtain a card. Requests are accepted at the discretion of the military governor. The giving and withholding of I.D. cards is used to punish activists and to try to bribe Palestinians into collaborating with the occupation authorities.

3. Until the Gulf crisis of 1990, there were an estimated 576,000 Palestinians living in the Gulf region. Kuwait has the largest population of Palestinians with roughly 350,000. Saudi Arabia has 170,000, and there are about 35,000 Palestinians in the United Arab Emirates (*The Christian Science Monitor*, 18 March 1988, 12).

Samiha Salameh Khalil (Umm Khalil)

1. Kuttab: a mosque school in which children were taught to read, write, do arithmetic, and recite the Quran.

2. In his memoirs, Akram Zuaiter notes that these lines came from a poem by Nouh (Noah) Ibrahim, a popular poet who recited his poetry in nationalist gatherings. The poem in question includes the following lines:

Mr. Commander Dill Do not think that the nation will tire/
but please take it easy, treat it with patience/
Perhaps it will be solved at your hands./ . . . Respect the
conditions set by the nation, independence and freedom. . . . /

You came to free Palestine, to put down the revolution/ . . .
For Britain to have peace with the Arab nation, it has to stop
immigration and the sale of land/ . . . Fix it etc.

Dill had heard his name repeated during demonstrations, so had the poem translated, and asked to see Nouh. Nouh was in prison, so Dill released him. The poet was later killed in battle (Zuaiter 1988: 500–501).

3. The Baghdad Pact, formed in February 1955, was a defense organization comprising Britain, Turkey, Iran, Pakistan, and Iraq. It was opposed by Saudi Arabia and Yemen and Egypt.

4. Mrs. Khalil enrolled at the Arab University of Beirut to study Arabic literature by correspondence. She passed her freshman and sophomore years, but the events of 1967 prevented her from leaving the country to sit for her yearly exams.

5. Zakaah is a specified portion of a Muslim's wealth that must be paid every year as alms on income that exceeds a certain amount, and on more than forty head of cattle. The rate is fixed for various forms of wealth. During the Ramadan feast in June 1985, for instance, In'ash al-Usra received the following as Zakaah: $9,051 cash and new clothes, shoes, and foodstuffs for the orphanage.

6. Mrs. Khalil felt that she was in a demographic race with the Israelis because of a number of statements the Israelis made about the Arab birthrate. Premier Golda Meir, for instance, said in early 1970 that she was afraid of a situation where she "would have to wake up every morning wondering how many Arab babies have been born during the night" (Yuval-Davis 1987: 61).

7. Mrs. Khalil has been imprisoned for the following reasons: (1) demonstrating to protest the torture of women prisoners at Ramleh Prison; (2) demonstrating against soldiers beating up youths; (3) demonstrating against soldiers entering girls' schools and beating up students; (4) demonstrating after the death of Abdul Nasser and staging a sit-in at a local mosque. She has been arrested for working with her husband and other families to pressure George Habash (leader of the Popular Front for the Liberation of Palestine) to release hostages from a hijacked plane in 1970 and for belonging to the National Guidance Committee (NGC) when the group, formed in 1978, was declared illegal.

8. According to the Kuwaiti News Agency, since 1967 the military authorities have issued 16,320 orders forbidding people from leaving the Occupied Territories (*Al Mithaq*, 3 March 1985).

9. Soldiers would not let the guard of In'ash al-Usra accompany them during their search. Because no one was there during the break-in, In'ash al-Usra lawyers protested that it is impossible to verify that what the police say was seized belonged to In'ash al-Usra. Mrs. Khalil announced a press conference at 1:00 P.M. the next day to complain about the way the raid was conducted and to defend the society. The military held a conference immediately preceding hers and showed journalists "an anti-Semitic tape" in which a Jew is shown beating a Palestinian student to death for refusing to call Palestine Israel. (See *New York Times*, 21 June 1988, 8).

10. Mrs. Khalil's trial was repeatedly postponed, and then authorities decided not to try her.

Samar Suleiman

1. Al-al-Shabiba (The Youth Committee) is a group of young men in the village affiliated with Fateh, the largest group within the PLO. Most of the young men are university and high school students who organize sports and cultural activities and volunteer work projects for the development of the community.

Najah Manasrah

1. Islamic legislation sets the marriage age on the basis of physical rather than psychological maturation. In the West, church leaders counsel abstinence, while liberals encourage sex education and safe sex through the provision of contraceptives. Unlike church leaders, Islamic legislators admit that teenage girls are sexual beings, find abstinence unrealistic, and premarital sex unacceptable, so offer marriage as the answer to teenage sexuality. In those early marriages, most of the women marry out of middle or high school, and college is not an option even for the brightest among them.

2: THE LAND, TWO FARMERS

Umm Ayyash

1. The Druze is an Arabic-speaking community living in South Lebanon, Syria, and North Israel. The Druze religion was founded in the tenth century A.D. as a splinter from Isma'ili Shi'a Islam. The Druze, who number about 350,000, play different roles in each of the countries they live in. In Syria, they serve in the Syrian army; in Israel, they serve in the Israeli army. See Robert Betts, *The Druze* (New Haven, Conn.: Yale University Press, 1988).

2. Although young brides were quite common, the parents of the bride often tried to delay the consummation of the marriage, sometimes by keeping the girl with them, sometimes by relying on the husband and his family. This was done so as not to create fear of sexual relations (See Granqvist 1935).

3. Umm Ayyash's mother lived with her all these years until Umm Ayyash moved to her new two-room house. But when the children were young, she was too ill to help, so Umm Ayyash had to depend more on her neighbor. Shortly after Umm Ayyash was interviewed, her mother died.

4. Update provided by Tahani Hussein Ali, 11 April 1990.

Aisheh Shamlawi

1. David Hirst notes that the 1950 Law for the Acquisition of Absentee Property was a very ingenious, retroactive device. "The absentees in question were for the most part the outsiders who could not return. . . . But insiders could become absentees too. They are known as 'absent-presents'; the precise number of these

Orwellian beings is a well-kept military secret, but they run into the tens of thousands." (Hirst 1977: 188, 189).

2. The Israeli government has confiscated almost half of the land belonging to the village of Hares (land previously taken from the village to set up Elkana settlement) in order to build a hotel and shopping complex to serve Israeli settlers in the area (*FE*, 22 July 1983, 15).

3. Israeli authorities have been uprooting trees since 1967. According to the Palestine Human Rights Information Center, Jerusalem, 110,646 trees have been uprooted between 8 December 1987, and 31 May 1991, *The Washington Report on the Middle East*, Aug-Sept, 1991, 31.

4. The Israeli High Court of Justice rarely takes on cases that have already been decided by the military government. During the first twenty years of occupation, the court examined 9 cases out of 416 submitted to it by people in the Occupied Territories (*Al-Usbu' al-Jadid*, 30 June 1989, 52).

5. Taking refuge has its roots in tribal custom. A fugitive on the run would literally throw himself at the mercy of someone, even someone from the family of his enemies, and expect protection because of the law of hospitality and the tradition of protecting the weak who ask for help.

3: *ENCOUNTERS WITH THE OCCUPATION AUTHORITIES*

Rawda al-Basiir
1. For information about the rape of Aisha Odeh and Rasmiyyeh Odeh (not related) and the torture of other women, see Soraya Antonius, "Prisoners for Palestine: A List of Women Political Prisoners," *JPS* (Spring 1980).

Haniyyeh Ghazawneh
1. In the first seven months of the Intifada forty-nine women were killed; of those, twenty-seven came from the West Bank, and the rest from Gaza (*Development Affairs* 1988: 20). By December 1990, the number had reached seventy (*FE*, 24 December 1990, 8).

2. A village near Jerusalem now considered a suburb of the city.

3. It is believed that in Ramadan, on one day a year, the sky opens up, and the prayers of some people will be answered.

4. On 21 March, the League of Palestinian Artists based in East Jerusalem held an exhibit called "The Intifada Martyrs," in which it exhibited fifty-three paintings by a number of Palestinian and Israeli artists of Palestinians killed in the uprising (*FE*, 27 March 1988, 3).

5. Initial reports by army officials acknowledged that military instructions had been violated. The soldier who killed Haniyyeh was found to have "lost control of himself" when he strayed from his comrades after he ran after the boy. But the army decided that the soldier would not face trial for the killing. Israel radio announced that the fact that the soldier in question lost his hand in an injury during army training five months later was taken into consideration when the

decision not to prosecute him was made. "Soldier Will Not Face Trial For Killing Ram Woman" (*FE*, 26 June 1988, 4).

Salima Kumsiyya
  1. "Cyprus"—a nonsense word to make the poem rhyme in Arabic.

4: INSTITUTION BUILDING ON THE WEST BANK

  1. Volunteer work started in 1972–73 with teaching activities; by 1976, it had started taking different forms including physical labor.
  2. This used to be true until 1988. Now charitable societies located in town are opening centers in villages.
  3. PUWWC was renamed Palestinian Federation of Women's Action Committees (PFWAC) in June 1987.
  4. Hiltermann observes that the Marxist-Leninist convictions of the first three of the committees are confined to the leadership level, and that the committees' nationalist bent has therefore worked in their favor, as long as they downplayed their ideological leanings (Hiltermann 1988: 469, 470).
  5. Debbie J. Gerner-Adams, "The Changing Status of Islamic Women in the Arab World," *Arab Studies Quarterly*, 1.4 (Fall 1979): 324–53.

Siham Barghuti
  1. Kassim Amin, an Egyptian, is the first Arab to be identified specifically as a feminist and as one "who transformed the women's cause into a full-blown feminist movement. Two of his books, *Tahrir-al-Mara'h* (The emancipation of women) [1900], and *Al-Mara'h-al-Jadidah* (The new woman) [1902], caused him to be vigorously attacked, as did his support of higher education for females" (Gerner-Adams 1979: 329).
  2. Munir Fasheh wrote about volunteer work in "Education as Praxis for Liberation: Birzeit University and the Community Work Program" (Ph.D. diss., Harvard University, 1987).
  3. A study conducted in 1981 revealed that the percentage of women's participation was as follows: Jerusalem, 20; Ramallah, 15; Hebron, 0; Bethlehem, 20; Nablus, 0; Jericho, 5. On further examination, it was revealed that most of the women who participated were in institutes of higher learning. Hasan al-Haj, "Some Issues of the Women's Movement in the Occupied Territories: A Study," *Al-Kateb*, September 1984.)
  4. Ali Abu Hilal was a leader of the Workers' Unity Block, which controls nine unions.
  5. Dr. Azmi Shu'aibi, a dentist, was a leading member of the al-Bireh municipal council before it was disbanded by the Israeli military government in 1982.
  6. Other women who were not allowed to go are: Samiha Khalil of In'ash al-Usra; Hanan Bannura, nurse, and member of the PUWWC; Na'ema el-Helou, Gaza; Fatmeh Jibreel, resident of Qalandia refugee camp and activist in WCSW;

Fatmeh el-Kurdi, teacher and activist in WCSW; Rabiha el-Kurdi of WCSW; Amal Wahdan, member of Abu Dis Public Institutions Workers' Union and PFWAC activist; Zahira Kamal of PFWAC (*FE*, 19 July 1985), and Amal Khreisheh of the PWWC.

Zahira Kamal

1. In 1987, the organization had thirty-two literacy classes in the West Bank and Gaza, serving 318 women, up from seventeen classes in 1986 serving 180 women.

2. The Executive Office is the body that supervises the organization in all districts on a daily basis. The office holds training sessions for other bodies and meets biweekly. Until 1985, the Executive Office had eight members. It now has fifteen to nineteen members, an increase designed to include representatives from new areas.

3. To allow girls to attend high schools, many villages have resorted to coeducational classes. This arrangement is not beneficial to women. Conservative parents reject coeducation and so pull their daughters out of school after the sixth grade. In some communities, religious authorities have accepted mixed schools only with the stipulation that girls wear the Shari'a dress. A curious situation is emerging where conservative dress is becoming a by-product of education.

4. Zahira Kamal was one of thirteen prominent Palestinians who met with Dennis Ross, U.S. State Department Policy Planning Staff, on 16 May 1989, and also met on 3 August 1989, with John Kelly, U.S. assistant secretary of state. William Quandt, a fellow at the Brookings Institute, described the meeting as Kelly's "first direct contact with leaders in the areas" (*FE*, 22 May 1989, 3, and 7 August 1989, 3). Zahira Kamal, identified by *JPS* as "close to DFLP [Democratic Front for the Liberation of Palestine] (Abd Rabbuh faction)," was chosen as a member of the steering committee for the Israeli-Palestinian Madrid Peace Conference (*JPS*, Vol XXI, No. 2, Winter 1992, p.123).

5. The refusal to meet with Israeli officials is designed to prevent the Israeli government from claiming that it has found negotiators other than the PLO. See *JPS* 18.4 (1989): 156. The tactics have now changed and a Palestinian delegation in meeting with Israelis,but it is still insisting that the PLO represents Palestinians.

Amal Khreisheh

1. Statistics from 1987 show that 1 percent of women are farmers where farming is their main profession. Farming constitutes a secondary source of income for 12 percent. Village women are more likely to work in paid labor than city women. Statistics from PFWAC publications show that in the West Bank, 13,500 village women work, as opposed to 9,500 from cities (*Development Affairs* 1988: 22).

2. Different women's committees have also been involved in securing that day as a paid holiday for female employees, but Amal Khreisheh says that her organization initially spearheaded the move.

3. For example, a UPWWC article advises women to write slogans on the wall, and suggests ways they could go about it:

The hands of women of my country also share in drawing these portraits and signs the name of different political groups as well as the General Unified command. . . . On February 10, [1989], the walls of my country drew the attention and hearts of women . . . "We salute the struggling Palestinian Women," "We Salute the Mothers of the Martyred and Wounded and arrestees," "Glory to the Female and Male martyrs." . . . We hope that this ex- perience will spread because it reflects a respect for the special revolutionary role women play, and will help place women in her correct place in the nation- alist movement (*Nisa' el Intifada* [Women of the Intifada], March 1989, 6).

4. Strikes were organized by women activists against "Tako" paper factory in Ramallah in 1976. UNRWA and government teachers organized a strike for higher salaries in 1981–82; workers at "Rania" biscuit factory organized a strike in 1982–83 in Ramallah; seamstresses of "Paris Fashions" in Ramallah went on strike in 1984; and a strike against the "Rai' " (Shepherd) company in Bethlehem was organized in 1985 to name only a few. (Amal Khreisheh, "Working Women in the Thicket of the National Palestinian Struggle," *Al-Kateb*, April 1985, 70.)

Rita Giacaman

1. Giacaman has since married Dr. Mustafa Barghouti, who founded the Union of Palestinian Medical Relief Committees (UPMRC) in 1979. They had a baby girl in 1990.

2. Gazans live in an area twenty-five miles long and six miles wide, making it the most densely populated part of the Occupied Territories and one of the most densely populated areas in the world (*ANERA Newsletter*, Fall 1989).

3. The average Israeli military governmental expenditure on health services in the West Bank and Gaza does not exceed $30 per person per year, in comparison to $350 per Israeli per year (Benvenisti 1986: 17).

4. The mother and child clinics are especially valuable because basic maternal and child health services are provided in only 29.4 percent of the localities in the West Bank, and 69 percent of the localities where the population is less than 3,000 have no modern services. No form of modern health services exist in 248 of the 489 localities in the West Bank (Union of Physicians, West Bank, *Primary Health Care in the West Bank*, Jerusalem, 1986, 4, 7).

5. See UPMRC's 1987 Report, 31.

6. Union of Palestinian Medical Relief Committees and Community Health Unit, Birzeit University, *Profile of Life and Health in Biddu: Interim Report*, Unpublished Data, 1987.

7. Between 8 December 1987, and 8 December 1990, curfew days (twenty-four hours) in areas with a population of over 10,000 totaled 8,676 for all areas (Palestine Human Rights Information Center, Jerusalem), *The Washington Report on Middle East Affairs*, January 1991, 29.

8. See Michal Sela, "The Intifada's Disabled," *New Outlook* (June 1988), 22,

translated from Koteret Rashit and Joel Brinkley, "The Palestinian Cost: To Be Young and Maimed," *New York Times* (International), 21 February 1989, Y5.

Mona Rishmawi

1. Mona was born in Gaza in 1958 and received an L.L.B. from Ain Shams University, Cairo (1981). She practiced law in the West Bank before the Israeli Military and Civil Courts between 1981 and 1988. She became a member of the Executive Committee of Law in the Service of Man in 1985 and its executive director in 1989. Mona received an L.L.M from Columbia University in 1989. She specialized in human rights and international law. In addition to writing a legal column in Arabic, Rishmawi has written some articles in English, for example, see "Land Use Planning as a Strategy of Judaization," *JPS* 16. 2 (Winter 1987): 105–16. "What Palestinians Want: Let Our People Go," *The Nation*, 19 March 1988, 368–70.

2. "Law in the Service of Man," later called al-Haq, was established in the West Bank city of Ramallah in 1979 to "promote the rule of law in Israeli occupied territories." The organization is the West Bank affiliate of the International Commission of Jurists, Geneva. In the West Bank, the organization lectures about human rights and law to university students and others and was, before the uprising, talking to at least one university to institute a course on human rights in cultural studies to prepare Palestinians for democracy in a future Palestinian state.

3. See "Law in the Service of Man" Newsletter of July 1984, 3 (Box 1413, Ramallah, West Bank, via Israel).

4. In 1946, lawyer Ya'acov Shapiro said: "The system established in Palestine since the issue of the Defence Laws is unparalleled in any civilized country; there were no such laws even in Nazi Germany. . . . It is our duty to tell the whole world that the Defence Laws passed by the British Mandatory government of Palestine destroy the very foundations of justice in this land." David Gilmour, who quoted Shapiro, noted, "Mr. Shapiro later became attorney-general and minister of justice in Israel but, curiously enough, he saw no need to repeal them. Laws, which are apparently so odious that they did not exist 'even in Nazi Germany' evidently became quite tolerable when applied to Arabs" (Gilmour 1980: 96).

5. There are four main schools of Islamic *fiqh* (jurisprudence): Hanafi, Shafi'i, Malki, and Hanbali.

Tahani Ali

1. The 1987 figures show that seven out of the ten best students in the scientific track and eight out of ten in the literary/art track in the country were girls. Khalil Touma, "Girls Excell in Tawjihi," *FE*, 26 July 1987, 2. The number of women in local universities in 1985–86: 38 percent (*Development Affairs* 1988: 43).

2. The military authorities placed some 8,000 West Bank government schoolteachers on mandatory unpaid vacation from 15 April to 23 May and from 6 October to 3 December 1988. Roughly 78 percent of all West Bank schools are govern-

ment schools, and during that period, teachers received only 50 percent of their salaries. At least 1,200 teachers with annual contracts did not receive new contracts for the 1988–89 school year (Zaroo 1989).

3. The Occupied Territories are the second biggest market (after the United States) for Israeli products. Israel annually sells $850 million in exports to a captive market next door. Israel annually realizes a surplus of $200 million through direct and indirect taxes, and that sum goes to the Israeli treasury (Siniora 1988: 6). The Intifada has cost Israel's food industry about $100 million over the past two years. The losses stem from the boycott of Israeli products in the territories and from the substantial increase in sales of West Bank Arab food products within the Green line (*JP* [Int], 11 November 1989, 21).

Mary Shehadeh

1. *Meraat Al Sherk* (also spelled Mirat al-Shark) was published between 1919 and 1939. It was "oppositionist," i.e., against the mainstream party of Haj Amin al-Husseini and his supporters. Although the paper criticized British policy in Palestine, it was not as strident as the other papers, and often called for cooperation with the British government to achieve self-rule. The newspaper offices were burned in 1925 by people opposed to the paper's political line, but it continued functioning (see Najjar 1975: 56, and Lesch 1979: 97).

2. Ahmad Khalil al-Akkad in his book *History of the Arabic Press* writes, "No females worked as editors or reporters but we can say that there were women who wrote for the press but did not work for it, among them, writer Samira Azzam, writer Mary Shehadeh, and writer Sathej Nassar, wife of Najeeb Nassar, owner of the Karmel newspaper [in Haifa] and it can be said the the last two were the most closely tied to journalism" (34).

3. The fourteen-member executive committee was entrusted with the execution of the resolutions of the congress and the administration of the Arab women's movement. Mogannam notes that "energetic steps were initiated at once to concentrate women's activities in all parts of the country . . . societies were immediately established in conformity with the resolutions of the Congress first at Jerusalem, and later at Acre, Nazareth, Haifa, Jaffa, Ramallah, Tulkarm, Safed and other important centers" (Mogannam 1937: 76, 77).

Wafa al-Baher Abu Ghosh

1. Percentage of women registered in professional unions in the West Bank and Gaza:

Pharmacists	22.92
Dentists	12.45
Doctors	8.06
Agricultural Engineers	7.89
Journalists	6.85
Lawyers	6.27

Engineers. 3.67
(Source: *Development Affairs* 1988: 21)

2. Akram Haniyyeh was deported on 27 December 1986, for allegedly being "a senior member of Fateh," the largest constituent group of the PLO. See Elaine Fletcher, "Editor Expelled," *JP*, 4 November 1986, and Mary Curtius, "Israelis, Palestinians Alike Decry Expulsion of Editor," *The Christian Science Monitor*, 20 December 1986, 1.

3. Faisal Husseini, head of the Arab Studies Society (Jerusalem) until its closure, is one of the leading political figures on the West Bank. Sufian al-Khatib is owner with his brother Mahmoud of *Al-Mithaq* newspaper, closed by the Israeli authorities on 12 August 1986, for allegedly being a mouth organ of the PFLP.

6. CONCLUSION

1. Interview with Islah Jad, Ramallah, August 1989.

2. For the best discussion on forcing women to wear the Hijab in Gaza, see (Hammami 1990).

 BIBLIOGRAPHY

In addition to titles of a general nature, this bibliography aims to include all material that takes Palestinian women as its primary subject. It includes only some material that refers to Palestinian women while dealing with broader subjects, containing small sections on village life, folklore, handicrafts, family, and health. Travelers' accounts, such as the recently published M. E. Rogers, *Domestic Life in Palestine* (New York: Kegan Paul, 1989) and G. Halsell, *Journey to Jerusalem* (New York: Macmillan, 1981), are not listed although both have good descriptions of Palestinian women. Also not listed are books about Palestinians in general except when they contain information about Palestinian women not found elsewhere (for example, work by Laurie Brand on the GUPW). Brief information is given only when the title does not reveal the subject matter or when there is material of special interest to researchers.

The bibliography is divided into the following sections:

General

Articles in *Al-Sha'ab* (an Arabic daily) by Wafa al-Baher Abu-Ghosh and Abla Yaeesh (arranged chronologically)

Articles about women in *Al-Fajr* (*FE*) (an English-language weekly paper; arranged chronologically)

Publications in English by the Palestinian Union of Women's Work Committees (PUWWC; now PFWAC)

Articles published in *Al-Kateb* (published in East Jerusalem, but not allowed to be distributed in the rest of the West Bank; arranged chronologically)

GENERAL

A'Amiri, Suad. See under Amiry, Suad

Abdel-Qader, Ghassan. "Al-Mar'a fi al-nidal al-watani al-Filastini." *Malaff al-Tali'a* 26 (1979).

Abdo-Zubi, Nahla. *Family, Women and Social Change in the Middle East: The Palestinian Case*. Toronto: Canadian Scholars Press, 1987.

Abdul Hadi, Ina'am. "Al'-mar'a wa qanoon al-ahwal al-shaksiyya." Paper presented at a GUPW colloqium in February 1981.

Abed Rabbu, Mohammad, and Salwa Abu Libdeh. "A Girl who 'Died' 17 years Ago in Ramallah turns out . . . to be imprisoned in her Father's House and Yesterday he killed her!" *Al-Fajr* (Arabic), 30 October 1985.

Abu Ali, Khadija. "Muqaddima hawl waqi' al-mar'a wa tajribatiha fi al-thawra al-Filastiniyya (Introduction to the Status of Women and Their Experience in the Palestinian Revolution). Beirut: GUPW, 1975. Report in Rosemary Sayigh, "Looking across the Mediterranean." *MERIP Reports* (June 1984), 24.

Abu-Daleb, Nuha. "Palestinian Women and Their Role in the Revolution." *Peuples Méditerranéens* 5 (October–December 1978).

Abu Omar, Abdel-Samih. *Traditional Palestinian Embroidery and Jewelry*. Jerusalem: Al-Sharq, 1986.

Abu Rizk. *Al-Mar'a hiya al-asl*. Nablus: al-Matba'a al-'Asriyyah, 1957. (Against the superficial imitation of Western women by Arab women.)

Abu-Shamsieh, Eisa. Review of *Wild Thorns* by Sahar Khalifeh. *Arab Studies Quarterly* 9 (Summer 1987):344–46.

Abu Yehya, Mohammad. *The Most Important Issues for the Muslim Woman*. Riyadh, Saudi Arabia: Dar er-Rashid, 1983. (Author affiliated with the Sharia' College, University of Jordan.)

Akel, Abdel-Latif. "The Whole Society Shares Guilt for [the murder of] this Girl." *Al-Fajr* (Arabic), 2 January 1985, 12. See also "Tragic End for 'the Prisoner of al-Bireh,' Father kills her with a knife, and the army saves him from Angry Crowd." 30 October 1985.

al-Akkad, Ahmad Khalil. *History of the Arabic Press in Palestine*. Damascus: al-Wafa'a, 1966.

al-Amed, Selwa. "Mulahazhat hawl waqi' al-mar'a fi al-thawra al-Filastiniyya." *Shu'un Filastiniyya* 113 (April 1981).

Amiry, Suad. "Space, Kinship and Gender: The Social Dimension of Peasant Architecture in Palestine." Ph.D. diss., Edinburgh University, 1987.

———, and Vera Tamari. *The Palestinian Village Home*. London: British Museum, 1989.

Amoretti, Biancamaria. "Assunzione politica del ruolo provato: La donna palestinese." *Nuova D/W/F (donnawomanfemme)* 1 (1976).

———. "De front al problema palestinese: Una questione di metodo." *Nuova D/W/F* 22 (1982).

"And Now Poison?" *MEI* 197 (1 April 1983):7–8.

Antonius, Soraya. "Fighting on Two Fronts: Conversations with Palestinian Women." *JPS* 8 (Spring 1979). Reprinted in M. Davies, ed., *Third World, Second Sex*. London: Zed Books, 1983.

———. "Prisoners for Palestine: A List of Women Political Prisoners." *JPS* 9 (Spring 1980).

Arab Women's Information Committee. *Facts about the Palestinian Problem: Women's Resistance*. Beirut, 1970.

Arafat, Ibtihaj, and James Gornwell. "The Palestinian Woman in the Labor Force." Paper presented at the Conference on Development in the Arab World, New York, 1–3 October 1976.

Ata, Ibrahim. *The West Bank Family*. London: Routledge & Kegan Paul, 1986.

Awwad, Hanan. *Arab Causes in the Fiction of Ghada al-Samman (1961–1975)*. Sherbrooke, Quebec: Editions Namaan, 1983.

Azad, Neda. "Long Journey through Three Prisons." *Big Mama Rag* (July 1981).

Azzam, Samirah. *Al-Sarah wa-al-insan*. Beirut: al-Muassassah al-Ahliyah lit-tiba'a wal-Nashr, 1963.

———. *Wa Qisas ukhra*. Beirut: Dar al-Tali'ah, 1960.

Az-Zamili, Mahdiyyah. *Women's Dress and Makeup in Islamic Fiqh*. Amman, Jordan: Dar al-Furkan, 1982.

Badr, Lilian, ed. "Madha anjazah al-'amal al-nissa'i wa ayna akhfaqa?" *Al-Hurriya*, 8 March 1982.

Badran, Nabil. "Tatawor ta'leem al-mar's al-Filastiniyya wa a'dadiha mahana." (Colloquium organized by the cultural subcommittee of the IAMF in February 1981.)

al-Bahr, Zahra. "Nabila Silbaq Breir: A True Martyr." *MEI* 293 (6 February 1987):21–22.

———. "Women of the Camps: A Special Way of Life." *MEI* 296 (20 March 1987): 13–14.

Bainerman, Joel. "Women Discuss Peace." *The Middle East* 180 (October 1989):50.

Baldensperger, Philip. "Birth, Marriage and Death among the Fellahin of Palestine." *Palestine Exploration Fund Quarterly Statement* (1894), 127–44.

Barbar, Aghil M. *The Study of Arab Women: A Bibliography of Bibliographies*. Monticello, Ill.: Vance Bibliographies. 1980.

Barbot, Michel. "Destin de femmes arabes." *Orient* 31 (1964):109–28. (Includes translation of the work of the Palestinian writer Samira Azzam.)

Baster, James. "Economic Aspects of the Palestine Refugees." *MEJ* 8 (1954).

Bauman, Pari, and Rima Hammami. *Annotated Bibliography on Palestinian Women*. Jerusalem: Arab Thought Forum, December 1989.

Bendt, Ingela, and James Downing. *We Shall Return: Women of Palestine*. London: Zed Books, 1982. Translated from the original edition in Swedish, *Vi ska tillbaka till var jord! Palestinska lägerkvinnor i Libanon*. Stockholm: Prisma, 1980.

Benvenisti, Meron. *1986 Report: Demographic, Economic, Legal, Social and Political Developments in the West Bank*. Boulder, Colo.: Westview Press, 1986.

Bernawi, Fatima. *Liqa' ma al-ukhwat*. Beirut: IAMF, n.d. (Distributed at the third general congress of the IAMF, Beirut, February 1980.)

Birzeit University. *Administrative Detention: Definition, Background and Implications*. Current Affairs Report, no. 1. Birzeit University Research Center, October 1985.

Boullata, Kamal, ed. "To Preserve and Persevere: The Women of Palestine." In *Palestine Today*. Washington D.C.: Palestine Center for the Study of Non-violence, 1990.

Brand, Laurie. "Nasir's Egypt and the Reemergence of the Palestinian National Movement." *JPS* 17 (Winter 1988):36–37.

———. *Palestinians in the Arab World: Institution Building and the Search for State*. New York: Columbia University Press, 1988.

Cainkar, Louise. "Palestinian Women in the U.S.: Who Are They and What Kind of Lives Do They Lead?" In *Images and Reality: Palestinian Women under Occupation and in the Diaspora*, edited by S. Sabbagh and G. Talhami. Washington, D.C.: Institute of Arab Women's Studies, 1990.

Canaan, T. "Unwritten Laws Affecting the Arab Woman of Palestine." *Journal of the Palestine Oriental Society* 11 (1931). (Reprinted as a booklet by the American University of Beirut.)

Canova, Giovanni. "Due poetesse: Fadwa Tuqan e Salma 'l-Khadra' al-gayyusi." *Orienti Moderno* (10 October 1973):876–93.

Cattan, Henry. *Jerusalem*. New York: St. Martin's Press, 1981.

"Close Encounter: Muna Hamzeh and Chaim Shur." *New Outlook* (August–September 1985):15–19.

Cohen, Mark. "U.S. Legal Involvement in Violations of Palestinian Rights." *JPS* 18 (Spring 1989):76–95.

Cooke, Miriam. *War's Other Voices: Women Writers on the Lebanese Civil War*. Cambridge: Cambridge University Press, 1988.

Cowell, Alan. "Israel Uses Tear Gas to Quell Palestinian Women's March." *New York Times*, 9 March 1988, A10.

Crowfoot, G. E. "Custom and Folktale in Palestine: The Dowry or Bride Price." *Folklore* 48 (1937):28–40.

Dagesh, Jamileh. "Hathi hiyya al-Mara'a al-Filastiniyyah!" (This is the Palestinian Woman!) *Al-Ghadd*, March 1989, 19–21. (Article about Amal Khreisheh, head of the UPWWC.)

Dakkak, Ibrahim. "Back to Square One: A Study of the Emergence of the Palestinian Identity in the West Bank 1967–1980." In *Palestinians over the Green Line*, edited by Alexander Schölch. London: Ithaca Press, 1983.

Dayan-Herzbrun, Sonia. "Femmes dans l'intifada: Le combat politique des Palestiniennes." *Peuples Méditerranéens* 48–49 (July–December 1989):241–56.

Dearden, Ann. Review of *My Home, My Prison* by Raymonda Hawa-Tawil. *The Middle East* 112 (February 1984):57.

———, ed. *Arab Women*. 2d ed. Report no. 27. London: Minority Rights Group, 1976.

Dearden, Sue. Review of *We Shall Return: Women of Palestine*, by Ingela Bendt and James Downing. *MEI* 190 (23 December 1982):19.

Deeb, Farajallah, and Nabila Breir. *Al-mar'a al-'arabiyya wa al-intaj (namoodhaj al-mar'a al-Filastiniyya)*. Beirut: Dar al-Hadatha lil Taba'a wa al-Nashara wa al-Towzi'a, 1981.

Dib, Farajallah, and Nabila Breir. "Al-mar'a al-Filastiniyya wa al-intaj." *Al-Fikr al-'Arabiya*, September–December 1980.

Dietl, Gulshan. "Portrait of a Revolutionary: Leila Khalid 20 Years On." *The Middle East* 171 (January 1989):59–60.

Ein-Gil, Ehud, and Ariyeh Finkelstein. "Changes in Palestinian Society." *Khamsin* 6 (1978).

Fahmawi, Kamel. "The Modern Literature of Palestinian Women from 1940–1970." M.A. thesis, al-Azhar University, 1978.

Fahum, Siba, ed. *Palestinian Political Women Prisoners and Detainees in Israeli Prisons*. Beirut: Women's International League for Peace and Freedom, Lebanese section, 1975.

Farah, Najwa. "Mendlebaum Gate." *New Outlook* 1 (January 1964):52–57.

Fasheh, Munir. "Education as Praxis for Liberation: Birzeit University and the Community Work Program." Ph.D. diss., Harvard University, 1987.

———. "Impact on Education." In *Occupation: Israel Over Palestine*, edited by Naseer Aruri. Belmont, Mass., 1983, 295–318.

Fawzia, Fawzia. "Palestine: Women and the Revolution." In *Sisterhood Is Global*, edited by Robin Morgan. Harmondsworth, Middlesex: Penguin Books, 1985.

Fawzy, Didar. "Palestiniennes de l'interieur." *Peuples Méditerranéens* 22–23 (January–June 1983).

Fiegerer, Celeste. "Courage in Adversity." *MEI* 61 (July 1976):22–25.

Fishman, Alex. "The Palestinian Woman and the Intifada." *New Outlook* (June–July 1989):7–9.

Fitch, Florence. *The Daughter of Abd Salam: The Life of a Palestinian Peasant Woman*. Boston: B. Humphries, 1934.

Flapan, Simha. *The Birth of Israel: Myths and Realities*. New York: Pantheon Books, 1987.

Fondazione Internazionale Lelio Basso per il Diritto e la Liberazione dei Popoli. *Fatime, Leila e Altre: Incontri con donne Palestinese*. Rome, 1985. (Contains interviews with women in Israel, the Occupied Territories, and Lebanon, some of whom are artists, writers, and intellectuals as well as activists.)

Gadant, Monique, ed. *Women of the Mediterranean*. London: Zed Books, 1986.

Galilee, Lily. "Rendezvous in Brussels." *New Outlook* (June–July 1989):27–29.

Gansekoele, Heleen, and Claartje van Well. "Ik Vecht Veel Maar Iedereen Vecht Veel . . . : Een Beschrijving van het Leven van Palestinjnse Vrouwen." Ph.D. diss., University of Nijmegen, 1979.

Georgetown University. Center for Contemporary Arab Studies. "Women and Arab Society: Old Boundaries, New Frontiers." Eleventh Annual Symposium, April 10–11, 1986, Washington, D.C. (Publication of papers in preparation.)

Gerbner, George. "Mass Media Discourse: Message System Analysis as a Component of Cultural Indicators." In *Discourse and Communication*, edited by Teun
van Dijk. Berlin and New York: Walter de Gruyter, 1985.

Ghabra, Shafeeq. *Palestinians in Kuwait: The Family and the Politics of Survival.*
Boulder, Colo.: Westview Press, 1987.

Ghandur, Muna Ahmad. *Al-fida'iat, um ahmad wa-banataha al-thalathah fi al-
mar'araka.* Beirut: Matba'at al-Wafa, 1969.

al-Ghazawi, Iazt. "The Woman Prisoner." *New Outlook* (December 1985):31–33.

el-Ghul, Mawwal. "A Woman's Problem: Those I Love Have Emigrated to
America." *Al-Sha'ab*, 12 November 1985, 10.

Giacaman, Rita. "Building Barricades and Breaking Barriers." In *Intifada: The Palestinian Uprising against Israeli Occupation*, edited by Zachary Lockman and Joel
Beinin. Boston: South End Press, 1989.

——. "Health as a Social Construction: The Debate in the Occupied
Territories." *Middle East Report* (November–December 1989):16–20.

——. *Life and Health in Three Palestinian Villages.* London: Ithaca Press, 1988.

——. "Palestinian Women and Development in the Occupied West Bank."
Unpub. ms, obtained from the author at Birzeit University, n.d. Mimeo.

——. "Palestinian Women and Development in the Occupied West Bank." Brief
no. 5. London: Council of Arab-British Understanding.

——. "Palestinian Women in the Uprising: From Followers to Leaders." Birzeit:
The Community Health Unit, Birzeit University, 1988.

——. "Reflections on the Palestinian Women's Movement in the Israeli-
Occupied Territories." Unpub. ms, May 1987.

——, and Penny Johnson. "Palestinian Women: Building Barricades and Breaking Barriers." In *Intifada: The Palestinian Uprising against the Israeli Occupation*,
edited by Zachary Lockman and Joel Beinin. Boston: South End Press, 1989.

——, and Muna Odeh. "Palestinian Women's Movement in the Israeli-
Occupied West Bank and Gaza Strip." In *Women of the Arab World*, edited by
Nahid Toubia, translated by Nahed El Gamal. London: Zed Books, 1988.

Gilmour, David. *Dispossessed.* London: Sidgwick and Jackson, 1980.

Ginat, Joseph. "A Rural Arab Community in Israel: Marriage Patterns and
Woman's Status." Ph.D. diss., University of Utah, 1975.

Gowen, Sara. "Women's Resistance under Occupation." *The Middle East* 165 (July
1988):44–45.

Graham-Brown, Sarah. "The Education of Palestinian Women on the West
Bank." In *Images and Reality: Palestinian Women under Occupation and in the
Diaspora*, edited by S. Sabbagh and G. Talhami. Washington, D.C.: Institute
of Arab Women's Studies, 1990.

——. *Images of Women: The Portrayal of Women in Photography of the Middle East,
1860–1950.* New York: Columbia University Press, 1988.

——. "Impact on the Social Structure of Palestinian Society." In *Occupation:
Israel over Palestine*, edited by Naseer Aruri. Belmont, Mass.: Association of
Arab-American University Graduates, 1983.

———. *Palestinians and Their Society, 1880–1946: A Photographic Essay*. London, New York: Quartet Books, 1980.

Granqvist, Hilma. *Birth and Childhood among the Arabs: Studies in a Muhammadan Village*. Helsinki: Societas Scientiarum Fennica, 1947.

———. *Marriage Conditions in a Palestinian Village*. 2 pts. Helsinki: Societas Scientiarum Fennica, 1931, 1935.

———. *Muslim Death and Burial: Arab Customs and Traditions Studied in a Village in Jordan*. Helsinki: Societas Scientiarum Fennica, 1965.

GUPW. *Political Report of the General Union of Palestinian Women, Third Congress*. Beirut: 1980. Reprinted for the "UN Decade for Women" Copenhagen Conference.

Haddad, Yvonne. "Palestinian Women: Patterns of Legitimation and Domination." In *The Sociology of the Palestinians*, edited by K. Nakhleh and Elia Zuriek. London: Croom/Helm, 1980.

Haddad, Yousef. *Society and Folklore in Palestine: A Study*. Acre: Dar al-Aswar, 1987. (Proverbs, 49–56; marriage, 67–110; pregnancy and children's songs, 111–26; elegies for men and women, 127–46; also other subjects.)

al-Haj, Majid. *Social Change and Family Processes: Arab Communities in Shefar 'Am*. Boulder, Colo.: Westview Press, 1987.

Hajjar, L., M. Rabbani, and J. Beinin. "Palestine and the Arab-Israeli Conflict for Beginners." In *Intifada: The Palestinian Uprising against Israeli Occupation*, edited by Zachary Lockman and Joel Beinin. Boston: South End Press, 1989.

Halabi, Rafik. *The West Bank Story*. New York: Harcourt Brace Jovanovich, 1981, 105–6, 278–84.

Halaby, Samia. "Profile: Sumayyah Samaha." In *Newsletter*, Association of Arab-American University Graduates, Inc. (May–June 1981), 14.

Halsell, Grace. "Nahla's Story: A Badge of Honor." *MEI* 147 (10 April 1981):19.

al-Hamdani, Laila. "A Palestinian Woman in Prison." In *Women in the Middle East*, edited by Khamsin Collective. London: Zed Books, 1987.

———. "Palestinian Women in the Occupied Territories." In *Women in the Middle East*, edited by Khamsin Collective. London: Zed Books, 1987.

Hammami, Rema. "Women, the Hijab and the Intifada." *Middle East Report* 20 (May–August 1990):24–28.

Harfouch, Samira. "An Assessment of the Status of Women in Education, Labor Force, and Development in the Case of Jordan." Report prepared for International Center for Research on Women, Washington, D.C., 1980.

Hassan, O. "Folk Crafts: Straw Weaving." *Turat wa al-Mjtama'* (Arabic), 16, 1982.

Hatta, Jihad. *Zikariyat 'an m'arikat aylul*. Beirut: Ittihad al-Kuttab, 1977.

Hijab, Nadia. *Womanpower: The Arab Debate on Women and Work*. Cambridge: Cambridge University Press, 1988, 94–115, 158–61.

Hilal, Jamil. "Mulahazat wa istintajat awaliyya hawl musharakat al-mar' al-Filastiniyya fi al-intaj." (GUPW 1981 colloquium.)

———. "The Palestinian Women's Movement in the Occupied Territories of 1967: The Reality and the Horizons" (Aafaq). *New Jordan* 3 (Spring 1986):77–94.

Hiltermann, Joost. "Before the Uprising: The Organization of Palestinian Workers and Women in the Israeli Occupied West Bank and Gaza Strip." Ph.D. diss., University of California, Santa Cruz, 1988.

———. *Behind the Intifada: Labor and Women's Movement in the Occupied Territories.* Princeton: Princeton University Press, 1991.

———. "Organizing Under Occupation." *MEI* 296 (20 March 1987):14–16.

———. "Trade Unions and Women's Committees: Sustaining Movement, Creating Space." *Middle East Report* 20 (May–August 1990):32–36.

Hirst, David. *The Gun and the Olive Branch: The Roots of Violence in the Middle East.* New York & London: Harcourt Brace Jovanovich, 1977.

Institut du Monde Arabe. *Memoire de Soie: Costumes et Parures de Palestine et de la Jordanie: Catalogue de la Collection Widad Kamel Kawar.* Paris, 1988.

"International Woman's Day." *PFLP Bulletin* 61 (April 1982). (Interviews with Jihan Helou.)

Ittihad al-Amm lil Mar'a al-Filastiniyya (IAMF). *Ihsa' al-mu'ataqalat al-Filastiniyya aladhina dakhalu sijoon al-ihtilal al-sahyooni.* Beirut, 1980.

———. *Mashrua' li helqa dirasiyya hawl awda' al-mar'a al-Filastiniyya ijtima'iyyan, iqtisadiyyan wa siyasiyyan.* Beirut, 1981.

———. *Al-mu'tamar al-thaniya: Tanzheem wa ta'bi'a taqat al-mar'a d' ama asasiyya fi m'arikat al-tahrir.* Beirut, August 1974.

———. *Tal al-Za'ter: al-shaheed wa al-shahad.* Beirut, April 1977.

al ittihad al-nisai' al arabi bil kuds fi yubeelihi eth-thahabi, 1980. (The Arab Women's Union in Its Golden Anniversary, 1980). Jerusalem, April 1983.

Jabbour, Hala. *A Woman from Nazareth.* New York: Olive Branch Press, 1989.

Jaber, Ahmad. *The Educational Standard of the Graduates of the Centers for Literacy in the West Bank.* Birzeit: Birzeit University, 1987.

Jad, Islah. "From Salons to Popular Committees: Palestinian Women, 1919–89." In *Intifada: Palestine at the Crossroads,* edited by Jamal Nassar and Roger Heacock. New York: Praeger, 1990.

Jafarey, S. A., et al. "Use of Medical, Para-Medical Personnel and Traditional Midwives in Palestine Family Planning Program." *Demography* 5 (1968):666–79.

Jammal, Laila. *Contributions by Palestinian Women to the National Struggle for Liberation.* Washington, D.C.: Middle East Public Relations, 1985.

Jaussen, A. J. *Costumes des Arabes au pays de Moab.* Paris: Adrien, 1948.

———. *Costumes palestiniennes: Vol. 1, Naplouse et son district.* Paris: Geuthner, 1927.

Jones, Christina. *The Ramallah Handicraft Cooperative.* Ramallah, 1962.

Jordanian Writers' Union. "Women's Commitee for International Women's Day: Recommendations of the Seminar on Women's Issues, 3–8 March 1986." *New Jordan* 3 (Spring 1986):74–76.

Joseph, Suad. "Women and Politics in the Middle East." *Middle East Reports* (January–February 1986).

Jouis, Jeanne. "Le Costume feminin dans l'Islam syro-palestinien." *Revue des Études Islamiques* 4 (1934):481–505.

Karmi, Ghada. "Liberation through Revolution for Palestinian Women." *The Guardian* (14 May 1976).

Kawar, Widad. *Costumes Dyed by the Sun: Palestinian Arab National Costumes*. Tokyo: Bunka Suppan, 1982.

Kazi, Hamida. "Palestinian Women and the National Liberation Movement: A Social Perspective." In *Women in the Middle East*, edited by Khamsin Collective. London: Zed Books, 1987.

Khader, Sami. *Critical Study of the Experience of Literacy Education in the West Bank and Gaza*. Jerusalem: Arab Thought Forum, 1987.

———. *Women, Education and Development in the Third World*. Birzeit: Birzeit University Literacy Office, 1986.

Khaled, Leila. *My People Shall Live: The Autobiography of a Revolutionary*. London: Hodder and Stoughton, 1973.

Khalidi, Walid, ed. *From Haven to Conquest*. Beirut: Institute of Palestine Studies, 1971.

Khalifah, Ijlal. *Al-Mara'a wa kadiyyat Falastine* (Women and the Palestine Cause). Cairo: Modern Arab Press, 1974. (A content analysis, with examples, of how Egyptian women's magazines reported the struggle of Palestinian women from the 1920s until the 1970s.)

Khalifeh, Sahar. "Our Fate, Our House." *Middle East Report* 20 (May–August 1990):30–31.

———. *The Sunflower*. Jerusalem: Dar al-Kateb, 1980.

———. *Wild Thorns*. Translated by Trevor Le Gassick and Elizabeth Fernea. London: Al Saqi Books, 1986. First published in 1976 as *Al-Subar* by Galileo Limited, Jerusalem. (A novel.)

al-Khalili, Ghazi. *Al-mar'a al-Filastiniyah wa al-thawra*. (The Palestinian Woman and the Revolution). Beirut: Markaz al-Abhath al-Filastiniyya, 1977; Acre: Dar al-Aswar, 1981.

———. "The Palestinian Woman and the Revolution." *JPS* 6 (Winter 1977):164–65. (Translated from "Al-mar'a al-Filastiniya wa al-thawra," *Shu'un Filastiniya*, October–November, 1976.)

al-Khayyat, Abd al-'Aziz. "An Islamic Viewpoint on the Concept of Association of Both Sexes and Its Rules." Seminar on the Status of Women in the Islamic Family, Cairo, 20–22 December 1975. (The author is Jordan's Minister of Islamic Affairs and Holy Places. Palestinian women in the West Bank are under Jordanian law.)

Kossman, I., and L. Scharenberg, eds. *Palastinensische Frauen: Der Alltagliche Kampf*. Berlin: Das Arabische Buch, 1982.

Kutschera, Chris. "Biting Truths behind Flowery Metaphors." *The Middle East* 64 (February 1980):44–45. (About Sahar Khalifah.)

Kuttab, Eileen, and al-Ratrout Khalidah. "Women's Cooperative Experience: The Cooperatives of Beitello and Sa'ir." *Developmental Affairs*. (East Jerusalem) 1 (December 1988):24–26.

Layish, Aharon. *Marriage, Divorce, and Succession in the Druze Family: A Study Based on Decisions of Druze Arbitrators and Religious Courts in Israel and the Golan Heights*. Leiden: Brill, 1982.

————. "Qadis and Sharia in Israel." *Asian and African Studies* 7 (1971):237–72.

————. *Women and Islamic Law in a Non-Muslim State: A Study Based on Decisions on the Sharia Courts in Israel*. New York: John Wiley, 1975.

————. "Women and Succession in the Druze Family in Israel." *Asian and African Studies* 11 (1976):101–19.

Lebanese Association for Information on Palestine. *Facts: Women's Resistance* (two parts). Beirut, 1975.

Lehn, Walter. "And the Fund Still Lives." *JPS* 3 (Summer 1974):74–96.

"Leila Khaled Answers Some Questions." *RISK* 7 (1971).

Lentin, Ronit. "Palestinian Women." *Women's View* 4 (Winter 1980).

Lesch, Ann Mosely. *Arab Politics in Palestine, 1917–1939: The Frustration of a Nationalist Movement*. Ithaca and London: Cornell University Press, 1979.

————. "Palestine: Land and People." In *Occupation: Israel over Palestine*, edited by Naseer Aruri. Belmont, Mass.: Association of Arab-American University Graduates, 1983.

————. *The Palestinian Uprising—Causes and Consequences*. Field Staff Reports, Africa/Middle East, no. 1, 1988–89.

————. *Political Perceptions of the Palestinians on the West Bank and the Gaza Strip*. Washington, D.C.: Middle East Institute, 1980.

Lev, Ilana. "Profile of an Arab Authoress: Najwa Farau." *New Outlook* 1 (January 1964):51–52.

Levy, Gideon. "Samiha Khalil: First Lady." *New Outlook* (June–July 1989):37–40.

Lewis, Harriet. "Palestinian Women, It Is Possible to Agree on Principles: An Interview with Hanan Mikhail-Ashrawi." *New Outlook* (June–July 1989):7–9.

Lipman, Beata. *Israel, the Embattled Land: Jewish and Palestinian Women Talk about Their Lives*. London: Allen and Unwin, 1988.

Lockman, Zachary, and Joel Beinin, eds. *Intifada: The Palestinian Uprising against Israeli Occupation*. Boston: South End Press, 1989.

Lutfiyya, L. M. "The Family." In *Readings in Arab Middle Eastern Societies and Cultures*, edited by A. M. Lutfiyya and C. W. Churchill. The Hague: Mouton, 1966.

McConnan, Isabel. "The Double Challenge Facing Gazan Women." *MEI* 315, (19 December 1987): 19–20.

McDonnell, Pat. "West Bankers: Iron Bars . . . " *The Middle East* 56 (June 1979), 48–49. (About exchanged prisoner Afifah Bannoura.)

Makdisi, J. S. *Beirut Fragments: A War Memoir*. New York: Persea Books, 1990.

Makhoul, Nejwa. "The Woman Question in Third World Development: Examples from the Palestinian Case." Conference on Development in the Arab World, New York, October 1–3, 1976. *Annals of the New York Academy*, 1976.

Malvi, Robin. "Women in Palestine." Women's Liberation Workshop, August 1970.

Mansour, Sylvie. "Identity among Palestinian Youth: Male and Female Differentials." *JPS* 6 (Summer 1977):71–89.

"A Meeting with a Girl Who Elicited the Praise of the Critics." *At-Talia* 26 January 1989, 5. (Artist Salwa Ibrahim.) Also see 19 January 1989, 7.

Merizian, Amal. *Description of Mother-Infant Interactions in Palestinian Women.* Ph.D. diss.,University of Illinois at Chicago, 1991.

Michael, B. "The Tale of Three Women." *MEI* 174 (7 May 1982):11. (Originally printed in *Ha'aretz* on 14 March 1982.)

Middle East Research and Information Project. *Arab Women Workers.* Washington, D.C., 1976.

"Mihwar Khass: Waqi' al-mar'a al-Filastiniya." *Samed al-Iqtisadi* 8 (July–August), 1986.

Mikhail-Ashrawi, Hanan. *From Intifada to Independence.* The Netherlands: The Palestine Information Office–Netherlands and the Arab League Office, 1989.

Miller, Ylana. *Government and Society in Rural Palestine 1920–1948.* Austin: University of Texas Press, 1985.

Minai, Naila. *Women in Islam: Tradition and Transition in the Middle East.* New York: Seaview Books, 1981.

Minces, Juliet. *Arab Women: From Oppression to Liberation.* London: Zed Books, 1981.

———. "Women in Algeria." In *Women in the Muslim World*, edited by Lois Beck and Nikki Keddie. Cambridge: Harvard University Press, 1980.

Mogannam, Matiel. *The Arab Woman and the Palestine Problem.* London: Herbert Joseph, 1937. Reprint, Westport, Conn.: Hyperion Press, 1976.

Mourad, K. "Palestiniennes: Elles luttes a mains nues." *Elle* (5 December 1988).

al-Nabulsi, Shakir. "Fadwa Toukan wa-al-shi'r al-urduni al muasir." Cairo: al-Dar al-Qawmi lil-Tiba'ah wa-al-Nashr, 1966.

Najjar, Aida. "The Arabic Press and Nationalism in Palestine, 1920–1948." Ph.D. diss., Syracuse University, 1975.

Najjar, Atallah, and Rafik al-Khatib. "Faisal Husseini: Home Is the Natural Place for a Woman." *Abeer* 1 (July 1986):14–15.

Najjar, Orayb. "Between Nationalism and Feminism: The Palestinian Answer." In *Women Transforming Politics: Worldwide Strategies for Empowerment*, edited by Jill Bystydzienski. Bloomington: Indiana University Press, 1992.

———. "The Coverage of Women in West Bank Newspapers." In *Images and Reality: Palestinian Women under Occupation and in the Diaspora*, edited by S. Sabbagh and G. Talhami. Washington, D.C.: Institute of Arab Women's Studies, 1990.

———. "Still 'A Difficult Journey up the Mountain'? " In *The Third Wave: Feminist Perspectives on Racism*, edited by N. Alarcon, L. Albrecht, J. Alexander, S. Day, and M. Sergest. Latham, New York: Kitchen Table, 1992.

Nashashibi, Nasir al-Din. *Nisa min al-sharq al-awsat: Al-Siyasah ismuha imraah* (Women from the Middle East: Politics Is Called Woman). London: Riyad al Rayyis lil-Kutub wa-al-Nashr, 1988.

Nasif, Munirah. "Madame Fatma Nimet Rachid recoit la delegation feminin Palestinienne." *La Reforme* (9 January 1946).

"Nedwa al-'adad: Waqi' al-mar'a al-Filastiniyya." *Samed al-Iqtisadi* 4 (March 1981).

Nye, Naomi. "One Village." *JPS* 13 (Winter 1984). (Contains portrait of author's grandmother.)

Ode-Vasileva, K. V. "Les coutumes relatives à l'accouchement de la traitement du nouveau ne chez les Arabes du nord de la Palestine." *Sovetskaya Etnografiya* 3 (1936):93–97.

Othman, Ali. "Palestinian Woman before the Start of the Twentieth Century 1880–1910." In *Afkar Falastini* (Thoughts of a Palestinian). Ramallah, 1976, 107–12. (Also contains articles about women's beauty, marriage and education, immigration, and involvement in public life.)

Otto, Ingeborg, and Schmidt-Dumont, Marianne. *Frauenfragen im Modernen Orient: Eine Auswahlbibliographie* (Women in the Middle East and North Africa: A Selected Bibliography). Hamburg: Deutsches Orient-Institut, Dokumentations-Leitstelle Moderner Orient, 1982.

Palestine Research Center. *The Struggle of Palestinian Women*. Beirut, 1975.

"Palestinian Women." *Hysteria* (November 1970).

"Palestinian Women Honor Huda Sha'rawi." *Al-Ahram*, 17 December 1974, 8.

Palestinian Yearbook, 1968. Beirut: Institute for Palestine Studies, 1968.

Pallas, Elfie. "Equal under Oppression." *MEI* 197 (3 April 1987):8.

Pedersen, Birgitte. "Oppressive and Liberating Elements in the Situation of the Palestinian Woman." In *Women in Islamic Societies*, edited by B. Utas. London and Malmo: Curzon Press, 1983.

Peretz, Don. "The Arab Minority of Israel." *MEJ* 8 (Spring 1954).

———. *Israel and the Palestine Arabs*. Washington, D.C.: Middle East Institute, 1958.

———. "Problems of Arab Refugee Compensation." *MEJ* 8 (Autumn 1954).

———. *The West Bank: History, Politics, Society, and Economy*. Boulder, Colo.: Westview Press, 1986.

Peteet, Julie Marie. *Gender in Crisis: Women and the Palestinian Resistance Movement*. New York: Columbia University Press, 1991.

———. "No Going Back: Women and the Palestinian Movement." *Middle East Report* 16 (January–February 1986):20–24, 44.

———. "Women and National Politics: The Palestinian Case." In *Class, Power and Stability in the Middle East*, edited by B. Berberoglu. London: Zed Press, 1989.

———. "Women and National Politics: The Palestinian Case." Ph.D. diss., Wayne State University, 1985.

———, and Rosemary Sayigh. "Between Two Fires: Palestinian Women in Lebanon." In *Caught Up in Conflict: Women's Responses to Political Strife*, edited by R. Ridd and H. Callaway. Basingstoke: Macmillan, 1986.

PFWAC. *Darb al-mar'a* (Woman's Path). June 1987.

———. *The Development of the Palestinian Women's Movement in the Territories Occupied in 1967: After 20 years of Israeli Occupation*. 1987.

———. *Hawl awda' al-mar'a al-Filastiniyya fi al-manataq al-muhtalla: Dirasa mayda-niyya.* Ramallah/al-Bireh: Lejnat al-Amal al-Nissa'i, 1980.

———. *Kifah al-mar'a* (Woman's Struggle). June 1984.

———. *Masirat al-mar'a* (Woman's March), 1986.

———. *The Program and Internal Platform of the Palestinian Federation of Women's Action Commmittees in the Occupied Territories.* 1988.

———. *Statistics about the Condition of the Palestinian Woman in Education, Work, and the Extent of Her Involvement in Nationalist Work.* N.d.

"A Picture of Fighting Palestinian Woman in the Mountain District of Lebanon." *Al-Ahram* (10 October 1976):5.

PLO. Department of Information. "Women under Occupation: Palestinian Women in the Occupied West Bank and Gaza Strip." Tunis, April 1988.

———. Department of National Information and Guidance. *The Woman's Role in the Palestine National Struggle.* Beirut, n.d.

"Poison: True or False?" *MEI* 198 (15 April 1983):8–9.

Popplewell, M. J. "Partnership or Isolation: Arab Women under Israeli Rule." *MEI* 87 (September 1978):25–26.

PWWC. *Nidal al-mar'a al-amila* (Struggle of the Working Woman). 1985.

———. *Nisa'a al-intifada* (Women of the Intifada). 8 March 1989, 46.

al-Qazzaz, Ayad. *Women in the Arab World: An Annotated Bibliography.* Detroit: Association of Arab-American University Graduates, 1975.

al-Qudsi-Ghabra, Taghreed. "City and Village in the Palestinian Wedding Song: The Palestinian Community in Kuwait." In *Images and Reality: Palestinian Women under Occupation and in the Diaspora*, edited by S. Sabbagh and G. Talhami. Washington, D.C.: Institute of Arab Women's Studies, 1990.

Quiring, Jane. "The Female Dimension of Palestinian Development." In *Which Way Women?*, edited by Dorothy Yoder Nyce. Akron, Penn.: Mennonite Central Committee Peace Section.

Raccagni, Michelle. *The Modern Arab Woman: A Bibliography.* London: Scarecrow Press, 1978, 195–98.

Rahbek, Birgitte. "Palestinian Women, Equality, Development and Peace." Paper prepared for Copenhagen World Conference ("UN Decade for Women"), 1980.

Rajab, Jehan S. *Palestinian Costume.* London: Kegan Paul, 1989.

Redelli, Pera. "Palestinian Working Women in the Occupied Territories." *Democratic Thought* 1 (Winter 1988):28–39. (Arabic)

Ricks, Thomas. "Palestinian Education: Directions and Areas of Research." *Birzeit Research Review* 1 (Spring 1985):3–14.

Rishmawi, Mona. "The Legal Status of Palestinian Women in the Occupied Territories." In *Women of the Arab World: The Coming Challenge*, edited by N. Toubia. London: Zed Books, 1988.

Roch, Dominique. "Femmes en exil." *Revue d'Études Palestiniennes* 14 (Winter 1986).

Rockwell, Susan. "Palestinian Women Workers in the Israel-Occupied Gaza Strip." *JPS* 14.2 (Winter 1985).

Rose, Sharon. "Interview with Eileen Kuttab: Women and the Intifada." *Palestine Focus* 8 (November–December 1989).

Rosenfeld, Henry. "An Analysis of Marriage and Marriage Statistics for a Muslim and Christian Arab Village." *International Archives of Ethnology* 1 (1957):32–62.

———. "Change, Barriers to Change, and Contradictions in the Arab Village Family." *American Anthropologist* 4 (August 1968):732–52. Reprint, *New Outlook* 2 (Fall 1970):28–44.

———. "On Determinants of the Status of Arab Village Women." *Man* 60 (1958).

Sabbagh, Suha. "Palestinian Women Writers and the Intifada." *Social Text: Theory/ Culture/Ideology* 22 (Spring 1989):62–78.

———, S., and G. Talhami, eds. *Images and Reality: Palestinian Women under Occupation and in the Diaspora*. Washington, D.C.: Institute of Arab Women's Studies, 1990.

Said, Edward. *The Question of Palestine*. New York: Vintage, 1980.

———, and Christopher Hitchens, eds. *Blaming the Victims: Spurious Scholarship and the Palestine Question*. London and New York: Verso, 1988.

Sakakini, Hala. *Jerusalem and I: A Personal Record*. Jerusalem: Habesch, The Commercial Press, 1987.

Salome, Louis. "Report by Israelis Is Critical of Army Actions in Territories." *The News and Observer*, 23 November 1989, 36A.

Samed, Amal. "The Proletarianization of Palestinian Women in Israel." *MERIP* 6 (August 1976).

Sarhan, Bassem. *Al-A'ila wa al-qaraba 'and al-Filastiniyeen fi Kuwait*. Kuwait: al-Mahad al-'Arabi lil Tahteen al-Iqtisadi wa al-Ijtima'i, n.d.

———. *Family and Kinship among Palestinians in Kuwait*. General Palestinian Union of Writers and Journalists. Proceedings of a Workshop on Family and Kinship held in Kuwait, November 1976.

———. "The Traditional Aspects of the Palestinian Woman in Lebanon and Her Participation in the Revolution; A Preliminary Study." *Shu'un Filastiniyah* 14 (January 1972):142–55.

al-Sarraj, Nadirah. "In Rememberance of Samira Azzam on the Fifth Anniversary [of her death]." *Shu'un Filastiniyah* 14 (October 1972):69–82.

Sayegh, May. *The Arab Palestinian Woman: Reality and Impediments*. Beirut: GUPW, 1980. (Published in English, French, and Arabic.)

———. "Choisir la revolution." *Peuples Méditerranéens* 22–23 (January–June 1983).

———. "Qiyadat al-thawra ma zalat maqsura tujah mawdoo' al-mar'a." *Al-Summood* (15 March 1980).

Sayigh, Rosemary. "Daily Life in Palestinian Camps." *Spare Rib* (January 1978).

———. "Encounters with Palestinian Women under Occupation." *JPS* 10 (Summer 1981).

———. "Femmes palestiniennes: Une histoire en quete d'historiens." *Revue d'études Palestiniennes* 23 (Spring 1987).

———. "Looking across the Mediterranean." *MERIP* 14 (June 1984): 22–26.

———. "The Mukhabarat State: Testimony of a Palestinian Woman Prisoner." *Race and Class* 26 (August 1984).

———. "Palestine." *Third World Quarterly* 5 (October 1983), in a section titled "Women in Struggle."

———. "Palestinian Women and Politics in Lebanon." In *Proceedings of a Symposium on Women and Arab Society: Old Boundaries, New Frontiers*, CCAS, Georgetown University, Washington, D.C., April 1986. (Publication in preparation.)

———. "Palestinian Women: Triple Burden, Single Struggle." *Peuples Méditerranéens* 44–45 (July–December 1988). Also in *Palestine: Profile of an Occupation*, edited by Khamsin Collective. London: Zed Books, 1989.

———. Review of *My Home, My Prison* by Raymonda Hawa-Tawil. *Arab Studies Quarterly* 3 (Spring 1981):215–20.

Schilling, Nancy Adams. "The Social and Political Research of Arab Women: A Study in Conflict." In *Women in Contemporary Muslim Societies*, edited by Jane Smith. London: Associated University Presses, 1980.

Seger, Karen, ed. *Portrait of a Palestinian Village: The Photographs of Hilma Granqvist*. London: Third World Publishing Center, 1981.

Seoudi, Fethiya. *Ahwal al-Filastiniyeen al-sahiya wa al-ijtima'iya fi Lubnan*. Beirut: Muessessa al-'Arabiya al-Dirasat wa al-Nashara, 1979.

Shaaban, Bouthaina. *Both Right and Left Handed: Arab Women Talk about Their Lives*. London: Women's Press, 1988.

Shadid, Myriam. "Femmes palestiniennes et politique." In *Femmes et politique autour de la Méditerranée*, edited by C. Souriau. Paris: L'Harmettan, 1980.

Shafiq, Munir. "Mawdoo'at hawl nidal al-mar'a." *Shu'un Filastiniyyah* 62 (1977).

Shami, Seteney Khalid. "Studying Your Own: The Complexities of Shared Culture." In *Arab Women in the Field*, edited by Soraya Altorki and Camillia El-Solh. Syracuse, N.Y.: Syracuse University Press, 1988.

———. *Women in Arab Society: Work Patterns and Gender Relations in Egypt, Jordan, and Sudan*. New York: St. Martin's Press for UNESCO, 1990.

Shehadeh, Raja. *Occupier's Law: Israel and the West Bank*. Washington, D.C.: Institute for Palestine Studies, 1985.

Shur, Chaim, and Liora Barash. Interview with Raymonda Tawil: "The PLO is the Conscience of the Palestinian People." *New Outlook*. (March/April 1984): 10–14.

Siddiq, Mohammed. "The Fiction of Sahar Khalifah: Between Defiance and Deliverance." *Arab Studies Quarterly* 8 (Spring 1986):143–60.

Siniora, Hanna. "An Analysis of the Current Revolt." *JPS* 17 (Spring 1988):3–13.

Siniora, Randa. "Palestinian Labor in a Dependent Economy: The Case of Women in Sub-Contracting Clothing Industry in the West Bank." M.A. thesis, American University in Cairo, 1987.

Sosebee, Stephen. "The Palestinian Women's Movement and the Intifada: A Historical and Current Analysis." *American Arab Affairs* 32 (Spring 1990):81–91.

"The Status of Arab Women in Israel." *Middle East Review* 2 (Winter 1976/77): 55–57.

Stillman, Yedida Kalfon. *Palestinian Costume and Jewelry*. Albuquerque: University of New Mexico Press, 1979.

———, and Serene Shadid. *Palestinian Embroidery: Cross-Stitch Patterns from the Traditional Costumes of Village Women of Palestine*. London: British Museum, 1988.

Stohl, Michael. "Une femme dans le siege des camps." *Revue d'études Palestiniennes* 24 (Summer 1987):57–66.

"A Struggle for Identity." *The Middle East* 134 (December 1985):38–39. (About Sahar Khalifah.)

Strum, Philippa. "Women and Peace." *New Outlook* (June–July 1989):30–33.

Swedenberg, Ted. "Palestinian Historiography." *Birzeit Research Review* 2 (Winter 1985–86).

al-Tal, Suheir. "Information Policy and Women's Issues" [in Jordan]. *New Jordan* (Cyprus), 3 (Spring 1986):73.

Talhami, Ghada. "Arab Women's Liberation." *Genesis* 12 (April 1981):8–9.

———. "The Human Rights of Women in Islam." *Journal of Social Philosophy* 16 (Winter 1985):1–7.

———. "One Woman's Ansar Story." Review of *Duet for Freedom* by Dina Abdel Hamid. *The Return* 1 (January 1989):30–31, 36–37.

———. "Palestinian Women: The Case for Political Liberation." *Arab Perspectives* 4 (January 1984):6–11.

———. "Women and the Question of Palestine." In UN *North American* NGO *Symposium on the Question of Palestine*, 25–27 June 1984. UN Document 84-25793, 130–43.

———. "Women as Revolutionaries." *JPS* 4 (Autumn 1974):169–71.

———. "The Women of Palestine." In *Palestine and the Palestinians*, edited by James A. Graff. Toronto: Near East Cultural and Educational Foundation of Canada, 1989.

———. "Women of the Intifada." Editorial, *Chicago Tribune*, 15 December 1989, 26.

———. "Women under Occupation: The Great Transformation." In *Images and Reality: Palestinian Women under Occupation and in the Diaspora*, edited by S. Sabbagh and G. Talhami. Washington, D.C.: Institute of Arab Women's Studies, 1990.

Tamari, Salim. "Building other People's Homes: The Palestinian Peasant's Household and Work in Israel." *JPS* 11 (Autumn 1981).

———. "Limited Rebellion and Civil Society: The Uprising's Dilemma." *Middle East Report* 164/165 (May–August 1990):4–8.

———. "The Palestinian Demand for Independence Cannot be Postponed Indefinitely." *MERIP* (October/December 1981).

———. "What the Uprising Means." In *Intifada: The Palestinian Uprising against Israeli Occupation*, edited by Zachary Lockman and Joel Beinin. Boston: South End Press, 1989.

Tawil, Raymonda. *My Home, My Prison*. New York: Rinehart and Winston, 1980. (Translated from the French edition, *Mon pays, mon prison*. Paris: Éditions de Seuil, 1979.)

———. "Return and Reminiscences of a Palestinian Woman." *New Outlook* 15 (November–December 1971).

Touby, Asma. *'Abir wa majd*. Beirut: Matba'at Qalalat, 1966. (Biographies of Palestinian women, mostly contemporary, prominent in art, literature, and social service.)

Touqan, Fadwa. See under Tuqan, Fadwa.

Tucker, Judith. "Women and the Politics of Patronage: Family Life in Nablus." Paper presented at the MESA annual conference, Boston, November 1986.

Tucker, Judith: "Ties that Bound: Women and Family in Eighteenth- and Nineteenth-Century Nablus." In *Women in Middle Eastern History: Shifting Boundaries in Sex and Gender*, edited by Nikki Keddie and Beth Baron. New Haven and London: Yale University Press, 1991.

Tuqan, Fadwa. "Constrained Adolescence from: *A Difficult Journey up the Mountain*." Translated by Hannah Amit-Kochavi. *New Outlook* (January–February 1987): 68–69.

———. *A Mountainous Journey*. St. Paul, Minn.: Graywolf Press, 1990.

———. *Al-Layl wa al-fursan*. Beirut: Dar al-Adab, 1969. (Poems in praise of the Palestinian Resistance.)

———. "Pages from My Diary." *Al-Tariq* 29 (February 1970).

———. "The Poetry of Fadwa Touqan." *New Middle East* (London) (April 1973): 11–12.

Turing, Penelope. "Women in Jordan: Progress and Participation." *MEI* 60 (June 1976):20–21.

al-Udwan, Andalib. "On the Occasion of Women's International Day . . . Where Is Woman in the Local Nationalist Press?" *Al-Mithaq* (7 March 1989):3.

UN. "The Conditions of Palestinian Women and Children in the Israeli Occupied Territories." International Conference on the Question of Palestine, Geneva, 1985.

———. "Regional Preparatory Meeting for the World Conference for the United Nations Decade for Women." E SDHS/CONF. 4/5, 4 December 1979. (Measures of assistance to Palestinian Women.)

———. "The Situation of Women and Children Living in the Occupied Arab Territories and Other Occupied Territories: Report of the Secretary-General." A/CONF. 116/6, 30 October 1984.

———. Economic Commission for Western Asia. "Social and Economic Conditions of Palestinian Women Inside and Outside the Occupied Territories." E/ECWA/SDHS/CONF. 4/65, February 1980.

UNESCO. "L'education du peuple arabe de Palestine." Conference of Arab Ministers of Education, UAE, 1977.

UPMRC. *The Union of Palestinian Medical Relief Committees: A Brief Review of Activities.* 1989.

UPWWC. *Women of the Intifada.* A one-time publication, March 1988 (in Arabic).

Van Arkadie, Brian. *Benefits and Burdens: A Report on the West Bank and Gaza Strip Economics Since 1967.* New York: Carnegie Endowment for International Peace, 1977.

Waddy, Chris. "New Opportunities for Jordan's Women." *MEI* 73 (July 1977): 29–31.

al-Wahidi, Maysoun al-Atawina. *La femme palestinienne et l'occupation israelienne.* Jerusalem: Ed. du Centre d'Études Arabes, 1986. (Reviewed in *Revue d'Études Palestiniennes* 24 (1987).

———. *Al-mar'a al-Filastiniyya wa al-ihtilal al-isra'eeli.* Al-Quds: Jami'at al-Dirasat al-Arabiyya, 1986.

———. *Women in the Occupied Territories.* Jerusalem: League of Arab States, 1985.

Wallach, John, and Janet Wallach. "The Liberation of Women: Mothering the Intifada." In *Still Small Voices: The Real Heroes of the Arab-Israeli Conflict.* San Diego: Harcourt Brace Jovanovich, 1989.

Warnock, Kitty. *Land before Honor.* New York: Monthly Review Press, 1990.

———. "Released Women Prisoners Speak." In *We Will Be Free in Our Homeland.* Committee Confronting the Iron Fist. Jerusalem: Arab Studies Society, 17 April 1986, 80–110.

Watad, Mohammad. "The War of Generations in the Arab Village." *New Outlook* (1964):29–33, 50.

WCSW *Fourth Issue of Accomplishments for the Year 1986.* March 1987:7, 17–18. (Arabic)

Weighert, Gideon. "Women Want Freedom." *New Outlook* 5 (June 1964), 60–62.

Weir, Shelagh. *Palestinian Costume.* Austin: University of Texas Press, 1989.

———. *Palestinian Embroidery.* London: British Museum, 1970.

———. *Spinning and Weaving in Palestine.* London: British Museum, 1970.

———, and Widad Kawar. "Costumes and Wedding Customs in Bayt Dajan." *Palestine Exploration Quarterly* (January–June 1975):39–52.

Wingate, R. O. "Moslem Women in Palestine and Syria." *World Dominion* (1934), 177–85.

"Women and Peace Conference." *New Outlook* (June–July 1989), 30.

"Women at Risk." *MEI* 195 (4 March 1983):7–8. (Palestinian women in Lebanon.)

"Women in the Palestinian Revolution." *PFLP Bulletin* 61 (April 1982).

"Women of Palestine." *ANERA Newsletter* 33 (1975).

"Women's Packet: A Collection of DataBase Project Documentation on Women and the Palestinian Uprising." The DataBase Project on Palestinian Human Rights, Chicago, 1989.

Yagi, Hashim, and Abdul-Rahman Yaghi, eds. *Shi'r Fadwa Tuqan.* Amman, 1970.

Yuval-Davis, Nira. *Women in the Middle East.* London: Zed Press, 1987.

Zaroo, Salah. *Education under the Shadow of the Intifada.* Translated by Adnan Shehadeh. Hebron: University Graduate Union Research Center, 1989. (Arabic and English)

Zerbe, Evelyne Accad. *Veil of Shame: The Role of Women in the Contemporary Fiction of North Africa and the Arab World.* Sherbrooke, Quebec: Editions Naaman, 1978.

Zuaiter, Akram. *The Palestine National Movement: 1935–1939.* 3d ed. Manshurat al-Yasar, Baka el-Gharbiyyah-Git, 1988.

Zycher, Augustine. "Palestinian Arab Women and the Vote." *Middle East Review* 2 (Winter 1976/77):52–54. (Excerpted from "Exercise in Democracy," *Jerusalem Post Weekly*, 4 May 1976.)

ARTICLES IN *AL-SHA'AB*, (AN ARABIC DAILY) BY WAFA AL-BAHER ABU-GHOSH AND ABLA YAEESH, OCTOBER 1985–JUNE 1986

"From the Old People's Home: Hajja Jamilah, and the Destiny of Lonliness." 22 October 1985, 10.

"Nursing: A Profession on the Move, But Difficulties Remain." 22 October 1985, 10.

"Aida Haddad: My Academic Ambition Is Timeless." 5 November 1985, 10.

"Angolan Women's March." 5 November 1985.

"Issues Regarding Women's Hostels." 5 November 1985, 10.

The Tribe Interrogates Ghada Samman." 12 November 1985.

"Women in the Village of Abu Falah." 12 November 1985, 10.

"Huda Nimr: A Teacher from my Country." 19 November 1985, 10.

"When a Woman Has a Choice of Working Away from Home." 19 November 1985, 10.

"Assia Habash: The Palestinian Woman Is Still inside the Bottle until Now." 17 December 1985, 10.

"Divorce: A New Look at a Permanent Problem." 17 December 1985, 10.

"Hala Nahhas [M.D.]: What Is Needed Is Effective Participation to Elevate the Condition of Palestinian Woman." 7 January 1986, 10.

"Women in Abu Ghosh Village." 14 January 1986, 10.

"A Face from My Country: Abstract Artist Ahlam Hijazi." 11 February 1986.

"The Old Question Still Stands, Boy or Girl? But They Ask about How the Mother Is Doing These Days." 11 February 1986, 10.

"Women As Engineers." 18 February 1986.

"Faizeh Abu Hilal: Blind Imitation Contradicts Women's Reality." 25 February 1986.

"Finding a Room: Al-Najah University Women Face a Chronic Problem." 25 February 1986.

"Re-drawing the Picture of Rural Women." 11 March 1986.

"The Mother: Ordinary Stories on a Special Day." 18 March 1986.

"Profession: Preserve Our Inheritance." 15 April 1986.

"Safa Odeh: Education Is an Indicator of Survival." 15 April 1986.

"Women in Kalandia Refugee Camp." 15 April 1986.

"When the Mother Is Absent, the Oldest Girl Performs More Than One Role." 13 May 1986.
"Faizeh Zalatimo: A Success Story in Administering a Medical Lab." 20 May 1986.
"Women as Dentists: Between the Sparkle of the Title, and the Problems of Work." 20 May 1986.
"Women in Balata Refugee Camp." 3 June 1986.
"Dr. Majida Nassar: An Ambition to Specialize . . . Belief in the Need for Women to Work." 17 June 1986.
"Woman as Artist." 17 June 1986.
"Dr. Fathiyyeh Nasru Writes about the Palestinian Child and Games." 24 June 1986.
"Woman as Lawyer." 24 June 1986.

ARTICLES ABOUT WOMEN IN *AL-FAJR (FE)* (ENGLISH-LANGUAGE WEEKLY PAPER)

1980
"Women in Palestinian Society." (First issue of English edition of *Al-Fajr*, April.)
"Halhul's Women's Work Committee Described." 23 April, p. 7.
"West Bank Nursing Conference." 18 May, p. 3.
"Women's Social Position in Palestinian Society." 25 May, p. 5; 11 August, p. 5.
"Bethlehem: Student Taghrid al Butmeh Killed." 22 June, p. 1; 29 June, p. 1; 6 July, p. 6; 14 September, p. 4.
"Ramallah Teacher Training College Raid." 22 June, p. 1."
"Copenhagen: UN Women's Conference." 20 July, p. 1.
"Women's Social Oppression in Arab World." 20 July, p. 8.
"Women Demonstrate in Support of Nafha Prison Strike." 27 July, p. 1.
"Anabta Charitable Women's Society Described." 3 August, p. 6.
"Copenhagen: International Women's Conference." 3 August, pp. 1, 4.
"Activist Leila Khalid Discusses Resistance Experience." 31 August, p. 3.
"Work Conditions in West Bank Factories." 31 August, p. 7.
"Women's Community Services Collectives." 14 September, p. 3.
"Positions in Fatah." 28 September, p. 5.
"Women's University Graduates Association Described." 2 November, p. 4.
"Increased Education in Camps." 30 November, p. 5.
"Secret Service Makes Collaboration Prerequisite for Reunion of Young Couple." 14 December, p. 3.

1981
"Arab College of Nursing: Students Strike for School Reform." 1 February, p. 4.
"Women's Work Committees in the West Bank Described." 22 February, p. 10.
"Women's Labor force." 1 March, p. 11.
"Artist Vera Tamari: Profile." 8 March, p. 13.
"General Union of Palestinian Women: History." 8 March, p. 9.
"Jerusalem: Women's World Day of Prayer Meeting." 8 March, p. 15.
"National Activism, History to Date." 8 March, p. 8.

"Women Lack Information to Manage Childbirth, Infant Care Problems." 8 March, p. 6.
"Women's Role in Unions of Occupied Territories." 8 March, p. 7.
"Working Conditions in Israeli Factory." 8 March, p. 7.
"Art Teachers Trained at Tireh UNRWA School." 15 March, p. 14.
"International Women's Day Celebrations." 15 March, pp. 1, 4.
"Kindergarten Programs in Camps." 15 March, p. 16.
"International Women's Day Celebrations at Birzeit University." 22 March, p. 15.
"Neve Tertza [Women's Prison] Prisoners Listed; Conditions Described." 19 April, p. 3.
"Al-Nahda Women's Association: Description." 3 May, p. 15.
"Jerusalem: Nurses' Day Celebrations." 17 May, p. 15.
"Women's Experiences in 1948." 27 May, p. 8.
"In'ash al-Usra: Projects Described." 7 June, p. 16.
"Soldiers Raid In'ash al-Usra Ceremony." 14 June, p. 13.
"Al-Khalili: The Palestinian Woman and the Revolution: Review." 12 July, p. 8.
"Women in Palestinian Economy: Employment; Work Conditions; Wages; Social Pressures." 2 August, p. 8.
"Women's Employment Opportunities, Industries, Problems." 2 August, p. 8.
"Arrabe: Liberation Efforts, Programs." 9 August, p. 14.
"Jerusalem: YWCA Exhibits Art on Village Theme." 23 August, p. 11.
"Women Restricted in Resistance Activities." 30 August, p. 16.
"Women's Health Deteriorates." 23 October, p. 5.
"Traditional Housework Difficult, Time-Consuming." 6 November, p. 15.

1982
"UNRWA Tireh Women's Institute Art Students' Show." 12 January, p. 11.
"Hebron: Young Women's Club Activities." 22 January, p. 14.
"[Birzeit University] Math Teacher Barred from Entering West Bank." 5 February, p. 4.
"Ramallah Women's Work Committee Activist Siham Barghouti: Orders Renewed." 5 March, 2.
"Gaza: Dress Changes; History." 12 March, p. 13.
"International Women's Day: History; Current Events." 12 March, pp. 3, 11.
"Women's Rights in the Arab World." 12 March, p. 11.
"Haifa Symposium Examines Oppression." 19 March, p. 13.
"Three Arab Women Profiled." 2 April, p. 10.
"Teacher Zahira Kamal: Order Renewed." 9 April, p. 2.
"Nuseirat: Arab Woman, 35, Body Found Buried in Sand." 23 April, p. 2.
"Silwan: Club Festival Held." 21 May, p. 15.
"Bethlehem Women's Work Committee Holds Fair." 4 June, p. 10.
"Women's Health Damaged by Frequent Pregnancies." 4 June, p. 16.
"Beit Hanina Daycare Center Opens." [PFWAC] 16 July, p. 13.
"In'ash al-Usra Provides Support to Large Families." October 8, p. 15.

1983

"Gaza; Women's Union Raided by Tax Officials." 18 February, p. 3.

"Palestinian Working Women's Federation Holds 1st Annual Conference." 18 February, p. 3.

"Women's Work Committee Holds Conference, International Women's Day Bazaar." 4 March, p. 4; 11 March, p. 3.

"Occupied Territories Committees Suffer from Factionalism." 11 March, p. 16.

"Um al-Fahm: Women's Conference Includes Speeches, Film, Arts." 25 March, p. 3.

"Kalandia Cooperative Teaches Vocational Skills." 22 April, p. 7.

"Palestinian Working Women Underpaid, Unprotected." 20 May, p. 8.

"Visiting Wife Beaten by Guards." 19 August, p. 15.

1984

"Abu Dis Women Describe Life as Arab Women." 7 March, p. 13.

"Women's Committees: Activities; Projects." 7 March, p. 16; 21 March, p. 16.

"Released Prisoner Shamout Reunited with Children in Algiers." 14 March, p. 15.

"Old Woman Jailed for Possessing Letter from Exiled Son." September 28, p. 3.

"Families Protest Bad Conditions [at Far'ah Prison]." 27 April, p. 15.

Abdel Fattah, Awad. "Kifah al-Mara'a: The WWC's [PUWWC] Magazine of Women's Struggle." 27 July, p. 7.

al-Ghazali, Said. "Muslim Brothers' Collision Course with Palestinian Nationalists." 27 July, pp. 8–9.

"Anabta, Women's Organization Members Rejected by Israeli Authorities." 21 March, p. 15.

"Women's Work Committee Holds 3rd General Conference." 18 May, p. 3.

"Women's Work Committee Publishes Annual Magazine *Kifah al-Mara'a* on Women's Conditions." 22 June, p. 4; Review, 27 July, p. 7.

"Beit Sahur's Women Reject Civil Administration." 13 July, p. 13.

1985

"History of Palestinian Women's Struggle," 8 March, p. 8; 15 March, p. 16.

Khalid, Usama. "A Palestinian History of Woman's Struggle." Part I, 8 March, pp. 8–9. Part II, 15 March, p. 16. (Translated from a 1984 *Al Hadaf* (Arabic weekly).

"March 8." 8 March, p. 5.

Pesa, Flavia. "The Straightjacket of Sex and Class." 8 March, pp. 15, 16.

"Rural Women: Labor; Living Conditions." 8 March, p. 16.

Said, Manar. "Maternity: High Risk in the West Bank." 8 March, pp. 7, 10.

"Women's Work Committee's 6th Annual Bazaar." 8 March, p. 3.

"Images of Women in Palestinian Literature Reviewed by Palestinian Critics." 15 March, p. 11.

"International Women's Day Celebrations." 15 March, p. 3.

Pesa, Flavia. "The Image of Women in Palestinian Literature." 15 March, p. 11.

Rouhana, Kate. "Occupied Territories Women Achieve Advancement in Education." 15 March, p. 7.

———. "West Bank Women Overcoming Obstacles to Education." 15 March, pp. 7, 10.

[PUWWC]. "Interview with Women's Work Committee Secretary Zahira-Kamal, Activities." 29 March, p. 10.

"Surif Needlework Cooperative; History, Products." 5 April, p. 7.

Kuttab, Daoud. "Women's Centre Principal Wins Case against UNRWA." 19 April, p. 7. (Article about Assia Habash.)

"Occupied Territories Women in Israeli Factories: Conditions, Wages; Israeli Contractors." 19 April, p. 8.

"Palestinian Women's Magazine Reviewed." 3 May, p. 16.

"A Long Awaited Wedding." 28 June, p. 3. (Bride waits for imprisoned fiancé for sixteen years.

"Military Block Khalil's Trip to Nairobi." 28 June, p. 1.

"Occupied Territories Women Forbidden to Attend Conference." 28 June, p. 1.

al-Ashhab, Baher. "Palestinian Women Prepare for Nairobi Showdown." 5 July, p.

"Objectives of Decade for Women." 5 July, p. 5.

"UN International Conference on Women: Preparations." 5 July, p. 1.

"UN Report on Women, Children in Occupied Territories." 12 July, p. 8.

"Palestinian Women's Committee Holds First Annual Conference." 13 July, p. 13.

"Palestinian Delegation Gains Conference's Support." 19 July, p. 2.

"Conference Ends." 2 August, p. 4.

"Women's Work Committee Children's Summer Camp." 10 August, p. 3.

"Incidents of Palestinian/Israeli Confrontation Recounted." 16 August, p. 16.

1986

Talhami, Ghada. "Women in the Movement: Their Long Uncelebrated History." 30 May, pp. 8–9.

Ashab, Baher. "Soldier Kills Pregnant Mother of Nine." 19 September, p. 1.

UNRWA Staff. "UNRWA's Education System: From Tents to Classrooms." 14 November.

1987

"Arab Women's Federation Strike." 6 February, p. 2.

Touma, Khalil. "The Human Side of Family Reunification." 6 February, pp. 8–9.

Al-Ghazali, Said. "An Interview with Artist Musician Antoinette Atwan." 6 March, p. 11.

———. "Women's Committees Could Provide a Model for Palestinian Unity." 6 March, p. 5. (Editorial, and see cartoon on p. 1.)

"Palestinian Women Call for Unity." 6 March, p. 3.

Touma, Khalil. "Women Struggle on Many Fronts." 13 March, pp. 8–9.

Safieh, Afif. "The Movement Should Try to Erect Bridges between Palestinian Women" (Interview with Ghada Talhami and Rima Salah), 5 July, pp. 8–9, 15.

1988

"Women Hold Sit-In Protest at UNRWA Gaza Office." 3 January, p. 2.

"Local Women's Groups Celebrate March 8." 15 March, p. 3.

Hamad, Saida. "About 90 Women in Detention." 31 July.

Nuseibeh, Reem. "Italian and Palestinian Women Protest Occupation." 4 September.

Touma, Khalil. "Interview with Freda Brown: I Was Moved Very Deeply by What I Saw." 19 December, p. 15.

1989

al-Helou, Nihaya. "Palestinian Women Have a History of Courage." 6 March, p. 9.

Hamad, Saida. "Intifada Transforms Palestinian Society, Especially the Role of Women." 13 March, pp. 8–9.

Mansour, Suleiman. "Happy International Women's Day." 13 March, p. 1. (Cartoon: woman removing barbed wire with a sickle.)

"Women Mark [International Women's] Day with Demonstrations." 13 March, p. 3.

Bishara, Ghassan. "Woman Relates Story behind Murder of Husband in Detention." 5 June, p. 6.

"Islamic Women Hold Charity Bazaar." 29 May, p. 7.

"Birzeit Professor Hanan Mikhail A. Ashrawi: International Conferences Are an Asset to Palestine." 12 June, p. 16.

"Palestinian Women Visit Druze Villages, Meet Their Counterparts." 26 June, p. 3.

"Zahira Kamal: Women Are in the First Rank of the Intifada." 26 June, p. 11.

Sanabel Press Service. "Experience of Women Is a 'Transfer' Policy in Disguise." 17 July, pp. 8, 15.

"Palestine and People." 31 July. (Journalist Amineh Odeh, 27, detained along with her sister.)

al-Ashhab, Baher. "Women Hold Sit-in [in support of prisoners]." 19 September, p. 2.

Edge, Simon. "The Situation of Palestinians in Israel." 16 October, p. 8.

"Hanan Awwad Brings International Women's Organization Home." 27 November, p. 9.

Awwad, Hanan. "Behind Every Great Palestinian Woman Stands a Great Palestinian Man." 4 December, p. 5.

"Military Tells Nablus Resident Wife Has to Leave Occupied Territories." 4 December, p. 16.

1990

Tawfiq, Basem. "Openness and Frankness Dominate Discussion of Women's Role." 24 December, pp. 8–9.

THE PALESTINIAN UNION OF WOMEN'S WORK COMMITTEES (PUWWC NOW PFWAC)
PUBLICATIONS (ENGLISH)

"The Development of the Palestinian Women's Movement in the Territories Occupied in 1967: After 20 Years of Israeli Occupation." 1987.
"The Program and Internal Platform of the Palestinian Federation of Women's Action Committees in the Occupied Territories." 1988.
"Special Issue: Women in the Uprising." *Newsletter*, 8 March 1988.

ARTICLES PUBLISHED IN *AL-KATEB* LITERARY-POLITICAL ARABIC JOURNAL
(Chronologically arranged. Published in East Jerusalem starting in 1979, but not allowed to be distributed in the rest of the West Bank).

Abu al-Hakam. "Woman and Work: Her Situation, Her Problems, and What Do We Do to Solve Them?" (discussion), June 1980, pp. 67–70.
Report of the Month. "Conditions of Working Women in Jordan." June 1980, pp. 64–66.
Bannura, Jamal. "Three Types of Women in Sahar Khalifa's Novel *The Sunflower*." January 1981, pp. 81–82.
Barghuti, Suha, and M. al-Sheikh. "Working Women and the Union Movement." March 1981, pp. 3–10.
Khalifah, Sahar. "Hulafa'a La Khulafa'a: A Review of the Reality of Palestinian Women through the experience of *The Sunflower*." July 1981, pp. 63–68; August 1981, pp. 57–64; September–October 1981, pp. 74–83. (Responds to the critics of her feminist book in three articles.)
Faris, Samia. "Azza and Omar." August 1981, p. 84. (A short feminist story for children.)
al-Sheikh, Mahmoud. "The Role of the Nursery Is a Symbol of the Suffering of Palestinian Women in the Occupied Territories." February 1982, pp. 59–65.
UPWWC in the West Bank and Gaza: Achievments and Hopes." February 1982, pp. 12–16.
Hawwash, Samar. "The Role of Women in Palestinian Society." September 1982, pp. 40–50.
Bader, Anwar. "Sahar Khalifah and the Narrative Structure of *The Sunflower*." March 1983, pp. 55–59.
Eleyyan, Hamad. "Women in Popular Palestinian Proverbs." October 1983, pp. 63–75.
Abu Hashish, Kayed. "Women in Bedouin Poetry." November 1983, pp. 92–94.
———. "Marriage in the Palestinian Desert." December 1983, pp. 56–63.
Hazboun, G., and B. al-Salihi. "The Workers and the Union Movement in the Occupied Territories 1967–1983, part 2." June 1984, pp. 23–35.
el-Haj, Hasan. "Some Issues of the Women's Movement in the Occupied Territories: A Study." September 1984.

UPWWC and Agricultural Relief Committee in Jericho. "Introduction to Understanding the Reality of Rural Women and Female Agricultural Workers in the Jordan Valley." January 1985, pp. 56–62.

"Working Women in the Thicket of the National Palestinian Struggle." April 1985, pp. 70–77. (Interviews with Amal Khreisheh of the UPWWC and Dr. Kathy Glavanis, Sociologist, Birzeit University.)

Doumani, Bishara. "The Role of the Vietnamese Woman and the Palestinian Woman in Nationalist Struggle: A Comparative Study." October 1985, pp. 23–37.

Khader, Sami. "Illiteracy among Palestinian Women: Its Incidence, Effects, and Suggested Remedies." September 1988, pp. 51-74.

Manasrah, Najah. "Has Woman's Status Kept up with Her Role in Events?" May 1989, pp. 54-58.

Abu Ghazaleh, Ilham. "Women in the Poetry of the Intifada." June 1989, pp. 65–76.

Manasrah, Najah. "Early Marriage: Temporary Retreat in the March of Palestinian Women." August 1989, pp. 24–31.

———. "Woman in the Palestinian Family." March 1990, pp. 20–29.

Abu Ghazaleh, Ilham. "Woman in the Literature of Ghassan Kanafani." August 1990, pp. 53–64.

 INDEX